Free as in Freedom

Richard Stallman's
Crusade for Free Software

FREE AS IN FREEDOM

*Richard Stallman's
Crusade for Free Software*

SAM WILLIAMS

O'REILLY®

BEIJING · CAMBRIDGE · FARNHAM · KÖLN · PARIS · SEBASTOPOL · TAIPEI · TOKYO

Free as in Freedom
Richard Stallman's Crusade for Free Software

by Sam Williams

Published by O'Reilly & Associates, Inc., 1005 Gravenstein Highway North, Sebastopol, CA 95472.

O'Reilly & Associates books may be purchased for educational, business, or sales promotional use. Online editions are also available for most titles (*safari.oreilly.com*). For more information, contact our corporate/institutional sales department: (800) 998-9938 or *corporate@oreilly.com*.

Editor: Laurie Petrycki

Production Editor: Jeffrey Holcomb

Cover Designers: Edie Freedman, Hanna Dyer, and Emma Colby

Interior Designers: Melanie Wang and David Futato

Printing History:

      March 2002:   First Edition.

ISBN: 0-596-00287-4

[M]

TO MY WIFE TRACY.

Table of Contents

PREFACE

The work of Richard M. Stallman literally speaks for itself. From the documented source code to the published papers to the recorded speeches, few people have expressed as much willingness to lay their thoughts and their work on the line.

Such openness—if one can pardon a momentary un-Stallman adjective—is refreshing. After all, we live in a society that treats information, especially personal information, as a valuable commodity. The question quickly arises. Why would anybody want to part with so much information and yet appear to demand nothing in return?

As we shall see in later chapters, Stallman does not part with his words or his work altruistically. Every program, speech, and on-the-record bon mot comes with a price, albeit not the kind of price most people are used to paying.

I bring this up not as a warning, but as an admission. As a person who has spent the last year digging up facts on Stallman's personal history, it's more than a little intimidating going up against the Stallman oeuvre. "Never pick a fight with a man who buys his ink by the barrel," goes the old Mark Twain adage. In the case of Stallman, never attempt the definitive biography of a man who trusts his every thought to the public record.

For the readers who have decided to trust a few hours of their time to exploring this book, I can confidently state that there are facts and quotes in here that one won't find in any Slashdot story or Google search. Gaining access to these facts involves paying a price, however. In the case of the book version, you can pay for these facts the traditional manner, i.e., by purchasing the book. In the case of the electronic versions, you can pay for these facts in the free software manner. Thanks to the folks at O'Reilly & Associates, this book is being distributed under the GNU Free Documentation License, meaning you can help to improve the work or create a personalized version and release that version under the same license.

If you are reading an electronic version and prefer to accept the latter payment option, that is, if you want to improve or expand this book for future readers, I welcome your input. Starting in June, 2002, I will be publishing a bare bones HTML version of the book on the web site, *http://www.faifzilla.org*. My aim is to update it regularly and expand the *Free as in Freedom* story as events warrant. If you choose to take the latter course, please review Appendix C of this book. It provides a copy of your rights under the GNU Free Documentation License.

For those who just plan to sit back and read, online or elsewhere, I consider your attention an equally valuable form of payment. Don't be surprised, though, if you, too, find yourself looking for other ways to reward the good will that made this work possible.

One final note: this is a work of journalism, but it is also a work of technical documentation. In the process of writing and editing this book, the editors and I have weighed the comments and factual input of various participants in the story, including Richard Stallman himself. We realize there are many technical details in this story that may benefit from additional or refined information. As this book is released under the GFDL, we are accepting patches just like we would with any free software program. Accepted changes will be posted electronically and will eventually be incorporated into future printed versions of this work. If you would like to contribute to the further improvement of this book, you can reach me at *sam@inow.com*.

Comments and Questions

Please address comments and questions concerning this book to the publisher:

O'Reilly & Associates, Inc.
1005 Gravenstein Highway North
Sebastopol, CA 95472
(800) 998-9938 (in the United States or Canada)
(707) 829-0515 (international/local)
(707) 829-0104 (fax)

There is a web page for this book, which lists errata, examples, or any additional information. The site also includes a link to a forum where you can discuss the book with the author and other readers. You can access this site at:

http://www.oreilly.com/catalog/freedom/

To comment or ask technical questions about this book, send email to:

bookquestions@oreilly.com

For more information about books, conferences, Resource Centers, and the O'Reilly Network, see the O'Reilly web site at:

http://www.oreilly.com

Acknowledgments

Special thanks to Henning Gutmann for sticking by this book. Special thanks to Aaron Oas for suggesting the idea to Tracy in the first place. Thanks to Laurie Petrycki, Jeffrey Holcomb, and all the others at O'Reilly & Associates. Thanks to Tim O'Reilly for backing this book. Thanks to all the first-draft reviewers: Bruce Perens, Eric Raymond, Eric Allman, Jon Orwant, Julie and Gerald Jay Sussman, Hal Abelson, and Guy Steele. I hope you enjoy this typo-free version. Thanks to Alice Lippman for the interviews, cookies, and photographs. Thanks to my family, Steve, Jane, Tish, and Dave. And finally, last but not least: thanks to Richard Stallman for having the guts and endurance to "show us the code."

—Sam Williams

CHAPTER I

FOR WANT OF A PRINTER

I fear the Greeks. Even when they bring gifts.

—Virgil
The Aeneid

The new printer was jammed, again.

Richard M. Stallman, a staff software programmer at the Massachusetts Institute of Technology's Artificial Intelligence Laboratory (AI Lab), discovered the malfunction the hard way. An hour after sending off a 50-page file to the office laser printer, Stallman, 27, broke off a productive work session to retrieve his documents. Upon arrival, he found only four pages in the printer's tray. To make matters even more frustrating, the four pages belonged to another user, meaning that Stallman's print job and the unfinished portion of somebody else's print job were still trapped somewhere within the electrical plumbing of the lab's computer network.

Waiting for machines is an occupational hazard when you're a software programmer, so Stallman took his frustration with a grain of salt. Still, the difference between waiting for a machine and waiting on a machine is a sizable one. It wasn't the first time he'd been forced to stand over the printer, watching pages print out one by one. As a person who spent the bulk of his days and nights improving the efficiency of machines and the software programs that controlled them, Stallman felt a natural urge to open up the machine, look at the guts, and seek out the root of the problem.

Unfortunately, Stallman's skills as a computer programmer did not extend to the mechanical-engineering realm. As freshly printed documents poured out of the machine, Stallman had a chance to reflect on other ways to circumvent the printing jam problem.

How long ago had it been that the staff members at the AI Lab had welcomed the new printer with open arms? Stallman wondered. The machine had been a donation from the Xerox Corporation. A cutting edge prototype, it was a modified version of the popular Xerox photocopier. Only instead of making copies, it relied on software data piped in over a computer network to turn that data into professional-looking documents. Created by engineers at the world-famous Xerox Palo Alto Research Facility, it was, quite simply, an early taste of the desktop-printing revolution that would seize the rest of the computing industry by the end of the decade.

Driven by an instinctual urge to play with the best new equipment, programmers at the AI Lab promptly integrated the new machine into the lab's sophisticated computing infrastructure. The results had been immediately pleasing. Unlike the lab's old laser printer, the new Xerox machine was fast. Pages came flying out at a rate of one per second, turning a 20-minute print job into a 2-minute print job. The new machine was also more precise. Circles came out looking like circles, not ovals. Straight lines came out looking like straight lines, not low-amplitude sine waves.

It was, for all intents and purposes, a gift too good to refuse.

It wasn't until a few weeks after its arrival that the machine's flaws began to surface. Chief among the drawbacks was the machine's inherent susceptibility to paper jams. Engineering-minded programmers quickly understood the reason behind the flaw. As a photocopier, the machine generally required the direct oversight of a human operator. Figuring that these human operators would always be on hand to fix a paper jam, if it occurred, Xerox engineers had devoted their time and energies to eliminating other pesky problems. In engineering terms, user diligence was built into the system.

In modifying the machine for printer use, Xerox engineers had changed the user-machine relationship in a subtle but profound way. Instead of making the machine subservient to an individual human operator, they made it subservient to an entire networked population of human operators. Instead of standing directly over the machine, a human user on one end of the network sent his print command through an extended bucket-brigade of machines, expecting the desired content to arrive at the targeted destination and in proper form. It wasn't until he finally went to check up on the final output that he realized how little of the desired content had made it through.

Stallman himself had been of the first to identify the problem and the first to suggest a remedy. Years before, when the lab was still using its old printer, Stallman had solved a similar problem by opening up the software program that regulated the printer on the lab's PDP-11 machine. Stallman couldn't eliminate paper jams, but he could insert a software command that ordered the PDP-11 to check the printer periodically and report back to the PDP-10, the lab's central computer. To ensure that one user's negligence didn't bog down an entire line of print jobs, Stallman also inserted a software command that instructed the PDP-10 to notify every user with a waiting print job that the printer was jammed. The notice was simple, something along the lines of "The printer is jammed, please fix it," and because it went out to the people with the most pressing need to fix the problem, chances were higher that the problem got fixed in due time.

As fixes go, Stallman's was oblique but elegant. It didn't fix the mechanical side of the problem, but it did the next best thing by closing the information loop between user and machine. Thanks to a few additional lines of software code, AI Lab employees could eliminate the 10 or 15 minutes wasted each week in running back and forth to check on the printer. In programming terms, Stallman's fix took advantage of the amplified intelligence of the overall network.

"If you got that message, you couldn't assume somebody else would fix it," says Stallman, recalling the logic. "You had to go to the printer. A minute or two after the printer got in trouble, the two or three people who got messages arrive to fix the machine. Of those two or three people, one of them, at least, would usually know how to fix the problem."

Such clever fixes were a trademark of the AI Lab and its indigenous population of programmers. Indeed, the best programmers at the AI Lab disdained the term programmer, preferring the more slangy occupational title of hacker instead. The job title covered a host of activities—everything from creative mirth making to the improvement of existing software and computer systems. Implicit within the title, however, was the old-fashioned notion of Yankee ingenuity. To be a hacker, one had to accept the philosophy that writing a software program was only the beginning. Improving a program was the true test of a hacker's skills.[1]

Such a philosophy was a major reason why companies like Xerox made it a policy to donate their machines and software programs to places where hackers typically congregated. If hackers improved the software, companies could borrow back the improvements, incorporating them into update versions for the commercial marketplace. In corporate terms, hackers were a leveragable community asset, an auxiliary research-and-development division available at minimal cost.

It was because of this give-and-take philosophy that when Stallman spotted the print-jam defect in the Xerox laser printer, he didn't panic. He simply looked for a way to update the old fix or "hack" for the new system. In the course of looking up the Xerox laser-printer software, however, Stallman made a troubling discovery. The printer didn't have any software, at least nothing Stallman or a fellow programmer could read. Until then, most companies had made it a form of courtesy to publish source-code files—readable text files that documented the individual software commands that told a machine what to do. Xerox, in this instance, had provided software files in precompiled, or binary, form. Programmers were free to open the files up if they wanted to, but unless they were an expert in deciphering an endless stream of ones and zeroes, the resulting text was pure gibberish.

Although Stallman knew plenty about computers, he was not an expert in translating binary files. As a hacker, however, he had other resources at his disposal. The notion of information sharing was so central to the hacker culture that Stallman knew it was only a matter of time before some hacker in some university lab or corporate computer room proffered a version of the laser-printer source code with the desired source-code files.

After the first few printer jams, Stallman comforted himself with the memory of a similar situation years before. The lab had needed a cross-network program to help the PDP-11 work more efficiently with the PDP-10. The lab's hackers were more than up to the task, but Stallman, a Harvard alumnus, recalled a similar program written by programmers at the Harvard computer-science department. The Harvard computer lab used the same model computer, the PDP-10, albeit with a different operating system. The Harvard computer lab also had a policy requiring that all programs installed on the PDP-10 had to come with published source-code files.

Taking advantage of his access to the Harvard computer lab, Stallman dropped in, made a copy of the cross-network source code, and brought it back to the AI Lab. He then rewrote the source code to make it more suitable for the AI Lab's operating system. With no muss and little fuss, the AI Lab shored up a major gap in its software infrastructure. Stallman even added a few features not found in the original Harvard program, making the program even more useful. "We wound up using it for several years," Stallman says.

From the perspective of a 1970s-era programmer, the transaction was the software equivalent of a neighbor stopping by to borrow a power tool or a cup of sugar from a neighbor. The only difference was that in borrowing a copy of the software for the AI Lab, Stallman had done nothing to deprive Harvard hackers the use of their original program. If anything, Harvard hackers gained in the process, because Stallman had introduced his own additional features to the program, features that hackers at Harvard were perfectly free to borrow in return. Although nobody at

Harvard ever came over to borrow the program back, Stallman does recall a programmer at the private engineering firm, Bolt, Beranek & Newman, borrowing the program and adding a few additional features, which Stallman eventually reintegrated into the AI Lab's own source-code archive.

"A program would develop the way a city develops," says Stallman, recalling the software infrastructure of the AI Lab. "Parts would get replaced and rebuilt. New things would get added on. But you could always look at a certain part and say, 'Hmm, by the style, I see this part was written back in the early 60s and this part was written in the mid-1970s.'"

Through this simple system of intellectual accretion, hackers at the AI Lab and other places built up robust creations. On the west coast, computer scientists at UC Berkeley, working in cooperation with a few low-level engineers at AT&T, had built up an entire operating system using this system. Dubbed Unix, a play on an older, more academically respectable operating system called Multics, the software system was available to any programmer willing to pay for the cost of copying the program onto a new magnetic tape and shipping it. Not every programmer participating in this culture described himself as a hacker, but most shared the sentiments of Richard M. Stallman. If a program or software fix was good enough to solve your problems, it was good enough to solve somebody else's problems. Why not share it out of a simple desire for good karma?

The fact that Xerox had been unwilling to share its source-code files seemed a minor annoyance at first. In tracking down a copy of the source-code files, Stallman says he didn't even bother contacting Xerox. "They had already given us the laser printer," Stallman says. "Why should I bug them for more?"

When the desired files failed to surface, however, Stallman began to grow suspicious. The year before, Stallman had experienced a blow up with a doctoral student at Carnegie Mellon University. The student, Brian Reid, was the author of a useful text-formatting program dubbed Scribe. One of the first programs that gave a user the power to define fonts and type styles when sending a document over a computer network, the program was an early harbinger of HTML, the lingua franca of the World Wide Web. In 1979, Reid made the decision to sell Scribe to a Pittsburgh-area software company called Unilogic. His graduate-student career ending, Reid says he simply was looking for a way to unload the program on a set of developers that would take pains to keep it from slipping into the public domain. To sweeten the deal, Reid also agreed to insert a set of time-dependent functions—"time bombs" in software-programmer parlance—that deactivated freely copied versions of the program after a 90-day expiration date. To avoid deactivation, users paid the software company, which then issued a code that defused the internal time-bomb feature.

For Reid, the deal was a win-win. Scribe didn't fall into the public domain, and Unilogic recouped on its investment. For Stallman, it was a betrayal of the programmer ethos, pure and simple. Instead of honoring the notion of share-and-share alike, Reid had inserted a way for companies to compel programmers to pay for information access.

As the weeks passed and his attempts to track down Xerox laser-printer source code hit a brick wall, Stallman began to sense a similar money-for-code scenario at work. Before Stallman could do or say anything about it, however, good news finally trickled in via the programmer grapevine. Word had it that a scientist at the computer-science department at Carnegie Mellon University had just departed a job at the Xerox Palo Alto Research Center. Not only had the scientist worked on the laser printer in question, but according to rumor, he was still working on it as part of his research duties at Carnegie Mellon.

Casting aside his initial suspicion, Stallman made a firm resolution to seek out the person in question during his next visit to the Carnegie Mellon campus.

He didn't have to wait long. Carnegie Mellon also had a lab specializing in artificial-intelligence research, and within a few months, Stallman had a business-related reason to visit the Carnegie Mellon campus. During that visit, he made sure to stop by the computer-science department. Department employees directed him to the office of the faculty member leading the Xerox project. When Stallman reached the office, he found the professor working there.

In true engineer-to-engineer fashion, the conversation was cordial but blunt. After briefly introducing himself as a visitor from MIT, Stallman requested a copy of the laser-printer source code so that he could port it to the PDP-11. To his surprise, the professor refused to grant his request.

"He told me that he had promised not to give me a copy," Stallman says.

Memory is a funny thing. Twenty years after the fact, Stallman's mental history tape is notoriously blank in places. Not only does he not remember the motivating reason for the trip or even the time of year during which he took it, he also has no recollection of the professor or doctoral student on the other end of the conversation. According to Reid, the person most likely to have fielded Stallman's request is Robert Sproull, a former Xerox PARC researcher and current director of Sun Laboratories, a research division of the computer-technology conglomerate Sun Microsystems. During the 1970s, Sproull had been the primary developer of the laser-printer software in question while at Xerox PARC. Around 1980, Sproull took a faculty research position at Carnegie Mellon where he continued his laser-printer work amid other projects.

"The code that Stallman was asking for was leading-edge state-of-the-art code that Sproull had written in the year or so before going to Carnegie Mellon," recalls Reid. "I suspect that Sproull had been at Carnegie Mellon less than a month before this request came in."

When asked directly about the request, however, Sproull draws a blank. "I can't make a factual comment," writes Sproull via email. "I have absolutely no recollection of the incident."

With both participants in the brief conversation struggling to recall key details—including whether the conversation even took place—it's hard to gauge the bluntness of Sproull's refusal, at least as recalled by Stallman. In talking to audiences, Stallman has made repeated reference to the incident, noting that Sproull's unwillingness to hand over the source code stemmed from a nondisclosure agreement, a contractual agreement between Sproull and the Xerox Corporation giving Sproull, or any other signatory, access the software source code in exchange for a promise of secrecy. Now a standard item of business in the software industry, the nondisclosure agreement, or NDA, was a novel development at the time, a reflection of both the commercial value of the laser printer to Xerox and the information needed to run it. "Xerox was at the time trying to make a commercial product out of the laser printer," recalls Reid. "They would have been insane to give away the source code."

For Stallman, however, the NDA was something else entirely. It was a refusal on the part of Xerox and Sproull, or whomever the person was that turned down his source-code request that day, to participate in a system that, until then, had encouraged software programmers to regard programs as communal resources. Like a peasant whose centuries-old irrigation ditch had grown suddenly dry, Stallman had followed the ditch to its source only to find a brand-spanking-new hydroelectric dam bearing the Xerox logo.

For Stallman, the realization that Xerox had compelled a fellow programmer to participate in this newfangled system of compelled secrecy took a while to sink in. At first, all he could focus on was the personal nature of the refusal. As a person who felt awkward and out of sync in most face-to-face encounters, Stallman's attempt to drop in on a fellow programmer unannounced had been intended as a demonstration of neighborliness. Now that the request had been refused, it felt like a major blunder. "I was so angry I couldn't think of a way to express it. So I just turned away and walked out without another word," Stallman recalls. "I might have slammed the door. Who knows? All I remember is wanting to get out of there."

Twenty years after the fact, the anger still lingers, so much so that Stallman has elevated the event into a major turning point. Within the next few months, a series of events would befall both Stallman and the AI Lab hacker community that would make 30 seconds worth of tension in a remote Carnegie Mellon office seem trivial by comparison. Nevertheless, when it comes time to sort out the events that would transform Stallman from a lone hacker, instinctively suspicious of centralized authority, to a crusading activist applying traditional notions of liberty, equality, and fraternity to the world of software development, Stallman singles out the Carnegie Mellon encounter for special attention.

"It encouraged me to think about something that I'd already been thinking about," says Stallman. "I already had an idea that software should be shared, but I wasn't sure how to think about that. My thoughts weren't clear and organized to the point where I could express them in a concise fashion to the rest of the world."

Although previous events had raised Stallman's ire, he says it wasn't until his Carnegie Mellon encounter that he realized the events were beginning to intrude on a culture he had long considered sacrosanct. As an elite programmer at one of the world's elite institutions, Stallman had been perfectly willing to ignore the compromises and bargains of his fellow programmers just so long as they didn't interfere with his own work. Until the arrival of the Xerox laser printer, Stallman had been content to look down on the machines and programs other computer users grimly tolerated. On the rare occasion that such a program breached the AI Lab's walls—when the lab replaced its venerable Incompatible Time Sharing operating system with a commercial variant, the TOPS 20, for example—Stallman and his hacker colleagues had been free to rewrite, reshape, and rename the software according to personal taste.

Now that the laser printer had insinuated itself within the AI Lab's network, however, something had changed. The machine worked fine, barring the occasional paper jam, but the ability to modify according to personal taste had disappeared. From the viewpoint of the entire software industry, the printer was a wake-up call. Software had become such a valuable asset that companies no longer felt the need to publicize source code, especially when publication meant giving potential competitors a chance to duplicate something cheaply. From Stallman's viewpoint, the printer was a Trojan Horse. After a decade of failure, privately owned software—future hackers would use the term "proprietary" software—had gained a foothold inside the AI Lab through the sneakiest of methods. It had come disguised as a gift.

That Xerox had offered some programmers access to additional gifts in exchange for secrecy was also galling, but Stallman takes pains to note that, if presented with such a quid pro quo bargain at a younger age, he just might have taken the Xerox Corporation up on its offer. The awkwardness of the Carnegie Mellon encounter, however, had a firming effect on Stallman's own moral lassitude. Not only did it give him the necessary anger to view all future entreaties with suspicion, it also forced him to ask the uncomfortable question: what if a fellow hacker dropped into Stallman's office someday and it suddenly became Stallman's job to refuse the hacker's request for source code?

"It was my first encounter with a nondisclosure agreement, and it immediately taught me that nondisclosure agreements have victims," says Stallman, firmly. "In this case I was the victim. [My lab and I] were victims."

It was a lesson Stallman would carry with him through the tumultuous years of the 1980s, a decade during which many of his MIT colleagues would depart the AI Lab and sign nondisclosure agreements of their own. Because most nondisclosure aggreements (NDAs) had expiration dates, few hackers who did sign them saw little need for personal introspection. Sooner or later, they reasoned, the software would become public knowledge. In the meantime, promising to keep the software secret during its earliest development stages was all a part of the compromise deal that allowed hackers to work on the best projects. For Stallman, however, it was the first step down a slippery slope.

"When somebody invited me to betray all my colleagues in that way, I remembered how angry I was when somebody else had done that to me and my whole lab," Stallman says. "So I said, 'Thank you very much for offering me this nice software package, but I can't accept it on the conditions that you're asking for, so I'm going to do without it.'"

As Stallman would quickly learn, refusing such requests involved more than personal sacrifice. It involved segregating himself from fellow hackers who, though sharing a similar distaste for secrecy, tended to express that distaste in a more morally flexible fashion. It wasn't long before Stallman, increasingly an outcast even within the AI Lab, began billing himself as "the last true hacker," isolating himself further and further from a marketplace dominated by proprietary software. Refusing another's request for source code, Stallman decided, was not only a betrayal of the scientific mission that had nurtured software development since the end of World War II, it was a violation of the Golden Rule, the baseline moral dictate to do unto others as you would have them do unto you.

Hence the importance of the laser printer and the encounter that resulted from it. Without it, Stallman says, his life might have followed a more ordinary path, one balancing the riches of a commercial programmer with the ultimate frustration of a life spent writing invisible software code. There would have been no sense of clarity, no urgency to address a problem others weren't addressing. Most importantly, there would have been no righteous anger, an emotion that, as we soon shall see, has propelled Stallman's career as surely as any political ideology or ethical belief.

"From that day forward, I decided this was something I could never participate in," says Stallman, alluding to the practice of trading personal liberty for the sake of convenience—Stallman's description of the NDA bargain—as well as the overall culture that encouraged such ethically suspect deal-making in the first place. "I decided never to make other people victims just like I had been a victim."

ENDNOTE

1. For more on the term "hacker," see Appendix B.

CHAPTER 2

2001:
A HACKER'S ODYSSEY

The New York University computer-science department sits inside Warren Weaver Hall, a fortress-like building located two blocks east of Washington Square Park. Industrial-strength air-conditioning vents create a surrounding moat of hot air, discouraging loiterers and solicitors alike. Visitors who breach the moat encounter another formidable barrier, a security check-in counter immediately inside the building's single entryway.

Beyond the security checkpoint, the atmosphere relaxes somewhat. Still, numerous signs scattered throughout the first floor preach the dangers of unsecured doors and propped-open fire exits. Taken as a whole, the signs offer a reminder: even in the relatively tranquil confines of pre–September 11, 2001, New York, one can never be too careful or too suspicious.

The signs offer an interesting thematic counterpoint to the growing number of visitors gathering in the hall's interior atrium. A few look like NYU students. Most look like shaggy-aired concert-goers milling outside a music hall in anticipation of the main act. For one brief morning, the masses have taken over Warren Weaver Hall, leaving the nearby security attendant with nothing better to do but watch Ricki Lake on TV and shrug her shoulders toward the nearby auditorium whenever visitors ask about "the speech."

Once inside the auditorium, a visitor finds the person who has forced this temporary shutdown of building security procedures. The person is Richard M. Stallman, founder of the GNU Project, original president of the Free Software Foundation, winner of the 1990 MacArthur Fellowship, winner of the Association of Computing Machinery's Grace Murray Hopper Award (also in 1990), corecipient of the Takeda Foundation's 2001 Takeda Award, and former AI Lab hacker. As announced over a host of hacker-related web sites, including the GNU Project's own *http://www.gnu.org* site, Stallman is in Manhattan, his former hometown, to deliver a much anticipated speech in rebuttal to the Microsoft Corporation's recent campaign against the GNU General Public License.

The subject of Stallman's speech is the history and future of the free software movement. The location is significant. Less than a month before, Microsoft senior vice president Craig Mundie appeared at the nearby NYU Stern School of Business, delivering a speech blasting the General Public License, or GPL, a legal device originally conceived by Stallman 16 years before. Built to counteract the growing wave of software secrecy overtaking the computer industry—a wave first noticed by Stallman during his 1980 troubles with the Xerox laser printer—the GPL has evolved into a central tool of the free software community. In simplest terms, the GPL locks software programs into a form of communal ownership—what today's legal scholars now call the "digital commons"—through the legal weight of copyright. Once locked, programs remain unremovable. Derivative versions must carry the same copyright protection—even derivative versions that bear only a small snippet of the original source code. For this reason, some within the software industry have taken to calling the GPL a "viral" license, because it spreads itself to every software program it touches.[1]

In an information economy increasingly dependent on software and increasingly beholden to software standards, the GPL has become the proverbial "big stick." Even companies that once laughed it off as software socialism have come around to recognize the benefits. Linux, the Unix-like kernel developed by Finnish college student Linus Torvalds in 1991, is licensed under the GPL, as are many of the world's most popular programming tools: GNU Emacs, the GNU Debugger, the GNU C Compiler, etc. Together, these tools form the components of a free software operating system developed, nurtured, and owned by the world-wide hacker community. Instead of viewing this community as a threat, high-tech companies like IBM, Hewlett Packard, and Sun Microsystems have come to rely upon it, selling software applications and services built to ride atop the ever-growing free software infrastructure.

They've also come to rely upon it as a strategic weapon in the hacker community's perennial war against Microsoft, the Redmond, Washington–based company that, for better or worse, has dominated the PC-software marketplace since the late 1980s. As owner of the popular Windows operating system, Microsoft stands to lose the most in an industry-wide shift to the GPL license. Almost every line of source code in the Windows colossus is protected by copyrights reaffirming the private nature of the underlying source code or, at the very least, reaffirming Microsoft's legal ability to treat it as such. From the Microsoft viewpoint, incorporating programs protected by the "viral" GPL into the Windows colossus would be the software equivalent of Superman downing a bottle of Kryptonite pills. Rival companies could suddenly copy, modify, and sell improved versions of Windows, rendering the company's indomitable position as the No. 1 provider of consumer-oriented software instantly vulnerable. Hence the company's growing concern over the GPL's rate of adoption. Hence the recent Mundie speech blasting the GPL and the "open source" approach to software development and sales. And hence Stallman's decision to deliver a public rebuttal to that speech on the same campus here today.

20 years is a long time in the software industry. Consider this: in 1980, when Richard Stallman was cursing the AI Lab's Xerox laser printer, Microsoft, the company modern hackers view as the most powerful force in the worldwide software industry, was still a privately held startup. IBM, the company hackers used to regard as the most powerful force in the worldwide software industry, had yet to to introduce its first personal computer,

thereby igniting the current low-cost PC market. Many of the technologies we now take for granted—the World Wide Web, satellite television, 32-bit video-game consoles—didn't even exist. The same goes for many of the companies that now fill the upper echelons of the corporate establishment, companies like AOL, Sun Microsystems, Amazon.com, Compaq, and Dell. The list goes on and on.

The fact that the high-technology marketplace has come so far in such little time is fuel for both sides of the GPL debate. GPL-proponents point to the short lifespan of most computer hardware platforms. Facing the risk of buying an obsolete product, consumers tend to flock to companies with the best long-term survival. As a result, the software marketplace has become a winner-take-all arena.[2] The current, privately owned software environment, GPL-proponents say, leads to monopoly abuse and stagnation. Strong companies suck all the oxygen out of the marketplace for rival competitors and innovative startups.

GPL-opponents argue just the opposite. Selling software is just as risky, if not more risky, than buying software, they say. Without the legal guarantees provided by private software licenses, not to mention the economic prospects of a privately owned "killer app" (i.e., a breakthrough technology that launches an entirely new market),[3] companies lose the incentive to participate. Once again, the market stagnates and innovation declines. As Mundie himself noted in his May 3 address on the same campus, the GPL's "viral" nature "poses a threat" to any company that relies on the uniqueness of its software as a competitive asset. Added Mundie:

> *It also fundamentally undermines the independent commercial software sector because it effectively makes it impossible to distribute software on a basis where recipients pay for the product rather than just the cost of distribution.*[4]

The mutual success of GNU/Linux, the amalgamated operating system built around the GPL-protected Linux kernel, and Windows over the last 10 years reveals the wisdom of both perspectives. Nevertheless, the battle for momentum is an important one in the software industry. Even powerful vendors such as Microsoft rely on the support of third-party software developers whose tools, programs, and computer games make an underlying software platform such as Windows more attractive to the mainstream consumer. Citing the rapid evolution of the technology marketplace over the last 20 years, not to mention his own company's admirable track record during that period, Mundie advised listeners to not get too carried away by the free software movement's recent momentum:

> *Two decades of experience have shown that an economic model that protects intellectual property and a business model that recoups research and development costs can create impressive economic benefits and distribute them very broadly.*[4]

Such admonitions serve as the backdrop for Stallman's speech today. Less than a month after their utterance, Stallman stands with his back to one of the chalk boards at the front of the room, edgy to begin.

If the last two decades have brought dramatic changes to the software marketplace, they have brought even more dramatic changes to Stallman himself. Gone is the skinny, clean-shaven hacker who once spent his entire days communing with his beloved PDP-10. In his place stands a heavy-set middle-aged man with long hair and rabbinical beard, a man who now spends the bulk of his time writing and answering email, haranguing fellow programmers, and giving speeches like the one today. Dressed in an aqua-colored T-shirt and brown polyester pants, Stallman looks like a desert hermit who just stepped out of a Salvation Army dressing room.

The crowd is filled with visitors who share Stallman's fashion and grooming tastes. Many come bearing laptop computers and cellular modems, all the better to record and transmit Stallman's words to a waiting Internet audience. The gender ratio is roughly 15 males to 1 female, and 1 of the 7 or 8 females in the room comes in bearing a stuffed penguin, the official Linux mascot, while another carries a stuffed teddy bear.

Richard Stallman, circa 2000. "I decided I would develop a free software operating system or die trying . . . of old age of course." Photo courtesy of http://www.stallman.org.

Agitated, Stallman leaves his post at the front of the room and takes a seat in a front-row chair, tapping a few commands into an already-opened laptop. For the next 10 minutes Stallman is oblivious to the growing number of students, professors, and fans circulating in front of him at the foot of the auditorium stage.

Before the speech can begin, the baroque rituals of academic formality must be observed. Stallman's appearance merits not one but two introductions. Mike Uretsky, codirector of the Stern School's Center for Advanced Technology, provides the first.

"The role of a university is to foster debate and to have interesting discussions," Uretsky says. "This particular presentation, this seminar falls right into that mold. I find the discussion of open source particularly interesting."

Before Uretsky can get another sentence out, Stallman is on his feet waving him down like a stranded motorist.

"I do free software," Stallman says to rising laughter. "Open source is a different movement."

The laughter gives way to applause. The room is stocked with Stallman partisans, people who know of his reputation for verbal exactitude, not to mention his much publicized 1998 falling out with the open source software proponents. Most have come to anticipate such outbursts the same way radio fans once waited for Jack Benny's trademark, "Now cut that out!" phrase during each radio program.

Uretsky hastily finishes his introduction and cedes the stage to Edmond Schonberg, a professor in the NYU computer-science department. As a computer programmer and GNU Project contributor, Schonberg knows which linguistic land mines to avoid. He deftly summarizes Stallman's career from the perspective of a modern-day programmer.

"Richard is the perfect example of somebody who, by acting locally, started thinking globally [about] problems concerning the unavailability of source code," says Schonberg. "He has developed a coherent philosophy that has forced all of us to reexamine our ideas of how software is produced, of what intellectual property means, and of what the software community actually represents."

Schonberg welcomes Stallman to more applause. Stallman takes a moment to shut off his laptop, rises out of his chair, and takes the stage.

At first, Stallman's address seems more Catskills comedy routine than political speech. "I'd like to thank Microsoft for providing me the opportunity to be on this platform," Stallman wisecracks. "For the past few weeks, I have felt like an author whose book was fortuitously banned somewhere."

For the uninitiated, Stallman dives into a quick free software warm-up analogy. He likens a software program to a cooking recipe. Both provide useful step-by-step instructions on how to complete a desired task and can be easily modified if a user has special desires or circumstances. "You don't have to follow a recipe exactly," Stallman notes. "You can leave out some ingredients. Add some mushrooms, 'cause you like mushrooms. Put in less salt because your doctor said you should cut down on salt—whatever."

Most importantly, Stallman says, software programs and recipes are both easy to share. In giving a recipe to a dinner guest, a cook loses little more than time and the cost of the paper the recipe was written on. Software programs require even less, usually a few mouse-clicks and a modicum of electricity. In both instances, however, the person giving the information gains two things: increased friendship and the ability to borrow interesting recipes in return.

"Imagine what it would be like if recipes were packaged inside black boxes," Stallman says, shifting gears. "You couldn't see what ingredients they're using, let alone change them, and imagine if you made a copy for a friend. They would call you a pirate and try to put you in prison for years. That world would create tremendous outrage from all the people who are used to sharing recipes. But that is exactly what the world of proprietary software is like. A world in which common decency towards other people is prohibited or prevented."

With this introductory analogy out of the way, Stallman launches into a retelling of the Xerox laser-printer episode. Like the recipe analogy, the laser-printer story is a useful rhetorical device. With its parable-like structure, it dramatizes just how quickly things can change in the software world. Drawing listeners back to an era before Amazon.com one-click shopping, Microsoft Windows, and Oracle databases, it asks the listener to examine the notion of software ownership free of its current corporate logos.

Stallman delivers the story with all the polish and practice of a local district attorney conducting a closing argument. When he gets to the part about the Carnegie Mellon professor refusing to lend him a copy of the printer source code, Stallman pauses.

"He had betrayed us," Stallman says. "But he didn't just do it to us. Chances are he did it to you."

On the word "you," Stallman points his index finger accusingly at an unsuspecting member of the audience. The targeted audience member's eyebrows flinch slightly, but Stallman's own eyes have moved on. Slowly and deliberately, Stallman picks out a second listener to nervous titters from the crowd. "And I think, mostly likely, he did it to you, too," he says, pointing at an audience member three rows behind the first.

By the time Stallman has a third audience member picked out, the titters have given away to general laughter. The gesture seems a bit staged, because it is. Still, when it comes time to wrap up the Xerox laser-printer story, Stallman does so with a showman's flourish. "He probably did it to most of the people here in this room—except a few, maybe, who weren't born yet in 1980," Stallman says, drawing more laughs. "[That's] because he had promised to refuse to cooperate with just about the entire population of the planet Earth."

Stallman lets the comment sink in for a half-beat. "He had signed a nondisclosure agreement," Stallman adds.

Richard Matthew Stallman's rise from frustrated academic to political leader over the last 20 years speaks to many things. It speaks to Stallman's stubborn nature and prodigious will. It speaks to the clearly articulated vision and values of the free software movement Stallman helped build. It speaks to the high-quality software programs Stallman has built, programs that have cemented Stallman's reputation as a programming legend. It speaks to the growing momentum of the GPL, a legal innovation that many Stallman observers see as his most momentous accomplishment.

Most importantly, it speaks to the changing nature of political power in a world increasingly beholden to computer technology and the software programs that power that technology.

Maybe that's why, even at a time when most high-technology stars are on the wane, Stallman's star has grown. Since launching the GNU Project in 1984,[5] Stallman has been at turns ignored, satirized, vilified, and attacked—both from within and without the free software movement. Through it all, the GNU Project has managed to meet its milestones, albeit with a few notorious delays, and stay relevant in a software marketplace several orders of magnitude more complex than the one it entered 18 years ago. So too has the free software ideology, an ideology meticulously groomed by Stallman himself.

To understand the reasons behind this currency, it helps to examine Richard Stallman both in his own words and in the words of the people who have collaborated and battled with him along the way. The Richard Stallman character sketch is not a complicated one. If any person exemplifies the old adage "what you see is what you get," it's Stallman.

"I think if you want to understand Richard Stallman the human being, you really need to see all of the parts as a consistent whole," advises Eben Moglen, legal counsel to the Free Software Foundation and professor of law at Columbia University Law School. "All those personal eccentricities that lots of people see as obstacles to getting to know Stallman really *are* Stallman: Richard's strong sense of personal frustration, his enormous sense of principled ethical commitment, his inability to compromise, especially on issues he considers fundamental. These are all the very reasons Richard did what he did when he did."

Explaining how a journey that started with a laser printer would eventually lead to a sparring match with the world's richest corporation is no easy task. It requires a thoughtful examination of the forces that have made software ownership so important in today's society. It also requires a thoughtful examination of a man who, like many political leaders before him, understands the malleability of human memory. It requires an ability to interpret the myths and politically laden code words that have built up around Stallman over time. Finally, it requires an understanding of Stallman's genius as a programmer and his failures and successes in translating that genius to other pursuits.

When it comes to offering his own summary of the journey, Stallman acknowledges the fusion of personality and principle observed by Moglen. "Stubbornness is my strong suit," he says. "Most people who attempt to do anything of any great difficulty eventually get discouraged and give up. I never gave up."

He also credits blind chance. Had it not been for that run-in over the Xerox laser printer, had it not been for the personal and political conflicts that closed out his career as an MIT employee, had it not been for a half dozen other timely factors, Stallman finds it very easy to picture his life following a different career path. That being said, Stallman gives thanks to the forces and circumstances that put him in the position to make a difference.

"I had just the right skills," says Stallman, summing up his decision for launching the GNU Project to the audience. "Nobody was there but me, so I felt like, 'I'm elected. I have to work on this. If not me, who?'"

ENDNOTES

1. Actually, the GPL's powers are not quite that potent. According to section 10 of the GNU General Public License, Version 2 (1991), the viral nature of the license depends heavily on the Free Software Foundation's willingness to view a program as a derivative work, not to mention the existing license the GPL would replace.

    If you wish to incorporate parts of the Program into other free programs whose distribution conditions are different, write to the author to ask for permission. For software that is copyrighted by the Free Software Foundation, write to the Free Software Foundation; we sometimes make exceptions for this. Our decision will be guided by the two goals of preserving the free status of all derivatives of our free software and of promoting the sharing and reuse of software generally.

    "To compare something to a virus is very harsh," says Stallman. "A spider plant is a more accurate comparison; it goes to another place if you actively take a cutting."

    For more information on the GNU General Public License, visit *http://www.gnu.org/copyleft/gpl.html.*

2. See Shubha Ghosh, "Revealing the Microsoft Windows Source Code," *Gigalaw.com* (January, 2000).

    http://www.gigalaw.com/articles/ghosh-2000-01-p1.html

3. Killer apps don't have to be proprietary. Witness, of course, the legendary Mosaic browser, a program whose copyright permits noncommercial derivatives with certain restrictions. Still, I think the reader gets the point: the software marketplace is like the lottery. The bigger the potential payoff, the more people want to participate. For a good summary of the killer-app phenomenon, see Philip Ben-David, "Whatever Happened to the 'Killer App'?" *e-Commerce News* (December 7, 2000).

    http://www.ecommercetimes.com/perl/story/5893.html

4. See Craig Mundie, "The Commercial Software Model," senior vice president, Microsoft Corp. Excerpted from an online transcript of Mundie's May 3, 2001, speech to the New York University Stern School of Business.

   http://www.microsoft.com/presspass/exec/craig/05-03sharedsource.asp

5. The acronym GNU stands for "GNU's not Unix." In another portion of the May 29, 2001, NYU speech, Stallman summed up the acronym's origin:

   > *We hackers always look for a funny or naughty name for a program, because naming a program is half the fun of writing the program. We also had a tradition of recursive acronyms, to say that the program that you're writing is similar to some existing program . . . I looked for a recursive acronym for Something Is Not UNIX. And I tried all 26 letters and discovered that none of them was a word. I decided to make it a contraction. That way I could have a three-letter acronym, for Something's Not UNIX. And I tried letters, and I came across the word "GNU." That was it.*

   Although a fan of puns, Stallman recommends that software users pronounce the "g" at the beginning of the acronym (i.e., "gah-new"). Not only does this avoid confusion with the word "gnu," the name of the African antelope, *Connochaetes gnou*, it also avoids confusion with the adjective "new." "We've been working on it for 17 years now, so it is not exactly new any more," Stallman says.

   Source: author notes and online transcript of "Free Software: Freedom and Cooperation," Richard Stallman's May 29, 2001, speech at New York University.

   http://www.gnu.org/events/rms-nyu-2001-transcript.txt

CHAPTER 3

A Portrait of the Hacker as a Young Man

Richard Stallman's mother, Alice Lippman, still remembers the moment she realized her son had a special gift.

"I think it was when he was eight," Lippman recalls.

The year was 1961, and Lippman, a recently divorced single mother, was wiling away a weekend afternoon within the family's tiny one-bedroom apartment on Manhattan's Upper West Side. Leafing through a copy of Scientific American, Lippman came upon her favorite section, the Martin Gardner–authored column titled "Mathematical Games." A substitute art teacher, Lippman always enjoyed Gardner's column for the brain-teasers it provided. With her son already ensconced in a book on the nearby sofa, Lippman decided to take a crack at solving the week's feature puzzle.

"I wasn't the best person when it came to solving the puzzles," she admits. "But as an artist, I found they really helped me work through conceptual barriers."

Lippman says her attempt to solve the puzzle met an immediate brick wall. About to throw the magazine down in disgust, Lippman was surprised by a gentle tug on her shirt sleeve.

"It was Richard," she recalls, "He wanted to know if I needed any help."

Looking back and forth, between the puzzle and her son, Lippman says she initially regarded the offer with skepticism. "I asked Richard if he'd read the magazine," she says. "He told me that, yes, he had and what's more he'd already solved the puzzle. The next thing I know, he starts explaining to me how to solve it." Hearing the logic of her son's approach, Lippman's skepticism quickly gave way to incredulity. "I mean, I always knew he was a bright boy," she says, "but this was the first time I'd seen anything that suggested how advanced he really was."

Thirty years after the fact, Lippman punctuates the memory with a laugh. "To tell you the truth, I don't think I ever figured out how to solve that puzzle," she says. "All I remember is being amazed he knew the answer."

Seated at the dining-room table of her second Manhattan apartment—the same spacious three-bedroom complex she and her son moved to following her 1967 marriage to Maurice Lippman, now deceased—Alice Lippman exudes a Jewish mother's mixture of pride and bemusement when recalling her son's early years. The nearby dining-room credenza offers an eight-by-ten photo of Stallman glowering in full beard and doctoral robes. The image dwarfs accompanying photos of Lippman's nieces and nephews, but before a visitor can make too much of it, Lippman makes sure to balance its prominent placement with an ironic wisecrack.

"Richard insisted I have it after he received his honorary doctorate at the University of Glasgow," says Lippman. "He said to me, 'Guess what, mom? It's the first graduation I ever attended.'"[1]

Such comments reflect the sense of humor that comes with raising a child prodigy. Make no mistake, for every story Lippman hears and reads about her son's stubbornness and unusual behavior, she can deliver at least a dozen in return.

"He used to be so conservative," she says, throwing up her hands in mock exasperation. "We used to have the worst arguments right here at this table. I was part of the first group of public city school teachers that struck to form a union, and Richard was very angry with me. He saw unions as corrupt. He was also very opposed to social security. He thought people could make much more money investing it on their own. Who knew that within 10 years he would become so idealistic? All I remember is his stepsister coming to me and saying, 'What is he going to be when he grows up? A fascist?'"

As a single parent for nearly a decade—she and Richard's father, Daniel Stallman, were married in 1948, divorced in 1958, and split custody of their son afterwards—Lippman can attest to her son's aversion to authority. She can also attest to her son's lust for knowledge. It was during the times when the two forces intertwined, Lippman says, that she and her son experienced their biggest battles.

"It was like he never wanted to eat," says Lippman, recalling the behavior pattern that set in around age eight and didn't let up until her son's high-school graduation in 1970. "I'd call him for dinner, and he'd never hear me. I'd have to call him 9 or 10 times just to get his attention. He was totally immersed."

Stallman, for his part, remembers things in a similar fashion, albeit with a political twist.

"I enjoyed reading," he says. "If I wanted to read, and my mother told me to go to the kitchen and eat or go to sleep, I wasn't going to listen. I saw no reason why I couldn't read. No reason why she should be able to tell me what to do, period. Essentially, what I had read about, ideas such as democracy and individual freedom, I applied to myself. I didn't see any reason to exclude children from these principles."

The belief in individual freedom over arbitrary authority extended to school as well. Two years ahead of his classmates by age 11, Stallman endured all the usual frustrations of a gifted public-school student. It wasn't long after the puzzle incident that his mother attended the first in what would become a long string of parent-teacher conferences.

"He absolutely refused to write papers," says Lippman, recalling an early controversy. "I think the last paper he wrote before his senior year in high school was an essay on the history of the number system in the west for a fourth-grade teacher."

Gifted in anything that required analytical thinking, Stallman gravitated toward math and science at the expense of his other studies. What some teachers saw as single-mindedness, however, Lippman saw as impatience. Math and science offered simply too much opportunity to learn, especially in comparison to subjects and pursuits for which her son seemed less naturally inclined. Around age 10 or 11, when the boys in Stallman's class began playing a regular game of touch football, she remembers her son coming home in a rage. "He wanted to play so badly, but he just didn't have the coordination skills," Lippman recalls. "It made him so angry."

The anger eventually drove her son to focus on math and science all the more. Even in the realm of science, however, her son's impatience could be problematic. Poring through calculus textbooks by age seven, Stallman saw little need to dumb down his discourse for adults. Sometime, during his middle-school years, Lippman hired a student from nearby Columbia University to play big brother to her son. The student left the family's apartment after the first session and never came back. "I think what Richard was talking about went over his head," Lippman speculates.

Another favorite maternal anecdote dates back to the early 1960s, shortly after the puzzle incident. Around age seven, two years after the divorce and relocation from Queens, Richard took up the hobby of launching model rockets in nearby Riverside Drive Park. What started as aimless fun soon took on an earnest edge as her son began recording the data from each launch. Like the interest in mathematical games, the pursuit drew little attention until one day, just before a major NASA launch, Lippman checked in on her son to see if he wanted to watch.

"He was fuming," Lippman says. "All he could say to me was, 'But I'm not published yet.' Apparently he had something that he really wanted to show NASA."

Such anecdotes offer early evidence of the intensity that would become Stallman's chief trademark throughout life. When other kids came to the table, Stallman stayed in his room and read. When other kids played Johnny Unitas, Stallman played Werner von Braun. "I was weird," Stallman says, summing up his early years succinctly in a 1999 interview. "After a certain age, the only friends I had were teachers."[1]

Although it meant courting more run-ins at school, Lippman decided to indulge her son's passion. By age 12, Richard was attending science camps during the summer and private school during the school year. When a teacher recommended her son enroll in the Columbia Science Honors Program, a post-Sputnik program designed for gifted middle- and high-school students in New York City, Stallman added to his extracurriculars and was soon commuting uptown to the Columbia University campus on Saturdays.

Dan Chess, a fellow classmate in the Columbia Science Honors Program, recalls Richard Stallman seeming a bit weird even among the students who shared a similar lust for math and science. "We were all geeks and nerds, but he was unusually poorly adjusted," recalls Chess, now a mathematics professor at Hunter College. "He was also smart as shit. I've known a lot of smart people, but I think he was the smartest person I've ever known."

Seth Breidbart, a fellow Columbia Science Honors Program alumnus, offers bolstering testimony. A computer programmer who has kept in touch with Stallman thanks to a shared passion for science fiction and science-fiction conventions, he recalls the 15-year-old, buzz-cut-wearing Stallman as "scary," especially to a fellow 15-year-old.

"It's hard to describe," Breidbart says. "It wasn't like he was unapproachable. He was just very intense. [He was] very knowledgeable but also very hardheaded in some ways."

Such descriptions give rise to speculation: are judgment-laden adjectives like "intense" and "hardheaded" simply a way to describe traits that today might be categorized under juvenile behavioral disorder? A December, 2001, *Wired* magazine article titled "The Geek Syndrome" paints the portrait of several scientifically gifted children diagnosed with high-functioning autism or Asperger Syndrome. In many ways, the parental recollections recorded in the *Wired* article are eerily similar to the ones offered by Lippman. Even Stallman has indulged in psychiatric revisionism from time to time. During a 2000 profile for the *Toronto Star*, Stallman described himself to an interviewer as "borderline autistic,"[2] a description that goes a long way toward explaining a lifelong tendency toward social and emotional isolation and the equally lifelong effort to overcome it.

Such speculation benefits from the fast and loose nature of most so-called "behavioral disorders" nowadays, of course. As Steve Silberman, author of "The Geek Syndrome," notes, American psychiatrists have only recently come to accept Asperger Syndrome as a valid umbrella term covering a wide set of behavioral traits. The traits range from poor motor skills and poor socialization to high intelligence and an almost obsessive affinity for numbers, computers, and ordered systems.[3] Reflecting on the broad nature of this umbrella, Stallman says its possible that, if born 40 years later, he might have merited just such a diagnosis. Then again, so would many of his computer-world colleagues.

"It's possible I could have had something like that," he says. "On the other hand, one of the aspects of that syndrome is difficulty following rhythms. I can dance. In fact, I love following the most complicated rhythms. It's not clear cut enough to know."

Chess, for one, rejects such attempts at back-diagnosis. "I never thought of him [as] having that sort of thing," he says. "He was just very unsocialized, but then, we all were."

Lippman, on the other hand, entertains the possibility. She recalls a few stories from her son's infancy, however, that provide fodder for speculation. A prominent symptom of autism is an oversensitivity to noises and colors, and Lippman recalls two anecdotes that stand out in this regard. "When Richard was an infant, we'd take him to the beach," she says. "He would start screaming two or three blocks before we reached the surf. It wasn't until the third time that we figured out what was going on: the sound of the surf was hurting his ears." She also recalls a similar screaming reaction in relation to color: "My mother had bright red hair, and every time she'd stoop down to pick him up, he'd let out a wail."

In recent years, Lippman says she has taken to reading books about autism and believes that such episodes were more than coincidental. "I do feel that Richard had some of the qualities of an autistic child," she says. "I regret that so little was known about autism back then."

Over time, however, Lippman says her son learned to adjust. By age seven, she says, her son had become fond of standing at the front window of subway trains, mapping out and memorizing the labyrinthian system of railroad tracks underneath the city. It was a hobby that relied on an ability to accommodate the loud noises that accompanied each train ride. "Only the initial noise seemed to bother him," says Lippman. "It was as if he got shocked by the sound but his nerves learned how to make the adjustment."

For the most part, Lippman recalls her son exhibiting the excitement, energy, and social skills of any normal boy. It wasn't until after a series of traumatic events battered the Stallman household, she says, that her son became introverted and emotionally distant.

The first traumatic event was the divorce of Alice and Daniel Stallman, Richard's father. Although Lippman says both she and her ex-husband tried to prepare their son for the blow, she says the blow was devastating nonetheless. "He sort of didn't pay attention when we first told him what was happening," Lippman recalls. "But the reality smacked him in the face when he and I moved into a new apartment. The first thing he said was, 'Where's Dad's furniture?'"

For the next decade, Stallman would spend his weekdays at his mother's apartment in Manhattan and his weekends at his father's home in Queens. The shuttling back and forth gave him a chance to study a pair of contrasting parenting styles that, to this day, leaves Stallman firmly opposed to the idea of raising children himself. Speaking about his father, a World War II vet who passed away in early 2001, Stallman balances respect with anger. On one hand, there is the man whose moral commitment led him to learn French just so he could be more helpful to Allies when they'd finally come. On the other hand, there was the parent who always knew how to craft a put-down for cruel effect.[4]

"My father had a horrible temper," Stallman says. "He never screamed, but he always found a way to criticize you in a cold, designed-to-crush way."

As for life in his mother's apartment, Stallman is less equivocal. "That was war," he says. "I used to say in my misery, 'I want to go home,' meaning to the nonexistent place that I'll never have."

For the first few years after the divorce, Stallman found the tranquility that eluded him in the home of his paternal grandparents. Then, around age 10 his grandparents passed away in short succession. For Stallman, the loss was devastating. "I used to go and visit and feel I was in a loving, gentle environment," Stallman recalls. "It was the only place I ever found one, until I went away to college."

Lippman lists the death of Richard's paternal grandparents as the second traumatic event. "It really upset him," she says. He was very close to both his grandparents. Before they died, he was very outgoing, almost a leader-of-the-pack type with the other kids. After they died, he became much more emotionally withdrawn."

From Stallman's perspective, the emotional withdrawal was merely an attempt to deal with the agony of adolescence. Labeling his teenage years a "pure horror," Stallman says he often felt like a deaf person amid a crowd of chattering music listeners.

"I often had the feeling that I couldn't understand what other people were saying," says Stallman, recalling the emotional bubble that insulated him from the rest of the adolescent and adult world. "I could understand the words, but something was going on underneath the conversations that I didn't understand. I couldn't understand why people were interested in the things other people said."

For all the agony it produced, adolescence would have a encouraging effect on Stallman's sense of individuality. At a time when most of his classmates were growing their hair out, Stallman preferred to keep his short. At a time when the whole teenage world was listening to rock and roll, Stallman preferred classical music. A devoted fan of science fiction, *Mad* magazine, and late-night TV, Stallman cultivated a distinctly off-the-wall personality that fed off the incomprehension of parents and peers alike.

"Oh, the puns," says Lippman, still exasperated by the memory of her son's teenage personality. "There wasn't a thing you could say at the dinner table that he couldn't throw back at you as a pun."

Outside the home, Stallman saved the jokes for the adults who tended to indulge his gifted nature. One of the first was a summer-camp counselor who handed Stallman a print-out manual for the IBM 7094 computer during his 12th year. To a preteenager fascinated with numbers and science, the gift was a godsend.[5] By the end of summer, Stallman was writing out paper programs according to the 7094's internal specifications, anxiously anticipating getting a chance to try them out on a real machine.

With the first personal computer still a decade away, Stallman would be forced to wait a few years before getting access to his first computer. His first chance finally came during his junior year of high school. Hired on at the IBM New York Scientific Center, a now-defunct research facility in downtown Manhattan, Stallman spent the summer after high-school graduation writing his first program, a pre-processor for the 7094 written in the programming language PL/I. "I first wrote it in PL/I, then started over in assembler language when the PL/I program was too big to fit in the computer," he recalls.

After that job at the IBM Scientific Center, Stallman had held a laboratory-assistant position in the biology department at Rockefeller University. Although he was already moving toward a career in math or physics, Stallman's analytical mind impressed the lab director enough that a few years after Stallman departed for college, Lippman received an unexpected phone call. "It was the professor at Rockefeller," Lippman says. "He wanted to know how Richard was doing. He was surprised to learn that he was working in computers. He'd always thought Richard had a great future ahead of him as a biologist."

Stallman's analytical skills impressed faculty members at Columbia as well, even when Stallman himself became a target of their ire. "Typically once or twice an hour [Stallman] would catch some mistake in the lecture," says Breidbart. "And he was not shy about letting the professors know it immediately. It got him a lot of respect but not much popularity."

Hearing Breidbart's anecdote retold elicits a wry smile from Stallman. "I may have been a bit of a jerk sometimes," he admits. "But I found kindred spirits among the teachers, because they, too, liked to learn. Kids, for the most part, didn't. At least not in the same way."

Hanging out with the advanced kids on Saturday nevertheless encouraged Stallman to think more about the merits of increased socialization. With college fast approaching, Stallman, like many in his Columbia Science Honors Program, had narrowed his list of desired schools down to two choices: Harvard and MIT. Hearing of her son's desire to move on to the Ivy League, Lippman became concerned. As a 15-year-old high-school junior, Stallman was still having run-ins with teachers and administrators. Only the year before, he had pulled straight A's in American History, Chemistry, French, and Algebra, but a glaring F in English reflected the ongoing boycott of writing assignments. Such miscues might draw a knowing chuckle at MIT, but at Harvard, they were a red flag.

During her son's junior year, Lippman says she scheduled an appointment with a therapist. The therapist expressed instant concern over Stallman's unwillingness to write papers and his run-ins with teachers. Her son certainly had the intellectual wherewithal to succeed at Harvard, but did he have the patience to sit through college classes that required a term paper? The therapist suggested a trial run. If Stallman could make it through a full year in New York City public schools, including an English class that required term papers, he could probably make it at Harvard. Following the completion of his junior year, Stallman promptly enrolled in summer school at Louis D. Brandeis High School, a public school located on 84th Street, and began making up the mandatory art classes he had shunned earlier in his high-school career.

By fall, Stallman was back within the mainstream population of New York City high-school students. It wasn't easy sitting through classes that seemed remedial in comparison with his Saturday studies at Columbia, but Lippman recalls proudly her son's ability to toe the line.

"He was forced to kowtow to a certain degree, but he did it," Lippman says. "I only got called in once, which was a bit of a miracle. It was the calculus teacher complaining that Richard was interrupting his lesson. I asked how he was interrupting. He said Richard was always accusing the teacher of using a false proof. I said, 'Well, is he right?' The teacher said, 'Yeah, but I can't tell that to the class. They wouldn't understand.'"

By the end of his first semester at Brandeis, things were falling into place. A 96 in English wiped away much of the stigma of the 60 earned 2 years before. For good measure, Stallman backed it up with top marks in American History, Advanced Placement Calculus, and Microbiology. The crowning touch was a perfect 100 in Physics. Though still a social outcast, Stallman finished his 11 months at Brandeis as the fourth-ranked student in a class of 789.

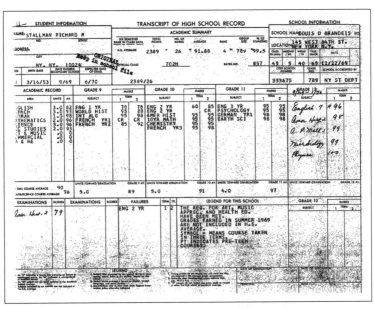

Stallman's senior-year transcript at Louis D. Brandeis H.S., November, 1969. Note turnaround in English class performance. "He was forced to kowtow to a certain degree," says his mother, "but he did it."

Outside the classroom, Stallman pursued his studies with even more diligence, rushing off to fulfill his laboratory-assistant duties at Rockefeller University during the week and dodging the Vietnam protesters on his way to Saturday school at Columbia. It was there, while the rest of the Science Honors Program students sat around discussing their college choices, that Stallman finally took a moment to participate in the preclass bull session.

Recalls Breidbart, "Most of the students were going to Harvard and MIT, of course, but you had a few going to other Ivy League schools. As the conversation circled the room, it became apparent that Richard hadn't said anything yet. I don't know who it was, but somebody got up the courage to ask him what he planned to do."

Thirty years later, Breidbart remembers the moment clearly. As soon as Stallman broke the news that he, too, would be attending Harvard University in the fall, an awkward silence filled the room. Almost as if on cue, the corners of Stallman's mouth slowly turned upward into a self-satisfied smile.

Says Breidbart, "It was his silent way of saying, 'That's right. You haven't got rid of me yet.'"

ENDNOTES

1. See Michael Gross, "Richard Stallman: High School Misfit, Symbol of Free Software, MacArthur-certified Genius" (1999). This interview is one of the most candid Stallman interviews on the record. I recommend it highly.

   http://www.mgross.com/interviews/stallman1.html

2. See Judy Steed, *Toronto Star*, BUSINESS, (October 9, 2000): C03.

   His vision of free software and social cooperation stands in stark contrast to the isolated nature of his private life. A Glenn Gould–like eccentric, the Canadian pianist was similarly brilliant, articulate, and lonely. Stallman considers himself afflicted, to some degree, by autism: a condition that, he says, makes it difficult for him to interact with people.

3. See Steve Silberman, "The Geek Syndrome," *Wired* (December, 2001).

   http://www.wired.com/wired/archive/9.12/aspergers_pr.html

4. Regrettably, I did not get a chance to interview Daniel Stallman for this book. During the early research for this book, Stallman informed me that his father suffered from Alzheimer's. When I resumed research in late 2001, I learned, sadly, that Daniel Stallman had died earlier in the year.

5. Stallman, an atheist, would probably quibble with this description. Suffice it to say, it was something Stallman welcomed. See previous note 1: "As soon as I heard about computers, I wanted to see one and play with one."

CHAPTER 4

IMPEACH GOD

Although their relationship was fraught with tension, Richard Stallman would inherit one noteworthy trait from his mother: a passion for progressive politics.

It was an inherited trait that would take several decades to emerge, however. For the first few years of his life, Stallman lived in what he now admits was a "political vacuum."[1] Like most Americans during the Eisenhower age, the Stallman family spent the 50s trying to recapture the normalcy lost during the wartime years of the 1940s.

"Richard's father and I were Democrats but happy enough to leave it at that," says Lippman, recalling the family's years in Queens. "We didn't get involved much in local or national politics."

That all began to change, however, in the late 1950s when Alice divorced Daniel Stallman. The move back to Manhattan represented more than a change of address; it represented a new, independent identity and a jarring loss of tranquility.

"I think my first taste of political activism came when I went to the Queens public library and discovered there was only a single book on divorce in the whole library," recalls Lippman. "It was very controlled by the Catholic church, at least in Elmhurst, where we lived. I think that was the first inkling I had of the forces that quietly control our lives."

Returning to her childhood neighborhood, Manhattan's Upper West Side, Lippman was shocked by the changes that had taken place since her departure to Hunter College a decade and a half before. The skyrocketing demand for postwar housing had turned the neighborhood into a political battleground. On one side stood the pro-development city-hall politicians and businessmen hoping to rebuild many of the neighborhood's blocks to accommodate the growing number of white-collar workers moving into the city. On the other side stood the poor Irish and Puerto Rican tenants who had found an affordable haven in the neighborhood.

At first, Lippman didn't know which side to choose. As a new resident, she felt the need for new housing. As a single mother with minimal income, however, she shared the poorer tenants' concern over the growing number of development projects catering mainly to wealthy residents. Indignant, Lippman began looking for ways to combat the political machine that was attempting to turn her neighborhood into a clone of the Upper East Side.

Lippman says her first visit to the local Democratic party headquarters came in 1958. Looking for a day-care center to take care of her son while she worked, she had been appalled by the conditions encountered at one of the city-owned centers that catered to low-income residents. "All I remember is the stench of rotten milk, the dark hallways, the paucity of supplies. I had been a teacher in private nursery schools. The contrast was so great. We took one look at that room and left. That stirred me up."

The visit to the party headquarters proved disappointing, however. Describing it as "the proverbial smoke-filled room," Lippman says she became aware for the first time that corruption within the party might actually be the reason behind the city's thinly disguised hostility toward poor residents. Instead of going back to the headquarters, Lippman decided to join up with one of the many clubs aimed at reforming the Democratic party and ousting the last vestiges of the Tammany Hall machine. Dubbed the Woodrow Wilson/FDR Reform Democratic Club, Lippman and her club began showing up at planning and city-council meetings, demanding a greater say.

"Our primary goal was to fight Tammany Hall, Carmine DeSapio and his henchman,"[2] says Lippman. "I was the representative to the city council and was very much involved in creating a viable urban-renewal plan that went beyond simply adding more luxury housing to the neighborhood."

Such involvement would blossom into greater political activity during the 1960s. By 1965, Lippman had become an "outspoken" supporter for political candidates like William Fitts Ryan, a Democratic elected to Congress with the help of reform clubs and one of the first U.S. representatives to speak out against the Vietnam War.

It wasn't long before Lippman, too, was an outspoken opponent of U.S. involvement in Indochina. "I was against the Vietnam war from the time Kennedy sent troops," she says. "I had read the stories by reporters and journalists sent to cover the early stages of the conflict. I really believed their forecast that it would become a quagmire."

Such opposition permeated the Stallman-Lippman household. In 1967, Lippman remarried. Her new husband, Maurice Lippman, a major in the Air National Guard, resigned his commission to demonstrate his opposition to the war. Lippman's stepson, Andrew Lippman, was at MIT and temporarily eligible for a student deferment. Still, the threat of induction should that deferment disappear, as it eventually did, made the risk of U.S. escalation all the more immediate. Finally, there was Richard who, though younger, faced the prospect of choosing between Vietnam or Canada when the war lasted into the 1970s.

"Vietnam was a major issue in our household," says Lippman. "We talked about it constantly: what would we do if the war continued, what steps Richard or his stepbrother would take if they got drafted. We were all opposed to the war and the draft. We really thought it was immoral."

For Stallman, the Vietnam War elicited a complex mixture of emotions: confusion, horror, and, ultimately, a profound sense of political impotence. As a kid who could barely cope in the mild authoritarian universe of private school, Stallman experienced a shiver whenever the thought of Army boot camp presented itself.

"I was devastated by the fear, but I couldn't imagine what to do and didn't have the guts to go demonstrate," recalls Stallman, whose March 18th birthday earned him a dreaded low number in the draft lottery when the federal government finally eliminated college deferments in 1971. "I couldn't envision moving to Canada or Sweden. The idea of getting up by myself and moving somewhere. How could I do that? I didn't know how to live by myself. I wasn't the kind of person who felt confident in approaching things like that."

Stallman says he was both impressed and shamed by the family members who did speak out. Recalling a bumper sticker on his father's car likening the My Lai massacre to similar Nazi atrocities in World War II, he says he was "excited" by his father's gesture of outrage. "I admired him for doing it," Stallman says. "But I didn't imagine that I could do anything. I was afraid that the juggernaut of the draft was going to destroy me."

Although descriptions of his own unwillingness to speak out carry a tinge of nostalgic regret, Stallman says he was ultimately turned off by the tone and direction of the anti-war movement. Like other members of the Science Honors Program, he saw the weekend demonstrations at Columbia as little more than a distracting spectacle.[3] Ultimately, Stallman says, the irrational forces driving the anti-war movement became indistinguishable from the irrational forces driving the rest of youth culture. Instead of worshiping the Beatles, girls in Stallman's age group were suddenly worshiping firebrands like Abbie Hoffman and Jerry Rubin. To a kid already struggling to comprehend his teenage peers, escapist slogans like "make love not war" had a taunting quality. Not only was it a reminder that Stallman, the short-haired outsider who hated rock 'n' roll, detested drugs, and didn't participate in campus demonstrations, wasn't getting it politically; he wasn't "getting it" sexually either.

"I didn't like the counter culture much," Stallman admits. "I didn't like the music. I didn't like the drugs. I was scared of the drugs. I especially didn't like the anti-intellectualism, and I didn't like the prejudice against technology. After all, I loved a computer.

And I didn't like the mindless anti-Americanism that I often encountered. There were people whose thinking was so simplistic that if they disapproved of the conduct of the U.S. in the Vietnam War, they had to support the North Vietnamese. They couldn't imagine a more complicated position, I guess."

Such comments alleviate feelings of timidity. They also underline a trait that would become the key to Stallman's own political maturation. For Stallman, political confidence was directly proportionate to personal confidence. By 1970, Stallman had become confident in few things outside the realm of math and science. Nevertheless, confidence in math gave him enough of a foundation to examine the anti-war movement in purely logical terms. In the process of doing so, Stallman had found the logic wanting. Although opposed to the war in Vietnam, Stallman saw no reason to disavow war as a means for defending liberty or correcting injustice. Rather than widen the breach between himself and his peers, however, Stallman elected to keep the analysis to himself.

In 1970, Stallman left behind the nightly dinnertime conversations about politics and the Vietnam War as he departed for Harvard. Looking back, Stallman describes the transition from his mother's Manhattan apartment to life in a Cambridge dorm as an "escape." Peers who watched Stallman make the transition, however, saw little to suggest a liberating experience.

"He seemed pretty miserable for the first while at Harvard," recalls Dan Chess, a classmate in the Science Honors Program who also matriculated at Harvard. "You could tell that human interaction was really difficult for him, and there was no way of avoiding it at Harvard. Harvard was an intensely social kind of place."

To ease the transition, Stallman fell back on his strengths: math and science. Like most members of the Science Honors Program, Stallman breezed through the qualifying exam for Math 55, the legendary "boot camp" class for freshman mathematics "concentrators" at Harvard. Within the class, members of the Science Honors Program formed a durable unit. "We were the math mafia," says Chess with a laugh. "Harvard was nothing, at least compared with the SHP."

To earn the right to boast, however, Stallman, Chess, and the other SHP alumni had to get through Math 55. Promising four years worth of math in two semesters, the course favored only the truly devout. "It was an amazing class," says David Harbater, a former "math mafia" member and now a professor of mathematics at the University of Pennsylvania. "It's probably safe to say there has never been a class for beginning college students that was that intense and that advanced. The phrase I say to people just to get it across is that, among other things, by the second semester we were discussing the differential geometry of Banach manifolds. That's usually when their eyes bug out, because most people don't start talking about Banach manifolds until their second year of graduate school."

Starting with 75 students, the class quickly melted down to 20 by the end of the second semester. Of that 20, says Harbater, "only 10 really knew what they were doing." Of that 10, 8 would go on to become future mathematics professors, 1 would go on to teach physics.

"The other one," emphasizes Harbater, "was Richard Stallman."

Seth Breidbart, a fellow Math 55 classmate, remembers Stallman distinguishing himself from his peers even then.

"He was a stickler in some very strange ways," says Breidbart. There is a standard technique in math which everybody does wrong. It's an abuse of notation where you have to define a function for something and what you do is you define a function and then you prove that it's well defined. Except the first time he did and presented it, he defined a relation and proved that it's a function. It's the exact same proof, but he used the correct terminology, which no one else did. That's just the way he was."

It was in Math 55 that Richard Stallman began to cultivate a reputation for brilliance. Breidbart agrees, but Chess, whose competitive streak refused to yield, says the realization that Stallman might be the best mathematician in the class didn't set in until the next year. "It was during a class on Real Analysis, which I took with Richard the next year," says Chess, now a math professor at

Hunter College. "I actually remember in a proof about complex valued measures that Richard came up with an idea that was basically a metaphor from the calculus of variations. It was the first time I ever saw somebody solve a problem in a brilliantly original way."

Chess makes no bones about it: watching Stallman's solution unfold on the chalkboard was a devastating blow. As a kid who'd always taken pride in being the smartest mathematician the room, it was like catching a glimpse of his own mortality. Years later, as Chess slowly came to accept the professional rank of a good-but-not-great mathematician, he had Stallman's sophomore-year proof to look back on as a taunting early indicator.

"That's the thing about mathematics," says Chess. "You don't have to be a first-rank mathematician to recognize first-rate mathematical talent. I could tell I was up there, but I could also tell I wasn't at the first rank. If Richard had chosen to be a mathematician, he would have been a first-rank mathematician."

For Stallman, success in the classroom was balanced by the same lack of success in the social arena. Even as other members of the math mafia gathered to take on the Math 55 problem sets, Stallman preferred to work alone. The same went for living arrangements. On the housing application for Harvard, Stallman clearly spelled out his preferences. "I said I preferred an invisible, inaudible, intangible roommate," he says. In a rare stroke of bureaucratic foresight, Harvard's housing office accepted the request, giving Stallman a one-room single for his freshman year.

Breidbart, the only math-mafia member to share a dorm with Stallman that freshman year, says Stallman slowly but surely learned how to interact with other students. He recalls how other dorm mates, impressed by Stallman's logical acumen, began welcoming his input whenever an intellectual debate broke out in the dining club or dorm commons.

"We had the usual bull sessions about solving the world's problems or what would be the result of something," recalls Breidbart. "Say somebody discovers an immortality serum. What do you do? What are the political results? If you give it to everybody, the world gets overcrowded and everybody dies. If you limit it, if you say everyone who's alive now can have it but their children can't, then you end up with an underclass of people without it. Richard was just better able than most to see the unforeseen circumstances of any decision."

Stallman remembers the discussions vividly. "I was always in favor of immortality," he says. "I was shocked that most people regarded immortality as a bad thing. How else would we be able to see what the world is like 200 years from now?"

Although a first-rank mathematician and first-rate debater, Stallman shied away from clear-cut competitive events that might have sealed his brilliant reputation. Near the end of freshman year at Harvard, Breidbart recalls how Stallman conspicuously ducked the Putnam exam, a prestigious test open to math students throughout the U.S. and Canada. In addition to giving students a chance to measure their knowledge in relation to their peers, the Putnam served as a chief recruiting tool for academic math departments. According to campus legend, the top scorer automatically qualified for a graduate fellowship at any school of his choice, including Harvard.

Like Math 55, the Putnam was a brutal test of merit. A six-hour exam in two parts, it seemed explicitly designed to separate the wheat from the chaff. Breidbart, a veteran of both the Science Honors Program and Math 55, describes it as easily the most difficult test he ever took. "Just to give you an idea of how difficult it was," says Breidbart, "the top score was a 120, and my score the first year was in the 30s. That score was still good enough to place me 101st in the country."

Surprised that Stallman, the best student in the class, had passed on the test, Breidbart says he and a fellow classmate cornered him in the dining common and demanded an explanation. "He said he was afraid of not doing well," Breidbart recalls.

Breidbart and the friend quickly wrote down a few problems from memory and gave them to Stallman. "He solved all of them," Breidbart says, "leading me to conclude that by not doing well, he either meant coming in second or getting something wrong."

Stallman remembers the episode a bit differently. "I remember that they did bring me the questions and it's possible that I solved one of them, but I'm pretty sure I didn't solve them all," he says. Nevertheless, Stallman agrees with Breidbart's recollection that fear was the primary reason for not taking the test. Despite a demonstrated willingness to point out the intellectual weaknesses of his peers and professors in the classroom, Stallman hated the notion of head-to-head competition.

"It's the same reason I never liked chess," says Stallman. "Whenever I'd play, I would become so consumed by the fear of making a single mistake that I would start making stupid mistakes very early in the game. The fear became a self-fulfilling prophecy."

Whether such fears ultimately prompted Stallman to shy away from a mathematical career is a moot issue. By the end of his freshman year at Harvard, Stallman had other interests pulling him away from the field. Computer programming, a latent fascination throughout Stallman's high-school years, was becoming a full-fledged passion. Where other math students sought occasional refuge in art and history classes, Stallman sought it in the computer-science laboratory.

For Stallman, the first taste of real computer programming at the IBM New York Scientific Center had triggered a desire to learn more. "Toward the end of my first year at Harvard school, I started to have enough courage to go visit computer labs and see what they had. I'd ask them if they had extra copies of any manuals that I could read."

Taking the manuals home, Stallman would examine machine specifications, compare them with other machines he already knew, and concoct a trial program, which he would then bring back to the lab along with the borrowed manual. Although some labs balked at the notion of a strange kid coming off the street and working on the lab machinery, most recognized competence when they saw it and let Stallman run the programs he had created.

One day, near the end of freshman year, Stallman heard about a special laboratory near MIT. The laboratory was located on the ninth floor an off-campus building in Tech Square, the newly built facility dedicated to advanced research. According to the rumors, the lab itself was dedicated to the cutting-edge science of artificial intelligence and boasted the cutting-edge machines and software programs to match.

Intrigued, Stallman decided to pay a visit.

The trip was short, about 2 miles on foot, 10 minutes by train, but as Stallman would soon find out, MIT and Harvard can feel like opposite poles of the same planet. With its maze-like tangle of interconnected office buildings, the Institute's campus offered an aesthetic yin to Harvard's spacious colonial-village yang. The same could be said for the student body, a geeky collection of ex–high school misfits known more for its predilection for pranks than its politically powerful alumni.

The yin-yang relationship extended to the AI Lab as well. Unlike Harvard computer labs, there was no grad-student gatekeeper, no clipboard waiting list for terminal access, no explicit atmosphere of "look but don't touch." Instead, Stallman found only a collection of open terminals and robotic arms, presumably the artifacts of some A.I. experiment.

Although the rumors said anybody could sit down at the terminals, Stallman decided to stick with the original plan. When he encountered a lab employee, he asked if the lab had any spare manuals it could loan to an inquisitive student. "They had some, but a lot of things weren't documented," Stallman recalls. "They were hackers after all."

Stallman left with something even better than a manual: a job. Although he doesn't remember what the first project was, he does remember coming back to the AI Lab the next week, grabbing an open terminal and writing software code.

Looking back, Stallman sees nothing unusual in the AI Lab's willingness to accept an unproven outsider at first glance. "That's the way it was back then," he says. "That's the way it still is now. I'll hire somebody when I meet him if I see he's good. Why wait? Stuffy people who insist on putting bureaucracy into everything really miss the point. If a person is good, he shouldn't have to go through a long, detailed hiring process; he should be sitting at a computer writing code."

To get a taste of "bureaucratic and stuffy," Stallman need only visit the computer labs at Harvard. There, access to the terminals was doled out according to academic rank. As an undergrad, Stallman usually had to sign up or wait until midnight, about the time most professors and grad students finished their daily work assignments. The waiting wasn't difficult, but it was frustrating. Waiting for a public terminal, knowing all the while that a half dozen equally usable machines were sitting idle inside professors' locked offices, seemed the height of illogic. Although Stallman paid the occasional visit to the Harvard computer labs, he preferred the more egalitarian policies of the AI Lab. "It was a breath of fresh air," he says. "At the AI Lab, people seemed more concerned about work than status."

Stallman quickly learned that the AI Lab's first-come, first-served policy owed much to the efforts of a vigilant few. Many were holdovers from the days of Project MAC, the Department of Defense–funded research program that had given birth to the first time-share operating systems. A few were already legends in the computing world. There was Richard Greenblatt, the lab's in-house Lisp expert and author of MacHack, the computer chess program that had once humbled A.I. critic Hubert Dreyfus. There was Gerald Sussman, original author of the robotic block-stacking program HACKER. And there was Bill Gosper, the in-house math whiz already in the midst of an 18-month hacking bender triggered by the philosophical implications of the computer game LIFE.[4]

Members of the tight-knit group called themselves "hackers." Over time, they extended the "hacker" description to Stallman as well. In the process of doing so, they inculcated Stallman in the ethical traditions of the "hacker ethic." To be a hacker meant more than just writing programs, Stallman learned. It meant writing the best possible programs. It meant sitting at a terminal for 36 hours straight if that's what it took to write the best possible programs. Most importantly, it meant having access to the best possible machines and the most useful information at all times. Hackers spoke openly about changing the world through software, and Stallman learned the instinctual hacker disdain for any obstacle that prevented a hacker from fulfilling this noble cause. Chief among these obstacles were poor software, academic bureaucracy, and selfish behavior.

Stallman also learned the lore, stories of how hackers, when presented with an obstacle, had circumvented it in creative ways. Stallman learned about "lock hacking," the art of breaking into professors' offices to "liberate" sequestered terminals. Unlike their pampered Harvard counterparts, MIT faculty members knew better than to treat the AI Lab's terminal as private property. If a faculty member made the mistake of locking away a terminal for the night, hackers were quick to correct the error. Hackers were equally quick to send a message if the mistake repeated itself. "I was actually shown a cart with a heavy cylinder of metal on it that had been used to break down the door of one professor's office,"[5] Stallman says.

Such methods, while lacking in subtlety, served a purpose. Although professors and administrators outnumbered hackers two-to-one inside the AI Lab, the hacker ethic prevailed. Indeed, by the time of Stallman's arrival at the AI Lab, hackers and the AI Lab administration had coevolved into something of a symbiotic relationship. In exchange for fixing the machines and keeping the software up and running, hackers earned the right to work on favorite pet projects. Often, the pet projects revolved around improving the machines and software programs even further. Like teenage hot-rodders, most hackers viewed tinkering with machines as its own form of entertainment.

Nowhere was this tinkering impulse better reflected than in the operating system that powered the lab's central PDP-6 mini-computer. Dubbed ITS, short for the Incompatible Time Sharing system, the operating system incorporated the hacking ethic into its very design. Hackers had built it as a protest to Project MAC's original operating system, the Compatible Time Sharing System, CTSS, and named it accordingly. At the time, hackers felt the CTSS design too restrictive, limiting programmers' power to modify and improve the program's own internal architecture if needed. According to one legend passed down by hackers, the decision to build ITS had political overtones as well. Unlike CTSS, which had been designed for the IBM 7094, ITS was built specifically for the PDP-6. In letting hackers write the systems themselves, AI Lab administrators guaranteed that only hackers would feel comfortable using the PDP-6. In the feudal world of academic research, the gambit worked. Although the PDP-6 was co-owned in conjunction with other departments, A.I. researchers soon had it to themselves.[6]

ITS boasted features most commercial operating systems wouldn't offer for years, features such as multitasking, debugging, and full-screen editing capability. Using it and the PDP-6 as a foundation, the Lab had been able to declare independence from Project MAC shortly before Stallman's arrival.[6]

As an apprentice hacker, Stallman quickly became enamored with ITS. Although forbidding to most newcomers, the program contained many built-in features that provided a lesson in software development to hacker apprentices such as himself.

"ITS had a very elegant internal mechanism for one program to examine another," says Stallman, recalling the program. "You could examine all sorts of status about another program in a very clean, well-specified way."

Using this feature, Stallman was able to watch how programs written by hackers processed instructions as they ran. Another favorite feature would allow the monitoring program to freeze the monitored program's job between instructions. In other operating systems, such a command would have resulted in half-computed gibberish or an automatic systems crash. In ITS, it provided yet another way to monitor the step-by-step performance.

"If you said, 'Stop the job,' it would always be stopped in user mode. It would be stopped between two user-mode instructions, and everything about the job would be consistent for that point," Stallman says. "If you said, 'Resume the job,' it would continue properly. Not only that, but if you were to change the status of the job and then change it back, everything would be consistent. There was no hidden status anywhere."

By the end of 1970, hacking at the AI Lab had become a regular part of Stallman's weekly schedule. From Monday to Thursday, Stallman devoted his waking hours to his Harvard classes. As soon as Friday afternoon arrived, however, he was on the T, heading down to MIT for the weekend. Stallman usually timed his arrival to coincide with the ritual food run. Joining five or six other hackers in their nightly quest for Chinese food, he would jump inside a beat-up car and head across the Harvard Bridge into nearby Boston. For the next two hours, he and his hacker colleagues would discuss everything from ITS to the internal logic of the Chinese language and pictograph system. Following dinner, the group would return to MIT and hack code until dawn.

For the geeky outcast who rarely associated with his high-school peers, it was a heady experience, suddenly hanging out with people who shared the same predilection for computers, science fiction, and Chinese food. "I remember many sunrises seen from a car coming back from Chinatown," Stallman would recall nostalgically, 15 years after the fact in a speech at the Swedish Royal Technical Institute. "It was actually a very beautiful thing to see a sunrise, 'cause that's such a calm time of day. It's a wonderful time of day to get ready to go to bed. It's so nice to walk home with the light just brightening and the birds starting to chirp; you can get a real feeling of gentle satisfaction, of tranquility about the work that you have done that night."[7]

The more Stallman hung out with the hackers, the more he adopted the hacker worldview. Already committed to the notion of personal liberty, Stallman began to infuse his actions with a sense of communal responsibility. When others violated the communal code, Stallman was quick to speak out. Within a year of his first visit, Stallman was the one breaking into locked offices, trying to recover the sequestered terminals that belonged to the lab community as a whole. In true hacker fashion, Stallman also sought to make his own personal contribution to the art of lock hacking. One of the most artful door-opening tricks, commonly attributed to Greenblatt, involved bending a stiff wire into a cane and attaching a loop of tape to the long end. Sliding the wire under the door, a hacker could twist and rotate the wire so that the long end touched the door knob. Provided the adhesive on the tape held, a hacker could open the doorknob with a few sharp twists.

When Stallman tried the trick, he found it good but wanting in a few places. Getting the tape to stick wasn't always easy, and twisting the wire in a way that turned the doorknob was similarly difficult. Stallman remembered that the hallway ceiling possessed tiles that could be slid away. Some hackers, in fact, had used the false ceiling as a way to get around locked doors, an approach that generally covered the perpetrator in fiberglass but got the job done.

Stallman considered an alternative approach. What if, instead of slipping a wire under the door, a hacker slid away one of the panels and stood over the door jamb?

Stallman took it upon himself to try it out. Instead of using a wire, Stallman draped out a long U-shaped loop of magnetic tape, fastening a loop of adhesive tape at the base of the U. Standing over the door jamb, he dangled the tape until it looped under the doorknob. Lifting the tape until the adhesive fastened, he then pulled on the left end of the tape, twisting the doorknob counter-clockwise. Sure enough, the door opened. Stallman had added a new twist to the art of lock hacking.

"Sometimes you had to kick the door after you turned the door knob," says Stallman, recalling the lingering bugginess of the new method. "It took a little bit of balance to pull it off."

Such activities reflected a growing willingness on Stallman's part to speak and act out in defense of political beliefs. The AI Lab's spirit of direct action had proved inspirational enough for Stallman to break out of the timid impotence of his teenage years. Breaking into an office to free a terminal wasn't the same as taking part in a protest march, but it was effective in ways that most protests weren't. It solved the problem at hand.

By the time of his last years at Harvard, Stallman was beginning to apply the whimsical and irreverent lessons of the AI Lab back at school.

"Did he tell you about the snake?" his mother asks at one point during an interview. "He and his dorm mates put a snake up for student election. Apparently it got a considerable number of votes."

Stallman verifies the snake candidacy with a few caveats. The snake was a candidate for election within Currier House, Stallman's dorm, not the campus-wide student council. Stallman does remember the snake attracting a fairly significant number of votes, thanks in large part to the fact that both the snake and its owner both shared the same last name. "People may have voted for it, because they thought they were voting for the owner," Stallman says. "Campaign posters said that the snake was 'slithering for' the office. We also said it was an 'at large' candidate, since it had climbed into the wall through the ventilating unit a few weeks before and nobody knew where it was."

Running a snake for dorm council was just one of several election-related pranks. In a later election, Stallman and his dorm mates nominated the house master's son. "His platform was mandatory retirement at age seven," Stallman recalls. Such pranks paled in comparison to the fake-candidate pranks on the MIT campus, however. One of the most successful fake-candidate pranks was a cat named Woodstock, which actually managed to outdraw most of the human candidates in a campus-wide election. "They never announced how many votes Woodstock got, and they treated those votes as spoiled ballots," Stallman recalls. "But the large number of spoiled ballots in that election suggested that Woodstock had actually won. A couple of years later, Woodstock was suspiciously run over by a car. Nobody knows if the driver was working for the MIT administration." Stallman says he had nothing to do with Woodstock's candidacy, "but I admired it."[8]

At the AI Lab, Stallman's political activities had a sharper-edged tone. During the 1970s, hackers faced the constant challenge of faculty members and administrators pulling an end-run around ITS and its hacker-friendly design. One of the first attempts came in the mid-1970s, as more and more faculty members began calling for a file security system to protect research data. Most other computer labs had installed such systems during late 1960s, but the AI Lab, through the insistence of Stallman and other hackers, remained a security-free zone.

For Stallman, the opposition to security was both ethical and practical. On the ethical side, Stallman pointed out that the entire art of hacking relied on intellectual openness and trust. On the practical side, he pointed to the internal structure of ITS being built to foster this spirit of openness, and any attempt to reverse that design required a major overhaul.

"The hackers who wrote the Incompatible Timesharing System decided that file protection was usually used by a self-styled system manager to get power over everyone else," Stallman would later explain. "They didn't want anyone to be able to get power over them that way, so they didn't implement that kind of a feature. The result was, that whenever something in the system was broken, you could always fix it."[9]

Through such vigilance, hackers managed to keep the AI Lab's machines security-free. Over at the nearby MIT Laboratory for Computer Sciences, however, security-minded faculty members won the day. The LCS installed its first password-based system in 1977. Once again, Stallman took it upon himself to correct what he saw as ethical laxity. Gaining access to the software code that controlled the password system, Stallman implanted a software command that sent out a message to any LCS user who attempted to choose a unique password. If a user entered "starfish," for example, the message came back something like:

I see you chose the password "starfish." I suggest that you switch to the password "carriage return." It's much easier to type, and also it stands up to the principle that there should be no passwords.[10]

Users who did enter "carriage return"—that is, users who simply pressed the Enter or Return button, entering a blank string instead of a unique password—left their accounts accessible to the world at large. As scary as that might have been for some users, it reinforced the hacker notion that Institute computers, and even

Institute computer files, belonged to the public, not private individuals. Stallman, speaking in an interview for the 1984 book *Hackers*, proudly noted that one-fifth of the LCS staff accepted this argument and employed the blank-string password.[11]

Stallman's null-string crusade would prove ultimately futile. By the early 1980s, even the AI Lab's machines were sporting password-based security systems. Even so, it represents a major milestone in terms of Stallman's personal and political maturation. To the objective observer familiar with Stallman's later career, it offers a convenient inflection point between the timid teenager afraid to speak out even on issues of life-threatening importance and the adult activist who would soon turn needling and cajoling into a full-time occupation.

In voicing his opposition to computer security, Stallman drew on many of the forces that had shaped his early life: hunger for knowledge, distaste for authority, and frustration over hidden procedures and rules that rendered some people clueless outcasts. He would also draw on the ethical concepts that would shape his adult life: communal responsibility, trust, and the hacker spirit of direct action. Expressed in software-computing terms, the null string represents the 1.0 version of the Richard Stallman political worldview—incomplete in a few places but, for the most part, fully mature.

Looking back, Stallman hesitates to impart too much significance to an event so early in his hacking career. "In that early stage there were a lot of people who shared my feelings," he says. "The large number of people who adopted the null string as their password was a sign that many people agreed that it was the proper thing to do. I was simply inclined to be an activist about it."

Stallman does credit the AI Lab for awakening that activist spirit, however. As a teenager, Stallman had observed political events with little idea as to how a single individual could do or say anything of importance. As a young adult, Stallman was speaking out on matters in which he felt supremely confident, matters such as software design, communal responsibility, and individual freedom. "I joined this community which had a way of life which involved respecting each other's freedom," he says. "It didn't take me long to figure out that that was a good thing. It took me longer to come to the conclusion that this was a moral issue."

Hacking at the AI Lab wasn't the only activity helping to boost Stallman's esteem. During the middle of his sophomore year at Harvard, Stallman had joined up with a dance troupe that specialized in folk dances. What began as a simple attempt to meet women and expand his social horizons soon expanded into yet another passion alongside hacking. Dancing in front of audiences dressed in the native garb of a Balkan peasant, Stallman no longer felt like the awkward, uncoordinated 10-year-old whose attempts to play football had ended in frustration. He felt confident, agile, and alive. For a brief moment, he even felt a hint of emotional connection. He soon found being in front of an audience fun, and it wasn't long thereafter that he began craving the performance side of dancing almost as much as the social side.

Although the dancing and hacking did little to improve Stallman's social standing, they helped him overcome the feelings of weirdness that had clouded his pre-Harvard life. Instead of lamenting his weird nature, Stallman found ways to celebrate it. In 1977, while attending a science-fiction convention, he came across a woman selling custom-made buttons. Excited, Stallman ordered a button with the words "Impeach God" emblazoned on it.

For Stallman, the "Impeach God" message worked on many levels. An atheist since early childhood, Stallman first saw it as an attempt to set a "second front" in the ongoing debate on religion. "Back then everybody was arguing about God being dead or alive," Stallman recalls. "'Impeach God' approached the subject of God from a completely different viewpoint. If God was so powerful as to create the world and yet do nothing to correct the problems in it, why would we ever want to worship such a God? Wouldn't it be better to put him on trial?"

At the same time, "Impeach God" was a satirical take on America and the American political system. The Watergate scandal of the 1970s affected Stallman deeply. As a child, Stallman had grown up mistrusting authority. Now, as an adult, his mistrust had been solidified by the culture of the AI Lab hacker community. To the hackers, Watergate was merely a Shakespearean rendition of the daily power struggles that made life such a hassle for those without privilege. It was an outsized parable for what happened when people traded liberty and openness for security and convenience.

Buoyed by growing confidence, Stallman wore the button proudly. People curious enough to ask him about it received the same well-prepared spiel. "My name is Jehovah," Stallman would say. "I have a special plan to save the universe, but because of heavenly security reasons I can't tell you what that plan is. You're just going to have to put your faith in me, because I see the picture and you don't. You know I'm good because I told you so. If you don't believe me, I'll throw you on my enemies list and throw you in a pit where Infernal Revenue Service will audit your taxes for eternity."

Those who interpreted the spiel as a word-for-word parody of the Watergate hearings only got half the message. For Stallman, the other half of the message was something only his fellow hackers seemed to be hearing. One hundred years after Lord Acton warned about absolute power corrupting absolutely, Americans seemed to have forgotten the first part of Acton's truism: power, itself, corrupts. Rather than point out the numerous examples of petty corruption, Stallman felt content voicing his outrage toward an entire system that trusted power in the first place.

"I figured why stop with the small fry," says Stallman, recalling the button and its message. "If we went after Nixon, why not going after Mr. Big. The way I see it, any being that has power and abuses it deserves to have that power taken away."

ENDNOTES

1. See Michael Gross, "Richard Stallman: High School Misfit, Symbol of Free Software, MacArthur-certified Genius" (1999).

2. Carmine DeSapio holds the dubious distinction of being the first Italian-American boss of Tammany Hall, the New York City political machine. For more information on DeSapio and the politics of post-war New York, see John Davenport, "Skinning the Tiger: Carmine DeSapio and the End of the Tammany Era," *New York Affairs* (1975): 3:1.

3. Chess, another Columbia Science Honors Program alum, describes the protests as "background noise." "We were all political," he says, "but the SHP was imporant. We would never have skipped it for a demonstration."

4. See Steven Levy, *Hackers* (Penguin USA [paperback], 1984): 144.

   Levy devotes about five pages to describing Gosper's fascination with LIFE, a math-based software game first created by British mathematician John Conway. I heartily recommend this book as a supplement, perhaps even a prerequisite, to this one.

5. Gerald Sussman, an MIT faculty member and hacker whose work at the AI Lab predates Stallman's, disputes this memory. According to Sussman, the hackers never broke any doors to retrieve terminals.

6. I apologize for the whirlwind summary of ITS' genesis, an operating system many hackers still regard as the epitome of the hacker ethos. For more information on the program's political significance, see Simson Garfinkel, *Architects of the Information Society: Thirty-Five Years of the Laboratory for Computer Science at MIT* (MIT Press, 1999).

7. See Richard Stallman, "RMS lecture at KTH (Sweden)," (October 30, 1986).

   http://www.gnu.org/philosophy/stallman-kth.html

8. In an email shortly after this book went into its final edit cycle, Stallman says he drew political inspiration from the Harvard campus as well. "In my first year of Harvard, in a Chinese History class, I read the story of the first revolt against the Chin dynasty," he says. "The story is not reliable history, but it was very moving."

9. See Richard Stallman (1986).

10. See Steven Levy, *Hackers* (Penguin USA [paperback], 1984): 417. I have modified this quote, which Levy also uses as an excerpt, to illustrate more directly how the program might reveal the false security of the system. Levy uses the placeholder "[such and such]."

11. See Steven Levy, *Hackers* (Penguin USA [paperback], 1984): 417.

CHAPTER 5

SMALL PUDDLE OF FREEDOM

Ask anyone who's spent more than a minute in Richard Stallman's presence, and you'll get the same recollection: forget the long hair. Forget the quirky demeanor. The first thing you notice is the gaze. One look into Stallman's green eyes, and you know you're in the presence of a true believer.

To call the Stallman gaze intense is an understatement. Stallman's eyes don't just look at you; they look through you. Even when your own eyes momentarily shift away out of simple primate politeness, Stallman's eyes remain locked-in, sizzling away at the side of your head like twin photon beams.

Maybe that's why most writers, when describing Stallman, tend to go for the religious angle. In a 1998 Salon.com article titled "The Saint of Free Software," Andrew Leonard describes Stallman's green eyes as "radiating the power of an Old Testament prophet."[1] A 1999 *Wired* magazine article describes the Stallman beard as "Rasputin-like,"[2] while a *London Guardian* profile describes the Stallman smile as the smile of "a disciple seeing Jesus."[3]

Such analogies serve a purpose, but they ultimately fall short. That's because they fail to take into account the vulnerable side of the Stallman persona. Watch the Stallman gaze for an extended period of time, and you will begin to notice a subtle change. What appears at first to be an attempt to intimidate or hypnotize reveals itself upon second and third viewing as a frustrated attempt to build and maintain contact. If, as Stallman himself has suspected from time to time, his personality is the product of autism or Asperger Syndrome, his eyes certainly confirm the diagnosis. Even at their most high-beam level of intensity, they have a tendency to grow cloudy and distant, like the eyes of a wounded animal preparing to give up the ghost.

My own first encounter with the legendary Stallman gaze dates back to the March, 1999, LinuxWorld Convention and Expo in San Jose, California. Billed as a "coming out party" for the Linux software community, the convention also stands out as the event that reintroduced Stallman to the technology media. Determined to push for his proper share of credit, Stallman used the event to instruct spectators and reporters alike on the history of the GNU Project and the project's overt political objectives.

As a reporter sent to cover the event, I received my own Stallman tutorial during a press conference announcing the release of GNOME 1.0, a free software graphic user interface. Unwittingly, I push an entire bank of hot buttons when I throw out my very first question to Stallman himself: do you think GNOME's maturity will affect the commercial popularity of the Linux operating system?

"I ask that you please stop calling the operating system Linux," Stallman responds, eyes immediately zeroing in on mine. "The Linux kernel is just a small part of the operating system. Many of the software programs that make up the operating system you call Linux were not developed by Linus Torvalds at all. They were created by GNU Project volunteers, putting in their own personal time so that users might have a free operating system like the one we have today. To not acknowledge the contribution of those programmers is both impolite and a misrepresentation of history. That's why I ask that when you refer to the operating system, please call it by its proper name, GNU/Linux."

Taking the words down in my reporter's notebook, I notice an eerie silence in the crowded room. When I finally look up, I find Stallman's unblinking eyes waiting for me. Timidly, a second reporter throws out a question, making sure to use the term "GNU/Linux" instead of Linux. Miguel de Icaza, leader of the GNOME project, fields the question. It isn't until halfway through de Icaza's answer, however, that Stallman's eyes finally unlock from mine. As soon as they do, a mild shiver rolls down my back. When Stallman starts lecturing another reporter over a perceived error in diction, I feel a guilty tinge of relief. At least he isn't looking at me, I tell myself.

For Stallman, such face-to-face moments would serve their purpose. By the end of the first LinuxWorld show, most reporters know better than to use the term "Linux" in his presence, and wired.com is running a story comparing Stallman to a pre-Stalinist revolutionary erased from the history books by hackers and entrepreneurs eager to downplay the GNU Project's overly political objectives.[2] Other articles follow, and while few reporters call the operating system GNU/Linux in print, most are quick to credit Stallman for launching the drive to build a free software operating system 15 years before.

I won't meet Stallman again for another 17 months. During the interim, Stallman will revisit Silicon Valley once more for the August, 1999 LinuxWorld show. Although not invited to speak, Stallman does managed to deliver the event's best line. Accepting the show's Linus Torvalds Award for Community Service—an award named after Linux creator Linus Torvalds—on behalf of the Free Software Foundation, Stallman wisecracks, "Giving the Linus Torvalds Award to the Free Software Foundation is a bit like giving the Han Solo Award to the Rebel Alliance."

This time around, however, the comments fail to make much of a media dent. Midway through the week, Red Hat, Inc., a prominent GNU/Linux vendor, goes public. The news merely confirms what many reporters such as myself already suspect: "Linux" has become a Wall Street buzzword, much like "e-commerce" and "dot-com" before it. With the stock market approaching the Y2K rollover like a hyperbola approaching its vertical asymptote, all talk of free software or open source as a political phenomenon falls by the wayside.

Maybe that's why, when LinuxWorld follows up its first two shows with a third LinuxWorld show in August, 2000, Stallman is conspicuously absent.

My second encounter with Stallman and his trademark gaze comes shortly after that third LinuxWorld show. Hearing that Stallman is going to be in Silicon Valley, I set up a lunch interview in Palo Alto, California. The meeting place seems ironic, not only because of the recent no-show but also because of the overall backdrop. Outside of Redmond, Washington, few cities offer a more direct testament to the economic value of proprietary software. Curious to see how Stallman, a man who has spent the better part of his life railing against our culture's predilection toward greed and selfishness, is coping in a city where even garage-sized bungalows run in the half-million-dollar price range, I make the drive down from Oakland.

I follow the directions Stallman has given me, until I reach the headquarters of Art.net, a nonprofit "virtual artists collective." Located in a hedge-shrouded house in the northern corner of the city, the Art.net headquarters are refreshingly run-down. Suddenly, the idea of Stallman lurking in the heart of Silicon Valley doesn't seem so strange after all.

I find Stallman sitting in a darkened room, tapping away on his gray laptop computer. He looks up as soon as I enter the room, giving me a full blast of his 200-watt gaze. When he offers a soothing "Hello," I offer a return greeting. Before the words come out, however, his eyes have already shifted back to the laptop screen.

"I'm just finishing an article on the spirit of hacking," Stallman says, fingers still tapping. "Take a look."

I take a look. The room is dimly lit, and the text appears as greenish-white letters on a black background, a reversal of the color scheme used by most desktop word-processing programs, so it takes my eyes a moment to adjust. When they do, I find myself reading Stallman's account of a recent meal at a Korean restaurant. Before the meal, Stallman makes an interesting discovery: the person setting the table has left six chopsticks instead of the usual two in front of Stallman's place setting. Where most restaurant goers would have ignored the redundant pairs, Stallman takes it as challenge: find a way to use all six chopsticks at once. Like many software hacks, the successful solution is both clever and silly at the same time. Hence Stallman's decision to use it as an illustration.

As I read the story, I feel Stallman watching me intently. I look over to notice a proud but child-like half smile on his face. When I praise the essay, my comment barely merits a raised eyebrow.

"I'll be ready to go in a moment," he says.

Stallman goes back to tapping away at his laptop. The laptop is gray and boxy, not like the sleek, modern laptops that seemed to be a programmer favorite at the recent LinuxWorld show. Above the keyboard rides a smaller, lighter keyboard, a testament to Stallman's aging hands. During the late 1980s, when Stallman was putting in 70- and 80-hour work weeks writing the first free software tools and programs for the GNU Project, the pain in Stallman's hands became so unbearable that he had to hire a typist. Today, Stallman relies on a keyboard whose keys require less pressure than a typical computer keyboard.

Stallman has a tendency to block out all external stimuli while working. Watching his eyes lock onto the screen and his fingers dance, one quickly gets the sense of two old friends locked in deep conversation.

The session ends with a few loud keystrokes and the slow disassembly of the laptop.

"Ready for lunch?" Stallman asks.

We walk to my car. Pleading a sore ankle, Stallman limps along slowly. Stallman blames the injury on a tendon in his left foot. The injury is three years old and has gotten so bad that Stallman, a huge fan of folk dancing, has been forced to give up all dancing activities. "I love folk dancing inherently," Stallman laments. "Not being able to dance has been a tragedy for me."

Stallman's body bears witness to the tragedy. Lack of exercise has left Stallman with swollen cheeks and a pot belly that was much less visible the year before. You can tell the weight gain has been dramatic, because when Stallman walks, he arches his back like a pregnant woman trying to accommodate an unfamiliar load. The walk is further slowed by Stallman's willingness to stop and smell the roses, literally. Spotting a particularly beautiful blossom, he tickles the innermost petals with his prodigious nose, takes a deep sniff and steps back with a contented sigh.

"Mmm, *rhinophytophilia*,"[4] he says, rubbing his back.

The drive to the restaurant takes less than three minutes. Upon recommendation from Tim Ney, former executive director of the Free Software Foundation, I have let Stallman choose the restaurant. While some reporters zero in on Stallman's monk-like lifestyle, the truth is, Stallman is a committed epicure when it comes to food. One of the fringe benefits of being a traveling missionary for the free software cause is the ability to sample delicious food from around the world. "Visit almost any major city in the world, and chances are Richard knows the best restaurant in town," says Ney. "Richard also takes great pride in knowing what's on the menu and ordering for the entire the table."

For today's meal, Stallman has chosen a Cantonese-style dim sum restaurant two blocks off University Avenue, Palo Alto's main drag. The choice is partially inspired by Stallman's recent visit to China, including a lecture stop in Guangdong province, in addition to Stallman's personal aversion to spicier Hunanese and Szechuan cuisine. "I'm not a big fan of spicy," Stallman admits.

We arrive a few minutes after 11 a.m. and find ourselves already subject to a 20-minute wait. Given the hacker aversion to lost time, I hold my breath momentarily, fearing an outburst. Stallman, contrary to expectations, takes the news in stride.

"It's too bad we couldn't have found somebody else to join us," he tells me. "It's always more fun to eat with a group of people."

During the wait, Stallman practices a few dance steps. His moves are tentative but skilled. We discuss current events. Stallman says his only regret about not attending LinuxWorld was missing out on a press conference announcing the launch of the GNOME Foundation. Backed by Sun Microsystems and IBM, the foundation is in many ways a vindication for Stallman, who has long championed that free software and free-market economics need not be mutually exclusive. Nevertheless, Stallman remains dissatisfied by the message that came out.

"The way it was presented, the companies were talking about Linux with no mention of the GNU Project at all," Stallman says.

Such disappointments merely contrast the warm response coming from overseas, especially Asia, Stallman notes. A quick glance at the Stallman 2000 travel itinerary bespeaks the growing popularity of the free software message. Between recent visits to India, China, and Brazil, Stallman has spent 12 of the last 115 days on United States soil. His travels have given him an opportunity to see how the free software concept translates into different languages of cultures.

"In India many people are interested in free software, because they see it as a way to build their computing infrastructure without spending a lot of money," Stallman says. "In China, the concept has been much slower to catch on. Comparing free software to free speech is harder to do when you don't have any free speech. Still, the level of interest in free software during my last visit was profound."

The conversation shifts to Napster, the San Mateo, California software company, which has become something of a media cause célèbre in recent months. The company markets a controversial software tool that lets music fans browse and copy the music files of other music fans. Thanks to the magnifying powers of the Internet, this so-called "peer-to-peer" program has evolved into a de facto online juke box, giving ordinary music fans a way to listen to MP3 music files over the computer without paying a royalty or fee, much to record companies' chagrin.

Although based on proprietary software, the Napster system draws inspiration from the long-held Stallman contention that once a work enters the digital realm—in other words, once making a copy is less a matter of duplicating sounds or duplicating atoms and more a matter of duplicating information—the natural human impulse to share a work becomes harder to restrict. Rather than impose additional restrictions, Napster execs have decided to take advantage of the impulse. Giving music listeners a central place to trade music files, the company has gambled on its ability to steer the resulting user traffic toward other commercial opportunities.

The sudden success of the Napster model has put the fear in traditional record companies, with good reason. Just days before my Palo Alto meeting with Stallman, U.S. District Court Judge Marilyn Patel granted a request filed by the Recording Industry Association of America for an injunction against the file-sharing service. The injunction was subsequently suspended by the U.S. Ninth District Court of Appeals, but by early 2001, the Court of Appeals, too, would find the San Mateo–based company in breach of copyright law,[5] a decision RIAA spokesperson Hillary Rosen would later proclaim proclaim a "clear victory for the creative content community and the legitimate online marketplace."[6]

For hackers such as Stallman, the Napster business model is scary in different ways. The company's eagerness to appropriate time-worn hacker principles such as file sharing and communal information ownership, while at the same time selling a service based on proprietary software, sends a distressing mixed message. As a person who already has a hard enough time getting his own carefully articulated message into the media stream, Stallman is understandably reticent when it comes to speaking out about the company. Still, Stallman does admit to learning a thing or two from the social side of the Napster phenomenon.

"Before Napster, I thought it might be OK for people to privately redistribute works of entertainment," Stallman says. "The number of people who find Napster useful, however, tells me that the right to redistribute copies not only on a neighbor-to-neighbor basis, but to the public at large, is essential and therefore may not be taken away."

No sooner does Stallman say this than the door to the restaurant swings open and we are invited back inside by the host. Within a few seconds, we are seated in a side corner of the restaurant next to a large mirrored wall.

The restaurant's menu doubles as an order form, and Stallman is quickly checking off boxes before the host has even brought water to the table. "Deep-fried shrimp roll wrapped in bean-curd skin," Stallman reads. "Bean-curd skin. It offers such an interesting texture. I think we should get it."

This comment leads to an impromptu discussion of Chinese food and Stallman's recent visit to China. "The food in China is utterly exquisite," Stallman says, his voice gaining an edge of emotion for the first time this morning. "So many different things that I've never seen in the U.S., local things made from local mushrooms and local vegetables. It got to the point where I started keeping a journal just to keep track of every wonderful meal."

The conversation segues into a discussion of Korean cuisine. During the same June, 2000, Asian tour, Stallman paid a visit to South Korea. His arrival ignited a mini-firestorm in the local media thanks to a Korean software conference attended by Microsoft founder and chairman Bill Gates that same week. Next to getting his photo above Gates's photo on the front page of the top Seoul newspaper, Stallman says the best thing about the trip was the food. "I had a bowl of naeng myun, which is cold noodles," says Stallman. "These were a very interesting feeling noodle. Most places don't use quite the same kind of noodles for your naeng myun, so I can say with complete certainty that this was the most exquisite naeng myun I ever had."

The term "exquisite" is high praise coming from Stallman. I know this, because a few moments after listening to Stallman rhapsodize about naeng myun, I feel his laser-beam eyes singeing the top of my right shoulder.

"There is the most exquisite woman sitting just behind you," Stallman says.

I turn to look, catching a glimpse of a woman's back. The woman is young, somewhere in her mid-20s, and is wearing a white sequinned dress. She and her male lunch companion are in the final stages of paying the check. When both get up from the table to leave the restaurant, I can tell without looking, because Stallman's eyes suddenly dim in intensity.

"Oh, no," he says. "They're gone. And to think, I'll probably never even get to see her again."

After a brief sigh, Stallman recovers. The moment gives me a chance to discuss Stallman's reputation vis-à-vis the fairer sex. The reputation is a bit contradictory at times. A number of hackers report Stallman's predilection for greeting females with a kiss on the back of the hand.[7] A May 26, 2000 Salon.com article, meanwhile, portrays Stallman as a bit of a hacker lothario. Documenting the free software–free love connection, reporter Annalee Newitz presents Stallman as rejecting traditional family values, telling her, "I believe in love, but not monogamy."[8]

Stallman lets his menu drop a little when I bring this up. "Well, most men seem to want sex and seem to have a rather contemptuous attitude towards women," he says. "Even women they're involved with. I can't understand it at all."

I mention a passage from the 1999 book *Open Sources* in which Stallman confesses to wanting to name the ill-fated GNU kernel after a girlfriend at the time. The girlfriend's name was Alix, a name that fit perfectly with the Unix developer convention of putting an "x" at the end of any new kernel name—e.g., "Linux." Because the woman was a Unix system administrator, Stallman says it would have been an even more touching tribute. Unfortunately, Stallman notes, the kernel project's eventual main developer renamed the kernel HURD.[9] Although Stallman and the girlfriend later broke up, the story triggers an automatic question: for all the media imagery depicting him as a wild-eyed fanatic, is Richard Stallman really just a hopeless romantic, a wandering Quixote tilting at corporate windmills in an effort to impress some as-yet-unidentified Dulcinea?

"I wasn't really trying to be romantic," Stallman says, recalling the Alix story. "It was more of a teasing thing. I mean, it was romantic, but it was also teasing, you know? It would have been a delightful surprise."

For the first time all morning, Stallman smiles. I bring up the hand kissing. "Yes, I do do that," Stallman says. "I've found it's a way of offering some affection that a lot of women will enjoy. It's a chance to give some affection and to be appreciated for it."

Affection is a thread that runs clear through Richard Stallman's life, and he is painfully candid about it when questions arise. "There really hasn't been much affection in my life, except in my mind," he says. Still, the discussion quickly grows awkward. After a few one-word replies, Stallman finally lifts up his menu, cutting off the inquiry.

"Would you like some shimai?" he asks.

When the food comes out, the conversation slaloms between the arriving courses. We discuss the oft-noted hacker affection for Chinese food, the weekly dinner runs into Boston's Chinatown district during Stallman's days as a staff programmer at the AI Lab, and the underlying logic of the Chinese language and its associated writing system. Each thrust on my part elicits a well-informed parry on Stallman's part.

"I heard some people speaking Shanghainese the last time I was in China," Stallman says. "It was interesting to hear. It sounded quite different [from Mandarin]. I had them tell me some cognate words in Mandarin and Shanghainese. In some cases you can see the resemblance, but one question I was wondering about was whether tones would be similar. They're not. That's interesting to me, because there's a theory that the tones evolved from additional syllables that got lost and replaced. Their effect survives in the tone. If that's true, and I've seen claims that that happened within historic times, the dialects must have diverged before the loss of these final syllables."

The first dish, a plate of pan-fried turnip cakes, has arrived. Both Stallman and I take a moment to carve up the large rectangular cakes, which smell like boiled cabbage but taste like potato latkes fried in bacon.

I decide to bring up the outcast issue again, wondering if Stallman's teenage years conditioned him to take unpopular stands, most notably his uphill battle since 1994 to get computer users and the media to replace the popular term "Linux" with "GNU/Linux."

"I believe it did help me," Stallman says, chewing on a dumpling. "I have never understood what peer pressure does to other people. I think the reason is that I was so hopelessly rejected that for me, there wasn't anything to gain by trying to follow any of the fads. It wouldn't have made any difference. I'd still be just as rejected, so I didn't try."

Stallman points to his taste in music as a key example of his contrarian tendencies. As a teenager, when most of his high school classmates were listening to Motown and acid rock, Stallman preferred classical music. The memory leads to a rare humorous episode from Stallman's middle-school years. Following the Beatles' 1964 appearance on the Ed Sullivan Show, most of Stallman's classmates rushed out to purchase the latest Beatles albums and singles. Right then and there, Stallman says, he made a decision to boycott the Fab Four.

"I liked some of the pre-Beatles popular music," Stallman says. "But I didn't like the Beatles. I especially disliked the wild way people reacted to them. It was like: who was going to have a Beatles assembly to adulate the Beatles the most?"

When his Beatles boycott failed to take hold, Stallman looked for other ways to point out the herd-mentality of his peers. Stallman says he briefly considered putting together a rock band himself dedicated to satirizing the Liverpool group.

"I wanted to call it Tokyo Rose and the Japanese Beetles."

Given his current love for international folk music, I ask Stallman if he had a similar affinity for Bob Dylan and the other folk musicians of the early 1960s. Stallman shakes his head. "I did like Peter, Paul and Mary," he says. "That reminds me of a great filk."

When I ask for a definition of "filk," Stallman explains the concept. A filk, he says, is a popular song whose lyrics have been replaced with parody lyrics. The process of writing a filk is called filking, and it is a popular activity among hackers and science-fiction aficionados. Classic filks include "On Top of Spaghetti," a rewrite of "On Top of Old Smokey," and "Yoda," filk-master "Weird" Al Yankovic's Star Wars–oriented rendition of the Kinks tune, "Lola."

Stallman asks me if I would be interested in hearing the folk filk. As soon as I say yes, Stallman's voice begins singing in an unexpectedly clear tone:

> *How much wood could a woodchuck chuck,*
> *If a woodchuck could chuck wood?*
> *How many poles could a polak lock,*
> *If a polak could lock poles?*
> *How many knees could a negro grow,*
> *If a negro could grow knees?*
> *The answer, my dear, is stick it in your ear.*
> *The answer is to stick it in your ear.*

The singing ends, and Stallman's lips curl into another child-like half smile. I glance around at the nearby tables. The Asian families enjoying their Sunday lunch pay little attention to the bearded alto in their midst.[10] After a few moments of hesitation, I finally smile too.

"Do you want that last cornball?" Stallman asks, eyes twinkling. Before I can screw up the punch line, Stallman grabs the corn-encrusted dumpling with his two chopsticks and lifts it proudly. "Maybe I'm the one who should get the cornball," he says.

The food gone, our conversation assumes the dynamics of a normal interview. Stallman reclines in his chair and cradles a cup of tea in his hands. We resume talking about Napster and its relation to the free software movement. Should the principles of free software be extended to similar arenas such as music publishing? I ask.

"It's a mistake to transfer answers from one thing to another," says Stallman, contrasting songs with software programs. "The right approach is to look at each type of work and see what conclusion you get."

When it comes to copyrighted works, Stallman says he divides the world into three categories. The first category involves "functional" works—e.g., software programs, dictionaries, and textbooks. The second category involves works that might best be described as "testimonial"—e.g., scientific papers and historical documents. Such works serve a purpose that would be undermined if subsequent readers or authors were free to modify the work at will. The final category involves works of personal expression—e.g., diaries, journals, and autobiographies. To modify such documents would be to alter a person's recollections or point of view—action Stallman considers ethically unjustifiable.

Of the three categories, the first should give users the unlimited right to make modified versions, while the second and third should regulate that right according to the will of the original author. Regardless of category, however, the freedom to copy and redistribute noncommercially should remain unabridged at all times, Stallman insists. If that means giving Internet users the right to generate a hundred copies of an article, image, song, or book and then email the copies to a hundred strangers, so be it. "It's clear that private occasional redistribution must be permitted, because only a police state can stop that," Stallman says. "It's antisocial to come between people and their friends. Napster has convinced me that we also need to permit, must permit, even noncommercial redistribution to the public for the fun of it. Because so many people want to do that and find it so useful."

When I ask whether the courts would accept such a permissive outlook, Stallman cuts me off.

"That's the wrong question," he says. "I mean now you've changed the subject entirely from one of ethics to one of interpreting laws. And those are two totally different questions in the same field. It's useless to jump from one to the other. How the courts would interpret the existing laws is mainly in a harsh way, because that's the way these laws have been bought by publishers."

The comment provides an insight into Stallman's political philosophy: just because the legal system currently backs up businesses' ability to treat copyright as the software equivalent of land title doesn't mean computer users have to play the game according to those rules. Freedom is an ethical issue, not a legal issue. "I'm looking beyond what the existing laws are to what they should be," Stallman says. "I'm not trying to draft legislation. I'm

thinking about what should the law do? I consider the law prohib-
iting the sharing of copies with your friend the moral equivalent of
Jim Crow. It does not deserve respect."

The invocation of Jim Crow prompts another question. How
much influence or inspiration does Stallman draw from past political leaders? Like the civil-rights movement of the 1950s and
1960s, his attempt to drive social change is based on an appeal to
timeless values: freedom, justice, and fair play.

Stallman divides his attention between my analogy and a particularly tangled strand of hair. When I stretch the analogy to the
point where I'm comparing Stallman with Dr. Martin Luther
King, Jr., Stallman, after breaking off a split end and popping it
into his mouth, cuts me off.

"I'm not in his league, but I do play the same game," he says,
chewing.

I suggest Malcolm X as another point of comparison. Like
the former Nation of Islam spokesperson, Stallman has built up a
reputation for courting controversy, alienating potential allies,
and preaching a message favoring self-sufficiency over cultural
integration.

Chewing on another split end, Stallman rejects the comparison. "My message is closer to King's message," he says. "It's a
universal message. It's a message of firm condemnation of certain
practices that mistreat others. It's not a message of hatred for
anyone. And it's not aimed at a narrow group of people. I invite
anyone to value freedom and to have freedom."

Even so, a suspicious attitude toward political alliances
remains a fundamental Stallman character trait. In the case of his
well-publicized distaste for the term "open source," the unwillingness to participate in recent coalition-building projects seems
understandable. As a man who has spent the last two decades
stumping on the behalf of free software, Stallman's political capital is deeply invested in the term. Still, comments such as the "Han
Solo" wisecrack at the 1999 LinuxWorld have only reinforced the
Stallman's reputation in the software industry as a disgruntled
mossback unwilling to roll with political or marketing trends.

"I admire and respect Richard for all the work he's done," says Red Hat president Robert Young, summing up Stallman's paradoxical political nature. "My only critique is that sometimes Richard treats his friends worse than his enemies."

Stallman's unwillingness to seek alliances seems equally perplexing when you consider his political interests outside of the free software movement. Visit Stallman's offices at MIT, and you instantly find a clearinghouse of left-leaning news articles covering civil-rights abuses around the globe. Visit his web site, and you'll find diatribes on the Digital Millennium Copyright Act, the War on Drugs, and the World Trade Organization.

Given his activist tendencies, I ask, why hasn't Stallman sought a larger voice? Why hasn't he used his visibility in the hacker world as a platform to boost rather than reduce his political voice.

Stallman lets his tangled hair drop and contemplates the question for a moment.

"I hesitate to exaggerate the importance of this little puddle of freedom," he says. "Because the more well-known and conventional areas of working for freedom and a better society are tremendously important. I wouldn't say that free software is as important as they are. It's the responsibility I undertook, because it dropped in my lap and I saw a way I could do something about it. But, for example, to end police brutality, to end the war on drugs, to end the kinds of racism we still have, to help everyone have a comfortable life, to protect the rights of people who do abortions, to protect us from theocracy, these are tremendously important issues, far more important than what I do. I just wish I knew how to do something about them."

Once again, Stallman presents his political activity as a function of personal confidence. Given the amount of time it has taken him to develop and hone the free software movement's core tenets, Stallman is hesitant to jump aboard any issues or trends that might transport him into uncharted territory.

"I wish I knew I how to make a major difference on those bigger issues, because I would be tremendously proud if I could, but they're very hard and lots of people who are probably better than I am have been working on them and have gotten only so far," he says. "But as I see it, while other people were defending against these big visible threats, I saw another threat that was unguarded. And so I went to defend against that threat. It may not be as big a threat, but I was the only one there."

Chewing a final split end, Stallman suggests paying the check. Before the waiter can take it away, however, Stallman pulls out a white-colored dollar bill and throws it on the pile. The bill looks so clearly counterfeit, I can't help but pick it up and read it. Sure enough, it is counterfeit. Instead of bearing the image of a George Washington or Abe Lincoln, the bill's front side bears the image of a cartoon pig. Instead of the United States of America, the banner above the pig reads "United Swines of Avarice." The bill is for zero dollars, and when the waiter picks up the money, Stallman makes sure to tug on his sleeve.

"I added an extra zero to your tip," Stallman says, yet another half smile creeping across his lips.

The waiter, uncomprehending or fooled by the look of the bill, smiles and scurries away.

"I think that means we're free to go," Stallman says.

ENDNOTES

1. See Andrew Leonard, "The Saint of Free Software," *Salon.com* (August 1998).

   http://www.salon.com/21st/feature/1998/08/cov_31feature.html

2. See Leander Kahney, "Linux's Forgotten Man," *Wired News* (March 5, 1999).

   http://www.wired.com/news/print/0,1294,18291,00.html

3. See "Programmer on moral high ground; Free software is a moral issue for Richard Stallman believes in freedom and free software." *London Guardian* (November 6, 1999).

   These are just a small sampling of the religious comparisons. To date, the most extreme comparison has to go to Linus Torvalds, who, in his autobiography—see Linus Torvalds and David Diamond, *Just For Fun: The Story of an Accidentaly Revolutionary* (HarperCollins Publishers, Inc., 2001): 58—writes "Richard Stallman is the God of Free Software."

Honorable mention goes to Larry Lessig, who, in a footnote description of Stallman in his book—see Larry Lessig, *The Future of Ideas* (Random House, 2001): 270—likens Stallman to Moses:

> ... *as with Moses, it was another leader, Linus Torvalds, who finally carried the movement into the promised land by facilitating the development of the final part of the OS puzzle. Like Moses, too, Stallman is both respected and reviled by allies within the movement. He is [an] unforgiving, and hence for many inspiring, leader of a critically important aspect of modern culture. I have deep respect for the principle and commitment of this extraordinary individual, though I also have great respect for those who are courageous enough to question his thinking and then sustain his wrath.*

In a final interview with Stallman, I asked him his thoughts about the religious comparisons. "Some people do compare me with an Old Testament prophet, and the reason is Old Testament prophets said certain social practices were wrong. They wouldn't compromise on moral issues. They couldn't be bought off, and they were usually treated with contempt."

4. At the time, I thought Stallman was referring to the flower's scientific name. Months later, I would learn that *rhinophytophilia* was in fact a humorous reference to the activity, i.e., Stallman sticking his nose into a flower and enjoying the moment. For another humorous Stallman flower incident, visit:

    http://www.stallman.org/texas.html

5. See Cecily Barnes and Scott Ard, "Court Grants Stay of Napster Injunction," *News.com* (July 28, 2000).

    http://news.cnet.com/news/0-1005-200-2376465.html

6. See "A Clear Victory for Recording Industry in Napster Case," RIAA press release (February 12, 2001).

    http://www.riaa.com/PR_story.cfm?id=372

7. See Mae Ling Mak, "Mae Ling's Story" (December 17, 1998).

    http://www.crackmonkey.org/pipermail/crackmonkey/1998q4/003006.htm

    So far, Mak is the only person I've found willing to speak on the record in regard to this practice, although I've heard this from a few other female sources. Mak, despite expressing initial revulsion at it, later managed to put aside her misgivings and dance with Stallman at a 1999 LinuxWorld show.

    http://www.linux.com/interact/potd.phtml?potd_id=44

8. See Annalee Newitz, "If Code is Free Why Not Me?" *Salon.com* (May 26, 2000).

    http://www.salon.com/tech/feature/2000/05/26/free_love/print.html

9. See Richard Stallman, "The GNU Operating System and the Free Software Movement," *Open Sources* (O'Reilly & Associates, Inc., 1999): 65.

10. For more Stallman filks, visit *http://www.stallman.org/doggerel.html*. To hear Stallman singing "The Free Software Song," visit *http://www.gnu.org/music/free-software-song.html*.

CHAPTER 6

THE EMACS COMMUNE

The AI Lab of the 1970s was by all accounts a special place. Cutting-edge projects and top-flight researchers gave it an esteemed position in the world of computer science. The internal hacker culture and its anarchic policies lent a rebellious mystique as well. Only later, when many of the lab's scientists and software superstars had departed, would hackers fully realize the unique and ephemeral world they had once inhabited.

"It was a bit like the Garden of Eden," says Stallman, summing up the lab and its software-sharing ethos in a 1998 Forbes article. "It hadn't occurred to us not to cooperate."[1]

Such mythological descriptions, while extreme, underline an important fact. The ninth floor of 545 Tech Square was more than a workplace for many. For hackers such as Stallman, it was home.

The word "home" is a weighted term in the Stallman lexicon. In a pointed swipe at his parents, Stallman, to this day, refuses to acknowledge any home before Currier House, the dorm he lived in during his days at Harvard. He has also been known to describe leaving that home in tragicomic terms. Once, while describing his years at Harvard, Stallman said his only regret was getting kicked out. It wasn't until I asked Stallman what precipitated his ouster, that I realized I had walked into a classic Stallman setup line.

"At Harvard they have this policy where if you pass too many classes they ask you to leave," Stallman says.

With no dorm and no desire to return to New York, Stallman followed a path blazed by Greenblatt, Gosper, Sussman, and the many other hackers before him. Enrolling at MIT as a grad student, Stallman rented an apartment in nearby Cambridge but soon viewed the AI Lab itself as his de facto home. In a 1986 speech, Stallman recalled his memories of the AI Lab during this period:

> *I may have done a little bit more living at the lab than most people, because every year or two for some reason or other I'd have no apartment and I would spend a few months living at the lab. And I've always found it very comfortable, as well as nice and cool in the summer. But it was not at all uncommon to find people falling asleep at the lab, again because of their enthusiasm; you stay up as long as you possibly can hacking, because you just don't want to stop. And then when you're completely exhausted, you climb over to the nearest soft horizontal surface. A very informal atmosphere.*[2]

The lab's home-like atmosphere could be a problem at times. What some saw as a dorm, others viewed as an electronic opium den. In the 1976 book *Computer Power and Human Reason,* MIT researcher Joseph Weizenbaum offered a withering critique of the "computer bum," Weizenbaum's term for the hackers who populated computer rooms such as the AI Lab. "Their rumpled clothes, their unwashed hair and unshaved faces, and their uncombed hair all testify that they are oblivious to their bodies and to the world in which they move," Weizenbaum wrote. "[Computer bums] exist, at least when so engaged, only through and for the computers."[3]

Almost a quarter century after its publication, Stallman still bristles when hearing Weizenbaum's "computer bum" description, discussing it in the present tense as if Weizenbaum himself was still in the room. "He wants people to be just professionals, doing it for the money and wanting to get away from it and forget about it as soon as possible," Stallman says. "What he sees as a normal state of affairs, I see as a tragedy."

Hacker life, however, was not without tragedy. Stallman characterizes his transition from weekend hacker to full-time AI Lab denizen as a series of painful misfortunes that could only be eased through the euphoria of hacking. As Stallman himself has said, the first misfortune was his graduation from Harvard. Eager to continue his studies in physics, Stallman enrolled as a graduate student at MIT. The choice of schools was a natural one. Not only did it give Stallman the chance to follow the footsteps of great MIT alumni: William Shockley ('36), Richard P. Feynman ('39), and Murray Gell-Mann ('51), it also put him two miles closer to the AI Lab and its new PDP-10 computer. "My attention was going toward programming, but I still thought, well, maybe I can do both," Stallman says.

Toiling in the fields of graduate-level science by day and programming in the monastic confines of the AI Lab by night, Stallman tried to achieve a perfect balance. The fulcrum of this geek teeter-totter was his weekly outing with the folk-dance troupe, his one social outlet that guaranteed at least a modicum of interaction with the opposite sex. Near the end of that first year at MIT, however, disaster struck. A knee injury forced Stallman to drop out of the troupe. At first, Stallman viewed the injury as a temporary problem, devoting the spare time he would have spent dancing to working at the AI Lab even more. By the end of the summer, when the knee still ached and classes reconvened, Stallman began to worry. "My knee wasn't getting any better," Stallman recalls, "which meant I had to stop dancing completely. I was heartbroken."

With no dorm and no dancing, Stallman's social universe imploded. Like an astronaut experiencing the aftereffects of zero-gravity, Stallman found that his ability to interact with non-hackers, especially female nonhackers, had atrophied significantly. After 16 weeks in the AI Lab, the self confidence he'd been quietly accumulating during his 4 years at Harvard was virtually gone.

"I felt basically that I'd lost all my energy," Stallman recalls. "I'd lost my energy to do anything but what was most immediately tempting. The energy to do something else was gone. I was in total despair."

Stallman retreated from the world even further, focusing entirely on his work at the AI Lab. By October, 1975, he dropped out of MIT, never to go back. Software hacking, once a hobby, had become his calling.

Looking back on that period, Stallman sees the transition from full-time student to full-time hacker as inevitable. Sooner or later, he believes, the siren's call of computer hacking would have overpowered his interest in other professional pursuits. "With physics and math, I could never figure out a way to contribute," says Stallman, recalling his struggles prior to the knee injury. "I would have been proud to advance either one of those fields, but I could never see a way to do that. I didn't know where to start. With software, I saw right away how to write things that would run and be useful. The pleasure of that knowledge led me to want to do it more."

Stallman wasn't the first to equate hacking with pleasure. Many of the hackers who staffed the AI Lab boasted similar, incomplete academic résumés. Most had come in pursuing degrees in math or electrical engineering only to surrender their academic careers and professional ambitions to the sheer exhilaration that came with solving problems never before addressed. Like St. Thomas Aquinas, the scholastic known for working so long on his theological summae that he sometimes achieved spiritual visions, hackers reached transcendent internal states through sheer mental focus and physical exhaustion. Although Stallman shunned drugs, like most hackers, he enjoyed the "high" that came near the end of a 20-hour coding bender.

Perhaps the most enjoyable emotion, however, was the sense of personal fulfillment. When it came to hacking, Stallman was a natural. A childhood's worth of late-night study sessions gave him the ability to work long hours with little sleep. As a social outcast since age 10, he had little difficulty working alone. And as a mathematician with built-in gift for logic and foresight, Stallman possessed the ability to circumvent design barriers that left most hackers spinning their wheels.

"He was special," recalls Gerald Sussman, an MIT faculty member and former AI Lab researcher. Describing Stallman as a "clear thinker and a clear designer," Sussman employed Stallman as a research-project assistant beginning in 1975. The project was complex, involving the creation of an AI program that could analyze circuit diagrams. Not only did it involve an expert's command of Lisp, a programming language built specifically for AI applications, but it also required an understanding of how a human might approach the same task.

When he wasn't working on official projects such as Sussman's automated circuit-analysis program, Stallman devoted his time to pet projects. It was in a hacker's best interest to improve the lab's software infrastructure, and one of Stallman's biggest pet projects during this period was the lab's editor program TECO.

The story of Stallman's work on TECO during the 1970s is inextricably linked with Stallman's later leadership of the free software movement. It is also a significant stage in the history of computer evolution, so much so that a brief recapitulation of that evolution is necessary. During the 1950s and 1960s, when computers were first appearing at universities, computer programming was an incredibly abstract pursuit. To communicate with the machine, programmers created a series of punch cards, with each card representing an individual software command. Programmers would then hand the cards over to a central system administrator who would then insert them, one by one, into the machine, waiting for the machine to spit out a new set of punch cards, which the programmer would then decipher as output. This process, known as "batch processing," was cumbersome and time consuming. It was also prone to abuses of authority. One of the motivating factors behind hackers' inbred aversion to centralization was the power held by early system operators in dictating which jobs held top priority.

In 1962, computer scientists and hackers involved in MIT's Project MAC, an early forerunner of the AI Lab, took steps to alleviate this frustration. Time-sharing, originally known as "time stealing," made it possible for multiple programs to take advantage of a machine's operational capabilities. Teletype interfaces also made it possible to communicate with a machine not through a series of punched holes but through actual text. A programmer typed in commands and read the line-by-line output generated by the machine.

During the late 1960s, interface design made additional leaps. In a famous 1968 lecture, Doug Engelbart, a scientist then working at the Stanford Research Institute, unveiled a prototype of the modern graphical interface. Rigging up a television set to the computer and adding a pointer device which Engelbart dubbed a "mouse," the scientist created a system even more interactive than the time-sharing system developed a MIT. Treating the video display like a high-speed printer, Engelbart's system gave a user the ability to move the cursor around the screen and see the cursor position updated by the computer in real time. The user suddenly had the ability to position text anywhere on the screen.

Such innovations would take another two decades to make their way into the commercial marketplace. Still, by the 1970s, video screens had started to replace teletypes as display terminals, creating the potential for full-screen—as opposed to line-by-line—editing capabilities.

One of the first programs to take advantage of this full-screen capability was the MIT AI Lab's TECO. Short for Text Editor and COrrector, the program had been upgraded by hackers from an old teletype line editor for the lab's PDP-6 machine.[4]

TECO was a substantial improvement over old editors, but it still had its drawbacks. To create and edit a document, a programmer had to enter a series of software commands specifying each edit. It was an abstract process. Unlike modern word processors, which update text with each keystroke, TECO demanded that the user enter an extended series of editing instructions followed by an "end of command" sequence just to change the text.

Over time, a hacker grew proficient enough to write entire documents in edit mode, but as Stallman himslef would later point out, the process required "a mental skill like that of blindfold chess."[5]

To facilitate the process, AI Lab hackers had built a system that displayed both the "source" and "display" modes on a split screen. Despite this innovative hack, switching from mode to mode was still a nuisance.

TECO wasn't the only full-screen editor floating around the computer world at this time. During a visit to the Stanford Artificial Intelligence Lab in 1976, Stallman encountered an edit program named E. The program contained an internal feature, which allowed a user to update display text after each command keystroke. In the language of 1970s programming, E was one of the first rudimentary WYSIWYG editors. Short for "what you see is what you get," WYSIWYG meant that a user could manipulate the file by moving through the displayed text, as opposed to working through a back-end editor program."[6]

Impressed by the hack, Stallman looked for ways to expand TECO's functionality in similar fashion upon his return to MIT. He found a TECO feature called Control-R, written by Carl Mikkelson and named after the two-key combination that triggered it. Mikkelson's hack switched TECO from its usual abstract command-execution mode to a more intuitive keystroke-by-keystroke mode. Stallman revised the feature in a subtle but significant way. He made it possible to trigger other TECO command strings, or "macros," using other, two-key combinations. Where users had once entered command strings and discarded them after entering then, Stallman's hack made it possible to save macro tricks on file and call them up at will. Mikkelson's hack had raised TECO to the level of a WYSIWYG editor. Stallman's hack had raised it to the level of a user-programmable WYSIWYG editor. "That was the real breakthrough," says Guy Steele, a fellow AI Lab hacker at the time.[6]

By Stallman's own recollection, the macro hack touched off an explosion of further innovation. "Everybody and his brother was writing his own collection of redefined screen-editor commands, a command for everything he typically liked to do," Stallman would later recall. "People would pass them around and improve them, making them more powerful and more general. The collections of redefinitions gradually became system programs in their own right."[6]

So many people found the macro innovations useful and had incorporated it into their own TECO programs that the TECO editor had become secondary to the macro mania it inspired. "We started to categorize it mentally as a programming language rather than as an editor," Stallman says. Users were experiencing their own pleasure tweaking the software and trading new ideas.[6]

Two years after the explosion, the rate of innovation began to exhibit dangerous side effects. The explosive growth had provided an exciting validation of the collaborative hacker approach, but it had also led to over-complexity. "We had a Tower of Babel effect," says Guy Steele.

The effect threatened to kill the spirit that had created it, Steele says. Hackers had designed ITS to facilitate programmers' ability to share knowledge and improve each other's work. That meant being able to sit down at another programmer's desk, open up a programmer's work and make comments and modifications directly within the software. "Sometimes the easiest way to show somebody how to program or debug something was simply to sit down at the terminal and do it for them," explains Steele.

The macro feature, after its second year, began to foil this capability. In their eagerness to embrace the new full-screen capabilities, hackers had customized their versions of TECO to the point where a hacker sitting down at another hacker's terminal usually had to spend the first hour just figuring out what macro commands did what.

Frustrated, Steele took it upon himself to the solve the problem. He gathered together the four different macro packages and began assembling a chart documenting the most useful macro commands. In the course of implementing the design specified by the chart, Steele says he attracted Stallman's attention.

"He started looking over my shoulder, asking me what I was doing," recalls Steele.

For Steele, a soft-spoken hacker who interacted with Stallman infrequently, the memory still sticks out. Looking over another hacker's shoulder while he worked was a common activity at the AI Lab. Stallman, the TECO maintainer at the lab, deemed Steele's work "interesting" and quickly set off to complete it.

"As I like to say, I did the first 0.001 percent of the implementation, and Stallman did the rest," says Steele with a laugh.

The project's new name, Emacs, came courtesy of Stallman. Short for "editing macros," it signified the evolutionary transcendence that had taken place during the macros explosion two years before. It also took advantage of a gap in the software programming lexicon. Noting a lack of programs on ITS starting with the letter "E," Stallman chose Emacs, making it possible to reference the program with a single letter. Once again, the hacker lust for efficiency had left its mark.[6]

In the course of developing a standard system of macro commands, Stallman and Steele had to traverse a political tightrope. In creating a standard program, Stallman was in clear violation of the fundamental hacker tenet—"promote decentralization." He was also threatening to hobble the very flexibility that had fueled TECO's explosive innovation in the first place.

"On the one hand, we were trying to make a uniform command set again; on the other hand, we wanted to keep it open ended, because the programmability was important," recalls Steele.

To solve the problem, Stallman, Steele, and fellow hackers David Moon and Dan Weinreib limited their standardization effort to the WYSIWYG commands that controlled how text appeared on-screen. The rest of the Emacs effort would be devoted to retaining the program's Tinker Toy–style extensibility.

Stallman now faced another conundrum: if users made changes but didn't communicate those changes back to the rest of the community, the Tower of Babel effect would simply emerge in other places. Falling back on the hacker doctrine of sharing innovation, Stallman embedded a statement within the source code that set the terms of use. Users were free to modify and redistribute the code on the condition that they gave back all the extensions they made. Stallman dubbed it the "Emacs Commune." Just as TECO had become more than a simple editor, Emacs had become more than a simple software program. To Stallman, it was a social contract. In an early memo documenting the project, Stallman spelled out the contract terms. "EMACS," he wrote, "was distributed on a basis of communal sharing, which means that all improvements must be given back to me to be incorporated and distributed."[7]

Not everybody accepted the contract. The explosive innovation continued throughout the decade, resulting in a host of Emacs-like programs with varying degrees of cross-compatibility. A few cited their relation to Stallman's original Emacs with humorously recursive names: Sine (Sine is not Emacs), Eine (Eine is not Emacs), and Zwei (Zwei was Eine initially). As a devoted exponent of the hacker ethic, Stallman saw no reason to halt this innovation through legal harassment. Still, the fact that some people would so eagerly take software from the community chest, alter it, and slap a new name on the resulting software displayed a stunning lack of courtesy.

Such rude behavior was reflected against other, unsettling developments in the hacker community. Brian Reid's 1979 decision to embed "time bombs" in Scribe, making it possible for Unilogic to limit unpaid user access to the software, was a dark omen to Stallman. "He considered it the most Nazi thing he ever saw in his life," recalls Reid. Despite going on to later Internet fame as the cocreator of the Usenet *alt* heirarchy, Reid says he still has yet to live down that 1979 decision, at least in Stallman's eyes. "He said that all software should be free and the prospect of charging money for software was a crime against humanity."[8]

Although Stallman had been powerless to head off Reid's sale, he did possess the ability to curtail other forms of behavior deemed contrary to the hacker ethos. As central source-code maintainer for the Emacs "commune," Stallman began to wield his power for political effect. During his final stages of conflict with the administrators at the Laboratory for Computer Science over password systems, Stallman initiated a software "strike,"[9] refusing to send lab members the latest version of Emacs until they rejected the security system on the lab's computers. The move did little to improve Stallman's growing reputation as an extremist, but it got the point across: commune members were expected to speak up for basic hacker values.

"A lot of people were angry with me, saying I was trying to hold them hostage or blackmail them, which in a sense I was," Stallman would later tell author Steven Levy. "I was engaging in violence against them because I thought they were engaging in violence to everyone at large."[9]

Over time, Emacs became a sales tool for the hacker ethic. The flexibility Stallman and built into the software not only encouraged collaboration, it demanded it. Users who didn't keep abreast of the latest developments in Emacs evolution or didn't contribute their contributions back to Stallman ran the risk of missing out on the latest breakthroughs. And the breakthroughs were many. Twenty years later, users had modified Emacs for so many different uses—using it as a spreadsheet, calculator, database, and web browser—that later Emacs developers adopted an overflowing sink to represent its versatile functionality. "That's the idea that we wanted to convey," says Stallman. "The amount of stuff it has contained within it is both wonderful and awful at the same time."

Stallman's AI Lab contemporaries are more charitable. Hal Abelson, an MIT grad student who worked with Stallman during the 1970s and would later assist Stallman as a charter board-member of the Free Software Foundation, describes Emacs as "an absolutely brilliant creation." In giving programmers a way to add new software libraries and features without messing up the system, Abelson says, Stallman paved the way for future large-scale collaborative software projects. "Its structure was robust enough that you'd have people all over the world who were loosely collaborating [and] contributing to it," Abelson says. "I don't know if that had been done before."[10]

Guy Steele expresses similar admiration. Currently a research scientist for Sun Microsystems, he remembers Stallman primarily as a "brilliant programmer with the ability to generate large quantities of relatively bug-free code." Although their personalities didn't exactly mesh, Steele and Stallman collaborated long enough for Steele to get a glimpse of Stallman's intense coding style. He recalls a notable episode in the late 1970s when the two programmers banded together to write the editor's "pretty print" feature.

Originally conceived by Steele, pretty print was another keystroke-triggerd feature that reformatted Emacs' source code so that it was both more readable and took up less space, further bolstering the program's WYSIWIG qualities. The feature was strategic enough to attract Stallman's active interest, and it wasn't long before Steele wrote that he and Stallman were planning an improved version.

"We sat down one morning," recalls Steele. "I was at the keyboard, and he was at my elbow," says Steele. "He was perfectly willing to let me type, but he was also telling me what to type.

The programming session lasted 10 hours. Throughout that entire time, Steele says, neither he nor Stallman took a break or made any small talk. By the end of the session, they had managed to hack the pretty print source code to just under 100 lines. "My fingers were on the keyboard the whole time," Steele recalls, "but it felt like both of our ideas were flowing onto the screen. He told me what to type, and I typed it."

The length of the session revealed itself when Steele finally left the AI Lab. Standing outside the building at 545 Tech Square, he was surprised to find himself surrounded by nighttime darkness. As a programmer, Steele was used to marathon coding sessions. Still, something about this session was different. Working with Stallman had forced Steele to block out all external stimuli and focus his entire mental energies on the task at hand. Looking back, Steele says he found the Stallman mind-meld both exhilarating and scary at the same time. "My first thought afterward was: it was a great experience, very intense, and that I never wanted to do it again in my life."

ENDNOTES

1. See Josh McHugh, "For the Love of Hacking," *Forbes* (August 10, 1998). *http://www.forbes.com/forbes/1998/0810/6203094a.html*

2. See Stallman (1986).

3. See Joseph Weizenbaum, *Computer Power and Human Reason: From Judgment to Calculation* (W. H. Freeman, 1976): 116.

4. According to the Jargon File, TECO's name originally stood for Tape Editor and Corrector. *http://www.tuxedo.org/~esr/jargon/html/entry/TECO.html*

5. See Richard Stallman, "EMACS: The Extensible, Customizable, Display Editor," AI Lab Memo (1979). An updated HTML version of this memo, from which I am quoting, is available at *http://www.gnu.org/software/emacs/emacs-paper.html*.

6. See Richard Stallman, "Emacs the Full Screen Editor" (1987). *http://www.lysator.liu.se/history/garb/txt/87-1-emacs.txt*

7. See Stallman (1979): #SEC34.

8. In a 1996 interview with online magazine *MEME*, Stallman cited Scribe's sale as irksome, but hesitated to mention Reid by name. "The problem was nobody censured or punished this student for what he did," Stallman said. "The result was other people got tempted to follow his example." See *MEME* 2.04. *http://memex.org/meme2-04.html*

9. See Steven Levy, *Hackers* (Penguin USA [paperback], 1984): 419.

10. In writing this chapter, I've elected to focus more on the social significance of Emacs than the software significance. To read more about the software side, I recommend Stallman's 1979 memo. I particularly recommend the section titled "Research Through Development of Installed Tools" (#SEC27). Not only is it accessible to the nontechnical reader, it also sheds light on how closely intertwined Stallman's political philosophies are with his software-design philosophies. A sample excerpt follows:

> *EMACS could not have been reached by a process of careful design, because such processes arrive only at goals which are visible at the outset, and whose desirability is established on the bottom line at the outset. Neither I nor anyone else visualized an extensible editor until I had made one, nor appreciated its value until he had experienced it. EMACS exists because I felt free to make individually useful small improvements on a path whose end was not in sight.*

CHAPTER 7

A STARK MORAL CHOICE

On September 27, 1983, computer programmers logging on to the Usenet newsgroup net.unix-wizards encountered an unusual message. Posted in the small hours of the morning, 12:30 a.m. to be exact, and signed by *rms@mit-oz*, the message's subject line was terse but attention-grabbing. "New UNIX implementation," it read. Instead of introducing a newly released version of Unix, however, the message's opening paragraph issued a call to arms:

> *Starting this Thanksgiving I am going to write a complete Unix-compatible software system called GNU (for Gnu's Not Unix), and give it away free to everyone who can use it. Contributions of time, money, programs and equipment are greatly needed.[1]*

To an experienced Unix developer, the message was a mixture of idealism and hubris. Not only did the author pledge to rebuild the already mature Unix operating system from the ground up, he also proposed to improve it in places. The new GNU system, the author predicted, would carry all the usual components—a text editor, a shell program to run Unix-compatible applications, a compiler, "and a few other things."[1] It would also contain many enticing features that other Unix systems didn't yet offer: a graphic user interface based on the Lisp programming language, a crash-proof file system, and networking protocols built according to MIT's internal networking system.

"GNU will be able to run Unix programs, but will not be identical to Unix," the author wrote. "We will make all improvements that are convenient, based on our experience with other operating systems."

Anticipating a skeptical response on some readers' part, the author made sure to follow up his operating-system outline with a brief biographical sketch titled, "Who am I?":

> I am Richard Stallman, inventor of the original much-imitated EMACS editor, now at the Artificial Intelligence Lab at MIT. I have worked extensively on compilers, editors, debuggers, command interpreters, the Incompatible Timesharing System and the Lisp Machine operating system. I pioneered terminal-independent display support in ITS. In addition I have implemented one crashproof file system and two window systems for Lisp machines.[1]

As fate would have it, Stallman's fanciful GNU Project missed its Thanksgiving launch date. By January, 1984, however, Stallman made good on his promise and fully immersed himself in the world of Unix software development. For a software architect raised on ITS, it was like designing suburban shopping malls instead of Moorish palaces. Even so, building a Unix-like operating system had its hidden advantages. ITS had been powerful, but it also possessed an Achilles' heel: MIT hackers had designed it to take specific advantage of the DEC-built PDP line. When AI Lab administrators elected to phase out the lab's powerful PDP-10 machine in the early 1980s, the operating system that hackers once likened to a vibrant city became an instant ghost town. Unix, on the other hand, was designed for mobility and long-term survival. Originally developed by junior scientists at AT&T, the program had slipped out under corporate-management radar, finding a happy home in the cash-strapped world of academic computer systems. With fewer resources than their MIT brethren, Unix developers had customized the software to ride atop a motley assortment of hardware systems: everything from the 16-bit PDP-11—a machine considered fit for only small tasks by most AI Lab hackers—to 32-bit mainframes such as the VAX 11/780. By 1983, a few companies, most notably Sun Microsystems, were even going so far as to develop a new generation of microcomputers, dubbed "workstations," to take advantage of the increasingly ubiquitous operating system. To facilitate this process, the developers in charge of designing the dominant Unix strains made sure to keep an extra layer of abstraction between the software and the machine. Instead of tailoring the operating system to take advantage of a specific machine's resources—as the AI Lab hackers had done with ITS and the PDP-10—Unix developers favored a more generic, off-the-rack approach. Focusing more on the interlocking standards and specifications that held the operating system's many subcomponents together, rather than the actual components themselves, they created a system that could be quickly modified to suit the tastes of any machine. If a user quibbled with a certain portion, the standards made it possible to pull out an individual subcomponent and either fix it or replace it with something better. Simply put, what the Unix approach lacked in terms of style or aesthetics, it more than made up for in terms of flexibility and economy, hence its rapid adoption.[2]

Stallman's decision to start developing the GNU system was triggered by the end of the ITS system that the AI Lab hackers had nurtured for so long. The demise of ITS had been a traumatic blow to Stallman. Coming on the heels of the Xerox laser printer episode, it offered further evidence that the AI Lab hacker culture was losing its immunity to business practices in the outside world.

Like the software code that composed it, the roots of ITS' demise stretched way back. Defense spending, long a major font for computer-science research, had dried up during the post-Vietnam years. In a desperate quest for new funds, laboratories and universities turned to the private sector. In the case of the AI Lab, winning over private investors was an easy sell. Home to some of the most ambitious computer-science projects of the post-war era, the lab became a quick incubator of technology. Indeed, by 1980, most of the lab's staff, including many hackers, were dividing its time between Institute and commercial projects.

What at first seemed like a win-win deal—hackers got to work on the best projects, giving the lab first look at many of the newest computer technologies coming down the pike—soon revealed itself as a Faustian bargain. The more time hackers devoted to cutting-edge commercial projects, the less time they had to devote to general maintenance on the lab's baroque software infrastructure. Soon, companies began hiring away hackers outright in an attempt to monopolize their time and attention. With fewer hackers to mind the shop, programs and machines took longer to fix. Even worse, Stallman says, the lab began to undergo a "demographic change." The hackers who had once formed a vocal minority within the AI Lab were losing membership while "the professors and the students who didn't really love the [PDP-10] were just as numerous as before."3

The breaking point came in 1982. That was the year the lab's administration decided to upgrade its main computer, the PDP-10. Digital, the corporation that manufactured the PDP-10, had discontinued the line. Although the company still offered a high-powered mainframe, dubbed the KL-10, the new machine required a drastic rewrite or "port" of ITS if hackers wanted to continue running the same operating system. Fearful that the lab had lost its critical mass of in-house programming talent, AI Lab faculty members pressed for Twenex, a commercial operating system developed by Digital. Outnumbered, the hackers had no choice but to comply.

"Without hackers to maintain the system, [faculty members] said, 'We're going to have a disaster; we must have commercial software,'" Stallman would recall a few years later. "They said, 'We can expect the company to maintain it.' It proved that they were utterly wrong, but that's what they did."3

At first, hackers viewed the Twenex system as yet another authoritarian symbol begging to be subverted. The system's name itself was a protest. Officially dubbed TOPS-20 by DEC, it was a successor to TOPS-10, a commercial operating system DEC marketed for the PDP-10. Bolt Beranek Newman had deveoped an improved version, dubbed Tenex, which TOPS-20 drew upon.4

Stallman, the hacker who coined the Twenex term, says he came up with the name as a way to avoid using the TOPS-20 name. "The system was far from tops, so there was no way I was going to call it that," Stallman recalls. "So I decided to insert a 'w' in the Tenex name and call it Twenex."

The machine that ran the Twenex/TOPS-20 system had its own derisive nickname: Oz. According to one hacker legend, the machine got its nickname because it required a smaller PDP-11 machine to power its terminal. One hacker, upon viewing the KL-10–PDP-11 setup for the first time, likened it to the wizard's bombastic onscreen introduction in the Wizard of Oz. "I am the great and powerful Oz," the hacker intoned. "Pay no attention to the PDP-11 behind that console."[5]

If hackers laughed when they first encountered the KL-10, their laughter quickly died when they encountered Twenex. Not only did Twenex boast built-in security, but the system's software engineers had designed the tools and applications with the security system in mind. What once had been a cat-and-mouse game over passwords in the case of the Laboratory for Computer Science's security system, now became an out-and-out battle over system management. System administrators argued that without security, the Oz system was more prone to accidental crashes. Hackers argued that crashes could be better prevented by overhauling the source code. Unfortunately, the number of hackers with the time and inclination to perform this sort of overhaul had dwindled to the point that the system-administrator argument prevailed.

Cadging passwords and deliberately crashing the system in order to glean evidence from the resulting wreckage, Stallman successfully foiled the system administrators' attempt to assert control. After one foiled "coup d'etat," Stallman issued an alert to the entire AI staff.[3]

"There has been another attempt to seize power," Stallman wrote. "So far, the aristocratic forces have been defeated." To protect his identity, Stallman signed the message "Radio Free OZ."

The disguise was a thin one at best. By 1982, Stallman's aversion to passwords and secrecy had become so well known that users outside the AI Laboratory were using his account as a stepping stone to the ARPAnet, the research-funded computer network that would serve as a foundation for today's Internet. One such "tourist" during the early 1980s was Don Hopkins, a California programmer who learned through the hacking grapevine that all an outsider needed to do to gain access to MIT's vaunted ITS system was to log in under the initials RMS and enter the same three-letter monogram when the system requested a password.

"I'm eternally grateful that MIT let me and many other people use their computers for free," says Hopkins. "It meant a lot to many people."

This so-called "tourist" policy, which had been openly tolerated by MIT management during the ITS years,[6] fell by the wayside when Oz became the lab's primary link to the ARPAnet. At first, Stallman continued his policy of repeating his login ID as a password so outside users could follow in his footsteps. Over time, however, the Oz's fragility prompted administrators to bar outsiders who, through sheer accident or malicious intent, might bring down the system. When those same administrators eventually demanded that Stallman stop publishing his password, Stallman, citing personal ethics, refused to do so and ceased using the Oz system altogether.[3]

"[When] passwords first appeared at the MIT AI Lab I [decided] to follow my belief that there should be no passwords," Stallman would later say. "Because I don't believe that it's really desirable to have security on a computer, I shouldn't be willing to help uphold the security regime."[3]

Stallman's refusal to bow before the great and powerful Oz symbolized the growing tension between hackers and AI Lab management during the early 1980s. This tension paled in comparison to the conflict that raged within the hacker community itself. By the time the KL-10 arrived, the hacker community had already divided into two camps. The first centered around a software company called Symbolics, Inc. The second centered around Symbolics chief rival, Lisp Machines, Inc. (LMI). Both companies were in a race to market the Lisp Machine, a device built to take full advantage of the Lisp programming language.

Created by artificial-intelligence research pioneer John McCarthy, a MIT artificial-intelligence researcher during the late 1950s, Lisp is an elegant language well-suited for programs charged with heavy-duty sorting and processing. The language's name is a shortened version of LISt Processing. Following McCarthy's departure to the Stanford Artificial Intelligence Laboratory, MIT hackers refined the language into a local dialect dubbed MACLISP. The "MAC" stood for Project MAC, the DARPA-funded research project that gave birth to the AI Lab and the Laboratory for Computer Science. Led by AI Lab arch-hacker Richard Greenblatt, AI Lab programmers during the 1970s built up an entire Lisp-based operating system, dubbed the Lisp Machine operating system. By 1980, the Lisp Machine project had generated two commercial spin-offs. Symbolics was headed by Russell Noftsker, a former AI Lab administrator, and Lisp Machines, Inc., was headed by Greenblatt.

The Lisp Machine software was hacker-built, meaning it was owned by MIT but available for anyone to copy as per hacker custom. Such a system limited the marketing advantage of any company hoping to license the software from MIT and market it as unique. To secure an advantage, and to bolster the aspects of the operating system that customers might consider attractive, the companies recruited various AI Lab hackers and set them working on various components of the Lisp Machine operating system outside the auspices of the AI Lab.

The most aggressive in this strategy was Symbolics. By the end of 1980, the company had hired 14 AI Lab staffers as part-time consultants to develop its version of the Lisp Machine. Apart from Stallman, the rest signed on to help LMI.[7]

At first, Stallman accepted both companies' attempt to commercialize the Lisp machine, even though it meant more work for him. Both licensed the Lisp Machine OS source code from MIT, and it was Stallman's job to update the lab's own Lisp Machine to keep pace with the latest innovations. Although Symbolics' license with MIT gave Stallman the right to review, but not copy, Symbolics' source code, Stallman says a "gentleman's agreement" between Symbolics management and the AI Lab made it possible to borrow attractive snippets in traditional hacker fashion.

On March 16, 1982, a date Stallman remembers well because it was his birthday, Symbolics executives decided to end this gentlemen's agreement. The move was largely strategic. LMI, the primary competition in the Lisp Machine marketplace, was essentially using a copy of the AI Lab Lisp Machine. Rather than subsidize the development of a market rival, Symbolics executives elected to enforce the letter of the license. If the AI Lab wanted its operating system to stay current with the Symbolics operating system, the lab would have to switch over to a Symbolics machine and sever its connection to LMI.

As the person responsible for keeping up the lab's Lisp Machine, Stallman was incensed. Viewing this announcement as an "ultimatum," he retaliated by disconnecting Symbolics' microwave communications link to the laboratory. He then vowed never to work on a Symbolics machine and pledged his immediate allegiance to LMI. "The way I saw it, the AI Lab was a neutral country, like Belgium in World War I," Stallman says. "If Germany invades Belgium, Belgium declares war on Germany and sides with Britain and France."

The circumstances of the so-called "Symbolics War" of 1982–1983 depend heavily on the source doing the telling. When Symbolics executives noticed that their latest features were still appearing in the AI Lab Lisp Machine and, by extension, the LMI Lisp machine, they installed a "spy" program on Stallman's computer terminal. Stallman says he was rewriting the features from scratch, taking advantage of the license's review clause but also taking pains to make the source code as different as possible. Symbolics executives argued otherwise and took their case to MIT administration. According to 1994 book, *The Brain Makers: Genius, Ego, and Greed, and the Quest for Machines That Think*, written by Harvey Newquist, the administration responded with a warning to Stallman to "stay away" from the Lisp Machine project.[8] According to Stallman, MIT administrators backed Stallman up. "I was never threatened," he says. "I did make changes in my practices, though. Just to be ultra safe, I no longer read their source code. I used only the documentation and wrote the code from that."

Whatever the outcome, the bickering solidified Stallman's resolve. With no source code to review, Stallman filled in the software gaps according to his own tastes and enlisted members of the AI Lab to provide a continuous stream of bug reports. He also made sure LMI programmers had direct access to the changes. "I was going to punish Symbolics if it was the last thing I did," Stallman says.

Such statements are revealing. Not only do they shed light on Stallman's nonpacifist nature, they also reflect the intense level of emotion triggered by the conflict. According to another Newquist-related story, Stallman became so irate at one point that he issued an email threatening to "wrap myself in dynamite and walk into Symbolics' offices."9 Although Stallman would deny any memory of the email and still describes its existence as a "vicious rumor," he acknowledges that such thoughts did enter his head. "I definitely did have fantasies of killing myself and destroying their building in the process," Stallman says. "I thought my life was over."5

The level of despair owed much to what Stallman viewed as the "destruction" of his "home"—i.e., the demise of the AI Lab's close-knit hacker subculture. In a later email interview with Levy, Stallman would liken himself to the historical figure Ishi, the last surviving member of the Yahi, a Pacific Northwest tribe wiped out during the Indian wars of the 1860s and 1870s. The analogy casts Stallman's survival in epic, almost mythical, terms. In reality, however, it glosses over the tension between Stallman and his fellow AI Lab hackers prior to the Symbolics-LMI schism. Instead of seeing Symbolics as an exterminating force, many of Stallman's colleagues saw it as a belated bid for relevance. In commercializing the Lisp Machine, the company pushed hacker principles of engineer-driven software design out of the ivory-tower confines of the AI Lab and into the corporate marketplace where manager-driven design principles held sway. Rather than viewing Stallman as a holdout, many hackers saw him as a troubling anachronism.

Stallman does not dispute this alternate view of historical events. In fact, he says it was yet another reason for the hostility triggered by the Symbolics "ultimatum." Even before Symbolics hired away most of the AI Lab's hacker staff, Stallman says many of the hackers who later joined Symbolics were shunning him. "I was no longer getting invited to go to Chinatown," Stallman recalls. "The custom started by Greenblatt was that if you went out to dinner, you went around or sent a message asking anybody at the lab if they also wanted to go. Sometime around 1980–1981, I stopped getting asked. They were not only not inviting me, but one person later confessed that he had been pressured to lie to me to keep their going away to dinner without me a secret."

Although Stallman felt anger toward the hackers who orchestrated this petty form of ostracism, the Symbolics controversy dredged up a new kind of anger, the anger of a person about to lose his home. When Symbolics stopped sending over its source-code changes, Stallman responded by holing up in his MIT offices and rewriting each new software feature and tool from scratch. Frustrating as it may have been, it guaranteed that future Lisp Machine users had unfettered access to the same features as Symbolics users.

It also guaranteed Stallman's legendary status within the hacker community. Already renowned for his work with Emacs, Stallman's ability to match the output of an entire team of Symbolics programmers—a team that included more than a few legendary hackers itself—still stands has one of the major human accomplishments of the Information Age, or of any age for that matter. Dubbing it a "master hack" and Stallman himself a "virtual John Henry of computer code," author Steven Levy notes that many of his Symbolics-employed rivals had no choice but to pay their idealistic former comrade grudging respect. Levy quotes Bill Gosper, a hacker who eventually went to work for Symbolics in the company's Palo Alto office, expressing amazement over Stallman's output during this period:

I can see something Stallman wrote, and I might decide it was bad (probably not, but somebody could convince me it was bad), and I would still say, "But wait a minute—Stallman doesn't have anybody to argue with all night over there. He's working alone! It's incredible anyone could do this alone!"[10]

For Stallman, the months spent playing catch up with Symbolics evoke a mixture of pride and profound sadness. As a dyed-in-the-wool liberal whose father had served in World War II, Stallman is no pacifist. In many ways, the Symbolics war offered the rite of passage toward which Stallman had been careening ever since joining the AI Lab staff a decade before. At the same time, however, it coincided with the traumatic destruction of the AI Lab hacker culture that had nurtured Stallman since his teenage years. One day, while taking a break from writing code, Stallman experienced a traumatic moment passing through the lab's equipment room. There, Stallman encountered the hulking, unused frame of the PDP-10 machine. Startled by the dormant lights, lights that once actively blinked out a silent code indicating the status of the internal program, Stallman says the emotional impact was not unlike coming across a beloved family member's well-preserved corpse.

"I started crying right there in the equipment room," he says. "Seeing the machine there, dead, with nobody left to fix it, it all drove home how completely my community had been destroyed."

Stallman would have little opportunity to mourn. The Lisp Machine, despite all the furor it invoked and all the labor that had gone into making it, was merely a sideshow to the large battles in the technology marketplace. The relentless pace of computer miniaturization was bringing in newer, more powerful microprocessors that would soon incorporate the machine's hardware and software capabilities like a modern metropolis swallowing up an ancient desert village.

Riding atop this microprocessor wave were hundreds—thousands—of commercial software programs, each protected by a patchwork of user licenses and nondisclosure agreements that made it impossible for hackers to review or share source code.

The licenses were crude and ill-fitting, but by 1983 they had become strong enough to satisfy the courts and scare away would-be interlopers. Software, once a form of garnish most hardware companies gave away to make their expensive computer systems more flavorful, was quickly becoming the main dish. In their increasing hunger for new games and features, users were putting aside the traditional demand to review the recipe after every meal.

Nowhere was this state of affairs more evident than in the realm of personal computer systems. Companies such as Apple Computer and Commodore were minting fresh millionaires selling machines with built-in operating systems. Unaware of the hacker culture and its distaste for binary-only software, many of these users saw little need to protest when these companies failed to attach the accompanying source-code files. A few anarchic adherents of the hacker ethic helped propel that ethic into this new marketplace, but for the most part, the marketplace rewarded the programmers speedy enough to write new programs and savvy enough to copyright them as legally protected works.

One of the most notorious of these programmers was Bill Gates, a Harvard dropout two years Stallman's junior. Although Stallman didn't know it at the time, seven years before sending out his message to the net.unix-wizards newsgroup, Gates, a budding entrepreneur and general partner with the Albuquerque-based software firm Micro-Soft, later spelled as Microsoft, had sent out his own open letter to the software-developer community. Written in response to the PC users copying Micro-Soft's software programs, Gates' "Open Letter to Hobbyists" had excoriated the notion of communal software development.

"Who can afford to do professional work for nothing?" asked Gates. "What hobbyist can put three man-years into programming, finding all bugs, documenting his product, and distributing it for free?"[11]

Although few hackers at the AI Lab saw the missive, Gates' 1976 letter nevertheless represented the changing attitude toward software both among commercial software companies and commercial software developers. Why treat software as a zero-cost commodity when the market said otherwise? As the 1970s gave way to the 1980s, selling software became more than a way to recoup costs; it became a political statement. At a time when the Reagan Administration was rushing to dismantle many of the federal regulations and spending programs that had been built up during the half century following the Great Depression, more than a few software programmers saw the hacker ethic as anticompetitive and, by extension, un-American. At best, it was a throwback to the anticorporate attitudes of the late 1960s and early 1970s. Like a Wall Street banker discovering an old tie-dyed shirt hiding between French-cuffed shirts and double-breasted suits, many computer programmers treated the hacker ethic as an embarrassing reminder of an idealistic age.

For a man who had spent the entire 1960s as an embarrassing throwback to the 1950s, Stallman didn't mind living out of step with his peers. As a programmer used to working with the best machines and the best software, however, Stallman faced what he could only describe as a "stark moral choice": either get over his ethical objection for "proprietary" software—the term Stallman and his fellow hackers used to describe any program that carried private copyright or end-user license that restricted copying and modification—or dedicate his life to building an alternate, nonproprietary system of software programs. Given his recent months-long ordeal with Symbolics, Stallman felt more comfortable with the latter option. "I suppose I could have stopped working on computers altogether," Stallman says. "I had no special skills, but I'm sure I could have become a waiter. Not at a fancy restaurant, probably, but I could've been a waiter somewhere."

Being a waiter—i.e., dropping out of programming altogether—would have meant completely giving up an activity, computer programming, that had given him so much pleasure. Looking back on his life since moving to Cambridge, Stallman finds it easy to identify lengthy periods when software programming provided the only pleasure. Rather than drop out, Stallman decided to stick it out.

An atheist, Stallman rejects notions such as fate, dharma, or a divine calling in life. Nevertheless, he does feel that the decision to shun proprietary software and build an operating system to help others do the same was a natural one. After all, it was Stallman's own personal combination of stubbornness, foresight, and coding virtuosity that led him to consider a fork in the road most others didn't know existed. In describing the decision in a chapter for the 1999 book, *Open Sources*, Stallman cites the spirit encapsulated in the words of the Jewish sage Hillel:

> *If I am not for myself, who will be for me?*
> *If I am only for myself, what am I?*
> *If not now, when?*[12]

Speaking to audiences, Stallman avoids the religious route and expresses the decision in pragmatic terms. "I asked myself: what could I, an operating-system developer, do to improve the situation? It wasn't until I examined the question for a while that I realized an operating-system developer was exactly what was needed to solve the problem."

Once he reached that decision, Stallman says, everything else "fell into place." He would abstain from using software programs that forced him to compromise his ethical beliefs, while at the same time devoting his life to the creation of software that would make it easier for others to follow the same path. Pledging to build a free software operating system "or die trying—of old age, of course," Stallman quips, he resigned from the MIT staff in January, 1984, to build GNU.

The resignation distanced Stallman's work from the legal auspices of MIT. Still, Stallman had enough friends and allies within the AI Lab to retain rent-free access to his MIT office. He also had the ability to secure outside consulting gigs to underwrite the early stages of the GNU Project. In resigning from MIT, however, Stallman negated any debate about conflict of interest or Institute ownership of the software. The man whose early adulthood fear of social isolation had driven him deeper and deeper into the AI Lab's embrace was now building a legal firewall between himself and that environment.

For the first few months, Stallman operated in isolation from the Unix community as well. Although his announcement to the net.unix-wizards group had attracted sympathetic responses, few volunteers signed on to join the crusade in its early stages. "The community reaction was pretty much uniform," recalls Rich Morin, leader of a Unix user group at the time. "People said, 'Oh, that's a great idea. Show us your code. Show us it can be done.'"

In true hacker fashion, Stallman began looking for existing programs and tools that could be converted into GNU programs and tools. One of the first was a compiler named VUCK, which converted programs written in the popular C programming language into machine-readable code. Translated from the Dutch, the program's acronym stood for the Free University Compiler Kit. Optimistic, Stallman asked the program's author if the program was free. When the author informed him that the words "Free University" were a reference to the Vrije Universiteit in Amsterdam, Stallman was chagrined.

"He responded derisively, stating that the university was free but the compiler was not," recalls Stallman. "I therefore decided that my first program for the GNU Project would be a multi-language, multi-platform compiler."[3]

Eventually Stallman found a Pastel language compiler written by programmers at Lawrence Livermore National Lab. According to Stallman's knowledge at the time, the compiler was free to copy and modify. Unfortunately, the program possessed a sizable design flaw: it saved each program into core memory, tying up precious space for other software activities. On mainframe systems this design flaw had been forgivable. On Unix systems it was a crippling barrier, since the machines that ran Unix were too small to handle the large files generated. Stallman made substantial progress at first, building a C-compatible frontend to the compiler. By summer, however, he had come to the conclusion that he would have to build a totally new compiler from scratch.

In September of 1984, Stallman shelved compiler development for the near term and began searching for lower-lying fruit. He began development of a GNU version of Emacs, the program he himself had been supervising for a decade. The decision was strategic. Within the Unix community, the two native editor programs were vi, written by Sun Microsystems cofounder Bill Joy, and ed, written by Bell Labs scientist (and Unix cocreator) Ken Thompson. Both were useful and popular, but neither offered the endlessly expandable nature of Emacs. In rewriting Emacs for the Unix audience, Stallman stood a better chance of showing off his skills. It also stood to reason that Emacs users might be more attuned to the Stallman mentality.

Looking back, Stallman says he didn't view the decision in strategic terms. "I wanted an Emacs, and I had a good opportunity to develop one."

Once again, the notion of reinventing the wheel grated on Stallman's efficient hacker sensibilities. In writing a Unix version of Emacs, Stallman was soon following the footsteps of Carnegie Mellon graduate student James Gosling, author of a C-based version dubbed Gosling Emacs or GOSMACS. Gosling's version of Emacs included an interpreter that exploited a simplified offshoot of the Lisp language called MOCKLISP. Determined to build GNU Emacs on a similar Lisp foundation, Stallman borrowed copiously from Gosling's innovations. Although Gosling had put GOSMACS under copyright and had sold the rights to UniPress, a privately held software company, Stallman cited the assurances of a fellow developer who had participated in the early MOCKLISP interpreter. According to the developer, Gosling, while a Ph.D. student at Carnegie Mellon, had assured early collaborators that their work would remain accessible. When UniPress caught wind of Stallman's project, however, the company threatened to enforce the copyright. Once again, Stallman faced the prospect of building from the ground up.

In the course of reverse-engineering Gosling's interpreter, Stallman would create a fully functional Lisp interpreter, rendering the need for Gosling's original interpreter moot. Nevertheless, the notion of developers selling off software rights—indeed, the very notion of developers having software rights to sell in the first place—rankled Stallman. In a 1986 speech at the Swedish Royal Technical Institute, Stallman cited the UniPress incident as yet another example of the dangers associated with proprietary software.

"Sometimes I think that perhaps one of the best things I could do with my life is find a gigantic pile of proprietary software that was a trade secret, and start handing out copies on a street corner so it wouldn't be a trade secret any more," said Stallman. "Perhaps that would be a much more efficient way for me to give people new free software than actually writing it myself; but everyone is too cowardly to even take it."[3]

Despite the stress it generated, the dispute over Gosling's innovations would assist both Stallman and the free software movement in the long term. It would force Stallman to address the weaknesses of the Emacs Commune and the informal trust system that had allowed problematic offshoots to emerge. It would also force Stallman to sharpen the free software movement's political objectives. Following the release of GNU Emacs in 1995, Stallman issued "The GNU Manifesto," an expansion of the original announcement posted in September, 1983. Stallman included within the document a lengthy section devoted to the many arguments used by commercial and academic programmers to justify the proliferation of proprietary software programs. One argument, "Don't programmers deserve a reward for their creativity," earned a response encapsulating Stallman's anger over the recent Gosling Emacs episode:

"If anything deserves a reward, it is social contribution," Stallman wrote. "Creativity can be a social contribution, but only in so far [sic] as society is free to use the results. If programmers deserve to be rewarded for creating innovative programs, by the same token they deserve to be punished if they restrict the use of these programs."[13]

With the release of GNU Emacs, the GNU Project finally had code to show. It also had the burdens of any software-based enterprise. As more and more Unix developers began playing with the software, money, gifts, and requests for tapes began to pour in. To address the business side of the GNU Project, Stallman drafted a few of his colleagues and formed the Free Software Foundation (FSF), a nonprofit organization dedicated to speeding the GNU Project towards its goal. With Stallman as president and various hacker allies as board members, the FSF helped provide a corporate face for the GNU Project.

Robert Chassell, a programmer then working at Lisp Machines, Inc., became one of five charter board members at the Free Software Foundation following a dinner conversation with Stallman. Chassell also served as the organization's treasurer, a role that started small but quickly grew.

"I think in '85 our total expenses and revenue were something in the order of $23,000, give or take," Chassell recalls. "Richard had his office, and we borrowed space. I put all the stuff, especially the tapes, under my desk. It wasn't until sometime later LMI loaned us some space where we could store tapes and things of that sort."

In addition to providing a face, the Free Software Foundation provided a center of gravity for other disenchanted programmers. The Unix market that had seemed so collegial even at the time of Stallman's initial GNU announcement was becoming increasingly competitive. In an attempt to tighten their hold on customers, companies were starting to close off access to Unix source code, a trend that only speeded the number of inquiries into ongoing GNU software projects. The Unix wizards who once regarded Stallman as a noisy kook were now beginning to see him as a software Cassandra.

"A lot of people don't realize, until they've had it happen to them, how frustrating it can be to spend a few years working on a software program only to have it taken away," says Chassell, summarizing the feelings and opinions of the correspondents writing in to the FSF during the early years. "After that happens a couple of times, you start to say to yourself, 'Hey, wait a minute.'"

For Chassell, the decision to participate in the Free Software Foundation came down to his own personal feelings of loss. Prior to LMI, Chassell had been working for hire, writing an introductory book on Unix for Cadmus, Inc., a Cambridge-area software company. When Cadmus folded, taking the rights to the book down with it, Chassell says he attempted to buy the rights back with no success.

"As far as I know, that book is still sitting on shelf somewhere, unusable, uncopyable, just taken out of the system," Chassell says. "It was quite a good introduction if I may say so myself. It would have taken maybe three or four months to convert [the book] into a perfectly usable introduction to GNU/Linux today. The whole experience, aside from what I have in my memory, was lost."

Forced to watch his work sink into the mire while his erstwhile employer struggled through bankruptcy, Chassell says he felt a hint of the anger that drove Stallman to fits of apoplexy. "The main clarity, for me, was the sense that if you want to have a decent life, you don't want to have bits of it closed off," Chassell says. "This whole idea of having the freedom to go in and to fix something and modify it, whatever it may be, it really makes a difference. It makes one think happily that after you've lived a few years that what you've done is worthwhile. Because otherwise it just gets taken away and thrown out or abandoned or, at the very least, you no longer have any relation to it. It's like losing a bit of your life."

ENDNOTES

1. See Richard Stallman, "Initial GNU Announcement" (September 1983).

    http://www.gnu.ai.mit.edu/gnu/initial-announcement.html

2. See Marshall Kirk McKusick, "Twenty Years of Berkeley Unix," *Open Sources* (O'Reilly & Associates, Inc., 1999): 38.

3. See Richard Stallman (1986).

4. Multiple sources: see Richard Stallman interview, Gerald Sussman email, and Jargon File 3.0.0.

    http://www.clueless.com/jargon3.0.0/TWENEX.html

5. See *http://www.as.cmu.edu/~geek/humor/See_Figure_1.txt*

6. See "MIT AI Lab Tourist Policy."

   http://catalog.com/hopkins/text/tourist-policy.html

7. See H. P. Newquist, *The Brain Makers: Genius, Ego, and Greed in the Quest for Machines that Think* (Sams Publishing, 1994): 172.

8. *Ibid.*: 196.

9. *Ibid.* Newquist, who says this anecdote was confirmed by several Symbolics executives, writes, "The message caused a brief flurry of excitement and speculation on the part of Symbolics' employees, but ultimately, no one took Stallman's outburst that seriously."

10. See Steven Levy, *Hackers* (Penguin USA [paperback], 1984): 426.

11. See Bill Gates, "An Open Letter to Hobbyists" (February 3, 1976).

   To view an online copy of this letter, go to *http://www.blinkenlights.com/classiccmp/gateswhine.html.*

12. See Richard Stallman, *Open Sources* (O'Reilly & Associates, Inc., 1999): 56.

   Stallman adds his own footnote to this statement, writing, "As an atheist, I don't follow any religious leaders, but I sometimes find I admire something one of them has said."

13. See Richard Stallman, "The GNU Manifesto" (1985).

   http://www.gnu.org/manifesto.html

CHAPTER 8

ST. IGNUCIUS

The Maui High Performance Computing Center is located in a single-story building in the dusty red hills just above the town of Kihei. Framed by million-dollar views and the multimillion dollar real estate of the Silversword Golf Course, the center seems like the ultimate scientific boondoggle. Far from the boxy, sterile confines of Tech Square or even the sprawling research metropolises of Argonne, Illinois and Los Alamos, New Mexico, the MHPCC seems like the kind of place where scientists spend more time on their tans than their post-doctoral research projects.

The image is only half true. Although researchers at the MHPCC do take advantage of the local recreational opportunities, they also take their work seriously. According to Top500.org, a web site that tracks the most powerful supercomputers in the world, the IBM SP Power3 supercomputer housed within the MHPCC clocks in at 837 billion floating-point operations per second, making it one of 25 most powerful computers in the world. Co-owned and operated by the University of Hawaii and the U.S. Air Force, the machine divides its computer cycles between the number crunching tasks associated with military logistics and high-temperature physics research.

Simply put, the MHPCC is a unique place, a place where the brainy culture of science and engineering and the laid-back culture of the Hawaiian islands coexist in peaceful equilibrium. A slogan on the lab's 2000 web site sums it up: "Computing in paradise."

It's not exactly the kind of place you'd expect to find Richard Stallman, a man who, when taking in the beautiful view of the nearby Maui Channel through the picture windows of a staffer's office, mutters a terse critique: "Too much sun." Still, as an emissary from one computing paradise to another, Stallman has a message to deliver, even if it means subjecting his pale hacker skin to the hazards of tropical exposure.

The conference room is already full by the time I arrive to catch Stallman's speech. The gender breakdown is a little better than at the New York speech, 85% male, 15% female, but not by much. About half of the audience members wear khaki pants and logo-encrusted golf shirts. The other half seems to have gone native. Dressed in the gaudy flower-print shirts so popular in this corner of the world, their faces are a deep shade of ochre. The only residual indication of geek status are the gadgets: Nokia cell phones, Palm Pilots, and Sony VAIO laptops.

Needless to say, Stallman, who stands in front of the room dressed in plain blue T-shirt, brown polyester slacks, and white socks, sticks out like a sore thumb. The fluorescent lights of the conference room help bring out the unhealthy color of his sun-starved skin. His beard and hair are enough to trigger beads of sweat on even the coolest Hawaiian neck. Short of having the words "mainlander" tattooed on his forehead, Stallman couldn't look more alien if he tried.

As Stallman putters around the front of the room, a few audience members wearing T-shirts with the logo of the Maui FreeBSD Users Group (MFUG) race to set up camera and audio equipment. FreeBSD, a free software offshoot of the Berkeley Software Distribution, the venerable 1970s academic version of Unix, is technically a competitor to the GNU/Linux operating system. Still, in the hacking world, Stallman speeches are documented with a fervor reminiscent of the Grateful Dead and its legendary army of amateur archivists. As the local free software heads, it's up to the MFUG members to make sure fellow programmers in Hamburg, Mumbai, and Novosibirsk don't miss out on the latest pearls of RMS wisdom.

The analogy to the Grateful Dead is apt. Often, when describing the business opportunities inherent within the free software model, Stallman has held up the Grateful Dead as an example. In refusing to restrict fans' ability to record live concerts, the Grateful Dead became more than a rock group. They became the center of a tribal community dedicated to Grateful Dead music. Over time, that tribal community became so large and so devoted that the band shunned record contracts and supported itself solely through musical tours and live appearances. In 1994, the band's last year as a touring act, the Grateful Dead drew $52 million in gate receipts alone.[1]

While few software companies have been able to match that success, the tribal aspect of the free software community is one reason many in the latter half of the 1990s started to accept the notion that publishing software source code might be a good thing. Hoping to build their own loyal followings, companies such as IBM, Sun Microsystems, and Hewlett Packard have come to accept the letter, if not the spirit, of the Stallman free software message. Describing the GPL as the information-technology industry's "Magna Carta," ZDNet software columnist Evan Leibovitch sees the growing affection for all things GNU as more than just a trend. "This societal shift is letting users take back control of their futures," Leibovitch writes. "Just as the Magna Carta gave rights to British subjects, the GPL enforces consumer rights and freedoms on behalf of the users of computer software."[2]

The tribal aspect of the free software community also helps explain why 40-odd programmers, who might otherwise be working on physics projects or surfing the Web for windsurfing buoy reports, have packed into a conference room to hear Stallman speak.

Unlike the New York speech, Stallman gets no introduction. He also offers no self-introduction. When the FreeBSD people finally get their equipment up and running, Stallman simply steps forward, starts speaking, and steamrolls over every other voice in the room.

"Most of the time when people consider the question of what rules society should have for using software, the people considering it are from software companies, and they consider the question from a self-serving perspective," says Stallman, opening his speech. "What rules can we impose on everybody else so they have to pay us lots of money? I had the good fortune in the 1970s to be part of a community of programmers who shared software. And because of this I always like to look at the same issue from a different direction to ask: what kind of rules make possible a good society that is good for the people who are in it? And therefore I reach completely different answers."

Once again, Stallman quickly segues into the parable of the Xerox laser printer, taking a moment to deliver the same dramatic finger-pointing gestures to the crowd. He also devotes a minute or two to the GNU/Linux name.

"Some people say to me, 'Why make such a fuss about getting credit for this system? After all, the important thing is the job is done, not whether you get recognition for it.' Well, this would be wise advice if it were true. But the job wasn't to build an operating system; the job is to spread freedom to the users of computers. And to do that we have to make it possible to do everything with computers in freedom."[3]

Adds Stallman, "There's a lot more work to do."

For some in the audience, this is old material. For others, it's a little arcane. When a member of the golf-shirt contingent starts dozing off, Stallman stops the speech and asks somebody to wake the person up.

"Somebody once said my voice was so soothing, he asked if I was some kind of healer," says Stallman, drawing a quick laugh from the crowd. "I guess that probably means I can help you drift gently into a blissful, relaxing sleep. And some of you might need that. I guess I shouldn't object if you do. If you need to sleep, by all means do."

The speech ends with a brief discussion of software patents, a growing issue of concern both within the software industry and within the free software community. Like Napster, software patents reflect the awkward nature of applying laws and concepts written for the physical world to the frictionless universe of information technology. The difference between protecting a program under copyright and protecting a program under software patents is subtle but significant. In the case of copyright, a software creator can restrict duplication of the source code but not duplication of the idea or functionality that the source code addresses. In other words, if a developer chooses not to use a software program under the original developer's terms, that second developer is still free to reverse-engineer the program—i.e., duplicate the software program's functionality by rewriting the source code from scratch. Such duplication of ideas is common within the commercial software industry, where companies often isolate reverse-engineering teams to head off accusations of corporate espionage or developer hanky-panky. In the jargon of modern software development, companies refer to this technique as "clean room" engineering.

Software patents work differently. According to the U.S. Patent Office, companies and individuals may secure patents for innovative algorithms provided they submit their claims to a public review. In theory, this allows the patent-holder to trade off disclosure of their invention for a limited monopoly of a minimum of 20 years after the patent filing. In practice, the disclosure is of limited value, since the operation of the program is often self-evident. Unlike copyright, a patent gives its holder the ability to head off the independent development of software programs with the same or similar functionality.

In the software industry, where 20 years can cover the entire life cycle of a marketplace, patents take on a strategic weight. Where companies such as Microsoft and Apple once battled over copyright and the "look and feel" of various technologies, today's Internet companies use patents as a way to stake out individual applications and business models, the most notorious example being Amazon.com's 2000 attempt to patent the company's "one-click" online shopping process. For most companies, however, software patents have become a defensive tool, with cross-licensing deals balancing one set of corporate patents against another in a tense form of corporate detente. Still, in a few notable cases of computer encryption and graphic imaging algorithms, software vendors have successfully stifled rival technologies.

For Stallman, the software-patent issue dramatizes the need for eternal hacker vigilance. It also underlines the importance of stressing the political benefits of free software programs over the competitive benefits. Pointing to software patents' ability to create sheltered regions in the marketplace, Stallman says competitive performance and price, two areas where free software operating systems such as GNU/Linux and FreeBSD already hold a distinct advantage over their proprietary counterparts, are red herrings compared to the large issues of user and developer freedom.

"It's not because we don't have the talent to make better software," says Stallman. "It's because we don't have the right. Somebody has prohibited us from serving the public. So what's going to happen when users encounter these gaps in free software? Well, if they have been persuaded by the open source movement that these freedoms are good because they lead to more-powerful reliable software, they're likely to say, 'You didn't deliver what you promised. This software's not more powerful. It's missing this feature. You lied to me.' But if they have come to agree with the free software movement, that the freedom is important in itself, then they will say, 'How dare those people stop me from having this feature and my freedom too.' And with that kind of response, we may survive the hits that we're going to take as these patents explode."

Such comments involve a hefty dose of spin, of course. Most open source advocates are equally, if not more, vociferous as Stallman when it comes to opposing software patents. Still, the underlying logic of Stallman's argument—that open source advocates emphasize the utilitarian advantages of free software over the political advantages—remains uncontested. Rather than stress the political significance of free software programs, open source advocates have chosen to stress the engineering integrity of the hacker development model. Citing the power of peer review, the open source argument paints programs such as GNU/Linux or FreeBSD as better built, better inspected and, by extension, more trushworthy to the average user.

That's not to say the term "open source" doesn't have its political implications. For open source advocates, the term open source serves two purposes. First, it eliminates the confusion associated with the word "free," a word many businesses interpret as meaning "zero cost." Second, it allows companies to examine the free software phenomenon on a technological, rather than ethical, basis. Eric Raymond, cofounder of the Open Source Initiative and one of the leading hackers to endorse the term, effectively summed up the frustration of following Stallman down the political path in a 1999 essay, titled "Shut Up and Show Them the Code":

> RMS's rhetoric is very seductive to the kind of people we are. We hackers are thinkers and idealists who readily resonate with appeals to "principle" and "freedom" and "rights." Even when we disagree with bits of his program, we want RMS's rhetorical style to work; we think it ought to work; we tend to be puzzled and disbelieving when it fails on the 95% of people who aren't wired like we are.[4]

Included among that 95%, Raymond writes, are the bulk of business managers, investors, and nonhacker computer users who, through sheer weight of numbers, tend to decide the overall direction of the commercial software marketplace. Without a way to win these people over, Raymond argues, programmers are doomed to pursue their ideology on the periphery of society:

> When RMS insists that we talk about "computer users' rights," he's issuing a dangerously attractive invitation to us to repeat old failures. It's one we should reject—not because his principles are wrong, but because that kind of language, applied to software, simply does not persuade anybody but us. In fact, it confuses and repels most people outside our culture.[4]

Watching Stallman deliver his political message in person, it is hard to see anything confusing or repellent. Stallman's appearance may seem off-putting, but his message is logical. When an audience member asks if, in shunning proprietary software, free software proponents lose the ability to keep up with the latest technological advancements, Stallman answers the question in terms of his own personal beliefs. "I think that freedom is more important than mere technical advance," he says. "I would always choose a less advanced free program rather than a more advanced nonfree program, because I won't give up my freedom for something like that. My rule is, if I can't share it with you, I won't take it."

Such answers, however, reinforce the quasi-religious nature of the Stallman message. Like a Jew keeping kosher or a Mormon refusing to drink alcohol, Stallman paints his decision to use free software in the place of proprietary in the color of tradition and personal belief. As software evangelists go, Stallman avoids forcing those beliefs down listeners' throats. Then again, a listener rarely leaves a Stallman speech not knowing where the true path to software righteousness lies.

As if to drive home this message, Stallman punctuates his speech with an unusual ritual. Pulling a black robe out of a plastic grocery bag, Stallman puts it on. Out of a second bag, he pulls a reflective yellow computer disk and places it on his head. The crowd lets out a startled laugh.

"I am St. Ignucius of the Church of Emacs," says Stallman, raising his right hand in mock-blessing. "I bless your computer, my child."

Stallman dressed as St. Ignucius. Photo by Wouter van Oortmerssen.

The laughter turns into full-blown applause after a few seconds. As audience members clap, the computer disk on Stallman's head catches the glare of an overhead light, eliciting a perfect halo effect. In the blink of an eye, Stallman goes from awkward *haole* to Russian religious icon.

"Emacs was initially a text editor," says Stallman, explaining the getup. "Eventually it became a way of life for many and a religion for some. We call this religion the Church of Emacs."

The skit is a lighthearted moment of self-pardoy, a humorous return-jab at the many people who might see Stallman's form of software asceticism as religious fanaticism in disguise. It is also the sound of the other shoe dropping—loudly. It's as if, in donning his robe and halo, Stallman is finally letting listeners of the hook, saying, "It's OK to laugh. I know I'm weird."

Discussing the St. Ignucius persona afterward, Stallman says he first came up with it in 1996, long after the creation of Emacs but well before the emergence of the "open source" term and the struggle for hacker-community leadership that precipitated it. At the time, Stallman says, he wanted a way to "poke fun at himself," to remind listeners that, though stubborn, Stallman was not the fanatic some made him out to be. It was only later, Stallman adds, that others seized the persona as a convenient way to play up his reputation as software ideologue, as Eric Raymond did in an 1999 interview with the linux.com web site:

> When I say RMS calibrates what he does, I'm not belittling or accusing him of insincerity. I'm saying that like all good communicators he's got a theatrical streak. Sometimes it's conscious— have you ever seen him in his St. Ignucius drag, blessing software with a disk platter on his head? Mostly it's unconscious; he's just learned the degree of irritating stimulus that works, that holds attention without (usually) freaking people out.[5]

Stallman takes issue with the Raymond analysis. "It's simply my way of making fun of myself," he says. "The fact that others see it as anything more than that is a reflection of their agenda, not mine."

That said, Stallman does admit to being a ham. "Are you kidding?" he says at one point. "I love being the center of attention." To facilitate that process, Stallman says he once enrolled in Toastmasters, an organization that helps members bolster their public-speaking skills and one Stallman recommends highly to others. He possesses a stage presence that would be the envy of most theatrical performers and feels a link to vaudevillians of years past. A few days after the Maui High Performance Computing Center speech, I allude to the 1999 LinuxWorld performace and ask Stallman if he has a Groucho Marx complex—i.e., the unwillingness to belong to any club that would have him as a member. Stallman's response is immediate: "No, but I admire Groucho Marx in a lot of ways and certainly have been in some things I say inspired by him. But then I've also been inspired in some ways by Harpo."

The Groucho Marx influence is certainly evident in Stallman's lifelong fondness for punning. Then again, punning and wordplay are common hacker traits. Perhaps the most Groucho-like aspect of Stallman's personality, however, is the deadpan manner in which the puns are delivered. Most come so stealthily—without even the hint of a raised eyebrow or upturned smile—you almost have to wonder if Stallman's laughing at his audience more than the audience is laughing at him.

Watching members of the Maui High Performance Computer Center laugh at the St. Ignucius parody, such concerns evaporate. While not exactly a standup act, Stallman certainly possesses the chops to keep a roomful of engineers in stitches. "To be a saint in the Church of Emacs does not require celibacy, but it does require making a commitment to living a life of moral purity," he tells the Maui audience. "You must exorcise the evil proprietary operating system from all your computer and then install a wholly [holy] free operating system. And then you must install only free software on top of that. If you make this commitment and live by it, then you too will be a saint in the Church of Emacs, and you too may have a halo."

The St. Ignucius skit ends with a brief inside joke. On most Unix systems and Unix-related offshoots, the primary competitor program to Emacs is vi, a text-editing program developed by former UC Berkeley student and current Sun Microsystems chief scientist, Bill Joy. Before doffing his "halo," Stallman pokes fun at the rival program. "People sometimes ask me if it is a sin in the Church of Emacs to use vi," he says. "Using a free version of vi is not a sin; it is a penance. So happy hacking."

After a brief question-and-answer session, audience members gather around Stallman. A few ask for autographs. "I'll sign this," says Stallman, holding up one woman's print out of the GNU General Public License, "but only if you promise me to use the term GNU/Linux instead of Linux and tell all your friends to do likewise."

The comment merely confirms a private observation. Unlike other stage performers and political figures, Stallman has no "off" mode. Aside from the St. Ignucius character, the ideologue you see onstage is the ideologue you meet backstage. Later that evening, during a dinner conversation in which a programmer mentions his affinity for "open source" programs, Stallman, between bites, upbraids his tablemate: "You mean free software. That's the proper way to refer to it."

During the question-and-answer session, Stallman admits to playing the pedagogue at times. "There are many people who say, 'Well, first let's invite people to join the community, and then let's teach them about freedom.' And that could be a reasonable strategy, but what we have is almost everybody's inviting people to join the community, and hardly anybody's teaching them about freedom once they come in."

The result, Stallman says, is something akin to a third-world city. People move in, hoping to strike it rich or at the very least to take part in a vibrant, open culture, and yet those who hold the true power keep evolving new tricks and strategies—i.e., software patents—to keep the masses out. "You have millions of people moving in and building shantytowns, but nobody's working on step two: getting them out of those shantytowns. If you think talking about software freedom is a good strategy, please join in doing step two. There are plenty working on step one. We need more people working on step two."

Working on "step two" means driving home the issue that freedom, not acceptance, is the root issue of the free software movement. Those who hope to reform the proprietary software industry from the inside are on a fool's errand. "Change from the inside is risky," Stallman stays. "Unless you're working at the level of a Gorbachev, you're going to be neutralized."

Hands pop up. Stallman points to a member of the golf shirt-wearing contingent. "Without patents, how would you suggest dealing with commercial espionage?"

"Well, those two questions have nothing to do with each other, really," says Stallman.

"But I mean if someone wants to steal another company's piece of software."

Stallman's recoils as if hit by a poisonous spray. "Wait a second," Stallman says. "Steal? I'm sorry, there's so much prejudice in that statement that the only thing I can say is that I reject that prejudice. Companies that develop nonfree software and other things keep lots and lots of trade secrets, and so that's not really likely to change. In the old days—even in the 1980s—for the most part programmers were not aware that there were even software patents and were paying no attention to them. What happened was that people published the interesting ideas, and if they were not in the free software movement, they kept secret the little details. And now they patent those broad ideas and keep secret the little details. So as far as what you're describing, patents really make no difference to it one way or another."

"But if it doesn't affect their publication," a new audience member jumps in, his voice trailing off almost as soon as he starts speaking.

"But it does," Stallman says. "Their publication is telling you that this is an idea that's off limits to the rest of the community for 20 years. And what the hell good is that? Besides, they've written it in such a hard way to read, both to obfuscate the idea and to make the patent as broad as possible, that it's basically useless looking at the published information to learn anything anyway. The only reason to look at patents is to see the bad news of what you can't do."

The audience falls silent. The speech, which began at 3:15, is now nearing the 5:00 whistle, and most listeners are already squirming in their seats, antsy to get a jump start on the weekend. Sensing the fatigue, Stallman glances around the room and hastily shuts things down. "So it looks like we're done," he says, following the observation with an auctioneer's "going, going, gone" to flush out any last-minute questioners. When nobody throws their hand up, Stallman signs off with a traditional exit line.

"Happy hacking," he says.

ENDNOTES

1. See "Grateful Dead Time Capsule: 1985–1995 North American Tour Grosses."

   http://www.accessplace.com/gdtc/1197.htm

2. See Evan Leibovitch, "Who's Afraid of Big Bad Wolves," *ZDNet Tech Update* (December 15, 2000).

   http://techupdate.zdnet.com/techupdate/stories/main/0,14179,2664992,00.html

3. For narrative purposes, I have hesitated to go in-depth when describing Stallman's full definition of software "freedom." The GNU Project web site lists four fundamental components:

   The freedom to run a program, for any purpose (freedom 0).

   The freedom to study how a program works, and adapt it to your needs (freedom 1).

   The freedom to redistribute copies of a program so you can help your neighbor (freedom 2).

   The freedom to improve the program, and release your improvements to the public, so that the whole community benefits (freedom 3).

   For more information, please visit "The Free Software Definition" at *http://www.gnu.org/philosophy/free-sw.html*.

4. See Eric Raymond, "Shut Up and Show Them the Code," online essay, (June 28, 1999).

5. See "Guest Interview: Eric S. Raymond," *Linux.com* (May 18, 1999).

   http://www.linux.com/interviews/19990518/8/

CHAPTER 9

THE GNU
GENERAL PUBLIC LICENSE

By the spring of 1985, Richard Stallman had settled on the GNU Project's first milestone—a Lisp-based free software version of Emacs. To meet this goal, however, he faced two challenges. First, he had to rebuild Emacs in a way that made it platform independent. Second, he had to rebuild the Emacs Commune in a similar fashion.

The dispute with UniPress had highlighted a flaw in the Emacs Commune social contract. Where users relied on Stallman's expert insight, the Commune's rules held. In areas where Stallman no longer held the position of alpha hacker—pre-1984 Unix systems, for example—individuals and companies were free to make their own rules.

The tension between the freedom to modify and the freedom to exert authorial privilege had been building before GOSMACS. The Copyright Act of 1976 had overhauled U.S. copyright law, extending the legal protection of copyright to software programs. According to Section 102(b) of the Act, individuals and companies now possessed the ability to copyright the "expression" of a software program but not the "actual processes or methods embodied in the program."[1] Translated, programmers and companies had the ability to treat software programs like a story or song. Other programmers could take inspiration from the work, but to make a direct copy or nonsatirical derivative, they first had to secure permission from the original creator. Although the new law guaranteed that even programs without copyright notices carried copyright protection, programmers quickly asserted their rights, attaching coypright notices to their software programs.

At first, Stallman viewed these notices with alarm. Rare was the software program that didn't borrow source code from past programs, and yet, with a single stroke of the president's pen, Congress had given programmers and companies the power to assert individual authorship over communally built programs. It also injected a dose of formality into what had otherwise been an informal system. Even if hackers could demonstrate how a given program's source-code bloodlines stretched back years, if not decades, the resources and money that went into battling each copyright notice were beyond most hackers' means. Simply put, disputes that had once been settled hacker-to-hacker were now settled lawyer-to-lawyer. In such a system, companies, not hackers, held the automatic advantage.

Proponents of software copyright had their counterarguments: without copyright, works might otherwise slip into the public domain. Putting a copyright notice on a work also served as a statement of quality. Programmers or companies who attached their name to the copyright attached their reputations as well. Finally, it was a contract, as well as a statement of ownership. Using copyright as a flexible form of license, an author could give away certain rights in exchange for certain forms of behavior on the part of the user. For example, an author could give away the right to suppress unauthorized copies just so long as the end user agreed not to create a commercial offshoot.

It was this last argument that eventually softened Stallman's resistance to software copyright notices. Looking back on the years leading up to the GNU Project, Stallman says he began to sense the beneficial nature of copyright sometime around the release of Emacs 15.0, the last significant pre–GNU Project upgrade of Emacs. "I had seen email messages with copyright notices plus simple 'verbatim copying permitted' licenses," Stallman recalls. "Those definitely were [an] inspiration."

For Emacs 15, Stallman drafted a copyright that gave users the right to make and distribute copies. It also gave users the right to make modified versions, but not the right to claim sole ownership of those modified versions, as in the case of GOSMACS. Although helpful in codifying the social contract of the Emacs Commune, the Emacs 15 license remained too "informal" for the purposes of the GNU Project, Stallman says. Soon after starting work on a GNU version of Emacs, Stallman began consulting with the other members of the Free Software Foundation on how to shore up the license's language. He also consulted with the attorneys who had helped him set up the Free Software Foundation.

Mark Fischer, a Boston attorney specializing in intellectual-property law, recalls discussing the license with Stallman during this period. "Richard had very strong views about how it should work," Fischer says, "He had two principles. The first was to make the software absolutely as open as possible. The second was to encourage others to adopt the same licensing practices."

Encouraging others to adopt the same licensing practices meant closing off the escape hatch that had allowed privately owned versions of Emacs to emerge. To close that escape hatch, Stallman and his free software colleagues came up with a solution: users would be free to modify GNU Emacs just so long as they published their modifications. In addition, the resulting "derivative" works would also have carry the same GNU Emacs License.

The revolutionary nature of this final condition would take a while to sink in. At the time, Fischer says, he simply viewed the GNU Emacs License as a simple contract. It put a price tag on GNU Emacs' use. Instead of money, Stallman was charging users access to their own later modifications. That said, Fischer does remember the contract terms as unique.

"I think asking other people to accept the price was, if not unique, highly unusual at that time," he says.

The GNU Emacs License made its debut when Stallman finally released GNU Emacs in 1985. Following the release, Stallman welcomed input from the general hacker community on how to improve the license's language. One hacker to take up the offer was future software activist John Gilmore, then working as a consultant to Sun Microsystems. As part of his consulting work, Gilmore had ported Emacs over to SunOS, the company's in-house version of Unix. In the process of doing so, Gilmore had published the changes as per the demands of the GNU Emacs License. Instead of viewing the license as a liability, Gilmore saw it as clear and concise expression of the hacker ethos. "Up until then, most licenses were very informal," Gilmore recalls.

As an example of this informality, Gilmore cites a copyright notice for trn, a Unix utility. Written by Larry Wall, future creator of the Perl programming language, patch made it simple for Unix programmers to insert source-code fixes—"patches" in hacker jargon—into any large program. Recognizing the utility of this feature, Wall put the following copyright notice in the program's accompanying README file:

Copyright (c) 1985, Larry Wall

You may copy the trn kit in whole or in part as long as you don't try to make money off it, or pretend that you wrote it.[2]

Such statements, while reflective of the hacker ethic, also reflected the difficulty of translating the loose, informal nature of that ethic into the rigid, legal language of copyright. In writing the GNU Emacs License, Stallman had done more than close up the escape hatch that permitted proprietary offshoots. He had expressed the hacker ethic in a manner understandable to both lawyer and hacker alike.

It wasn't long, Gilmore says, before other hackers began discussing ways to "port" the GNU Emacs License over to their own programs. Prompted by a conversation on Usenet, Gilmore sent an email to Stallman in November, 1986, suggesting modification:

You should probably remove "EMACS" from the license and replace it with "SOFTWARE" or something. Soon, we hope, Emacs will not be the biggest part of the GNU system, and the license applies to all of it.[3]

Gilmore wasn't the only person suggesting a more general approach. By the end of 1986, Stallman himself was at work with GNU Project's next major milestone, a source-code debugger, and was looking for ways to revamp the Emacs license so that it might apply to both programs. Stallman's solution: remove all specific references to Emacs and convert the license into a generic copyright umbrella for GNU Project software. The GNU General Public License, GPL for short, was born.

In fashioning the GPL, Stallman followed the software convention of using decimal numbers to indicate prototype versions and whole numbers to indicate mature versions. Stallman published Version 1.0 of the GPL in 1989 (a project Stallman was developing in 1985), almost a full year after the release of the GNU Debugger, Stallman's second major foray into the realm of Unix programming. The license contained a preamble spelling out its political intentions:

> The General Public License is designed to make sure that you have the freedom to give away or sell copies of free software, that you receive source code or can get it if you want it, that you can change the software or use pieces of it in new free programs; and that you know you can do these things.
>
> To protect your rights, we need to make restrictions that forbid anyone to deny you these rights or to ask you to surrender the rights. These restrictions translate to certain responsibilities for you if you distribute copies of the software, or if you modify it.[4]

In fashioning the GPL, Stallman had been forced to make an additional adjustment to the informal tenets of the old Emacs Commune. Where he had once demanded that Commune members publish any and all changes, Stallman now demanded publication only in instances when programmers circulated their derivative versions in the same public manner as Stallman. In other words, programmers who simply modified Emacs for private use no longer needed to send the source-code changes back to Stallman. In what would become a rare compromise of free software doctrine, Stallman slashed the price tag for free software. Users could innovate without Stallman looking over their shoulders just so long as they didn't bar Stallman and the rest of the hacker community from future exchanges of the same program.

Looking back, Stallman says the GPL compromise was fueled by his own dissatisfaction with the Big Brother aspect of the original Emacs Commune social contract. As much as he liked peering into other hackers' systems, the knowledge that some future source-code maintainer might use that power to ill effect forced him to temper the GPL.

"It was wrong to require people to publish all changes," says Stallman. "It was wrong to require them to be sent to one privileged developer. That kind of centralization and privilege for one was not consistent with a society in which all had equal rights."

As hacks go, the GPL stands as one of Stallman's best. It created a system of communal ownership within the normally proprietary confines of copyright law. More importantly, it demonstrated the intellectual similarity between legal code and software code. Implicit within the GPL's preamble was a profound message: instead of viewing copyright law with suspicion, hackers should view it as yet another system begging to be hacked.

"The GPL developed much like any piece of free software with a large community discussing its structure, its respect or the opposite in their observation, needs for tweaking and even to compromise it mildly for greater acceptance," says Jerry Cohen, another attorney who helped Stallman with the creation of the license. "The process worked very well and GPL in its several versions has gone from widespread skeptical and at times hostile response to widespread acceptance."

In a 1986 interview with *Byte* magazine, Stallman summed up the GPL in colorful terms. In addition to proclaiming hacker values, Stallman said, readers should also "see it as a form of intellectual jujitsu, using the legal system that software hoarders have set up against them."[5] Years later, Stallman would describe the GPL's creation in less hostile terms. "I was thinking about issues that were in a sense ethical and in a sense political and in a sense legal," he says. "I had to try to do what could be sustained by the legal system that we're in. In spirit the job was that of legislating the basis for a new society, but since I wasn't a government, I couldn't actually change any laws. I had to try to do this by building on top of the existing legal system, which had not been designed for anything like this."

About the time Stallman was pondering the ethical, political, and legal issues associated with free software, a California hacker named Don Hopkins mailed him a manual for the 68000 microprocessor. Hopkins, a Unix hacker and fellow science-fiction buff, had borrowed the manual from Stallman a while earlier. As a display of gratitude, Hopkins decorated the return envelope with a number of stickers obtained at a local science-fiction convention. One sticker in particular caught Stallman's eye. It read, "Copyleft (L), All Rights Reversed." Following the release of the first version of GPL, Stallman paid tribute to the sticker, nicknaming the free software license "Copyleft." Over time, the nickname and its shorthand symbol, a backwards "C," would become an official Free Software Foundation synonym for the GPL.

The German sociologist Max Weber once proposed that all great religions are built upon the "routinization" or "institutionalization" of charisma. Every successful religion, Weber argued, converts the charisma or message of the original religious leader into a social, political, and ethical apparatus more easily translatable across cultures and time.

While not religious per se, the GNU GPL certainly qualifies as an interesting example of this "routinization" process at work in the modern, decentralized world of software development. Since its unveiling, programmers and companies who have otherwise expressed little loyalty or allegiance to Stallman have willingly accepted the GPL bargain at face value. A few have even accepted the GPL as a preemptive protective mechanism for their own software programs. Even those who reject the GPL contract as too compulsory, still credit it as influential.

One hacker falling into this latter group was Keith Bostic, a University of California employee at the time of the GPL 1.0 release. Bostic's department, the Computer Systems Research

Group (SRG), had been involved in Unix development since the late 1970s and was responsible for many key parts of Unix, including the TCP/IP networking protocol, the cornerstone of modern Internet communications. By the late 1980s, AT&T, the original owner of the Unix brand name, began to focus on commercializing Unix and began looking to the Berkeley Software Distribution, or BSD, the academic version of Unix developed by Bostic and his Berkeley peers, as a key source of commercial technology.

Although the Berkeley BSD source code was shared among researchers and commercial programmers with a source-code license, this commercialization presented a problem. The Berkeley code was intermixed with proprietary AT&T code. As a result, Berkeley distributions were available only to institutions that already had a Unix source license from AT&T. As AT&T raised its license fees, this arrangement, which had at first seemed innocuous, became increasingly burdensome.

Hired in 1986, Bostic had taken on the personal project of porting BSD over to the Digital Equipment Corporation's PDP-11 computer. It was during this period, Bostic says, that he came into close interaction with Stallman during Stallman's occasional forays out to the west coast. "I remember vividly arguing copyright with Stallman while he sat at borrowed workstations at CSRG," says Bostic. "We'd go to dinner afterward and continue arguing about copyright over dinner."

The arguments eventually took hold, although not in the way Stallman would have liked. In June, 1989, Berkeley separated its networking code from the rest of the AT&T-owned operating system and distributed it under a University of California license. The contract terms were liberal. All a licensee had to do was give credit to the university in advertisements touting derivative programs.[6] In contrast to the GPL, proprietary offshoots were permissible. Only one problem hampered the license's rapid adoption: the BSD Networking release wasn't a complete operating system. People could study the code, but it could only be run in conjunction with other proprietary-licensed code.

Over the next few years, Bostic and other University of California employees worked to replace the missing components and turn BSD into a complete, freely redistributable operating system. Although delayed by a legal challenge from Unix Systems Laboratories—the AT&T spin-off that retained ownership of the Unix brand name—the effort would finally bear fruit in the early 1990s. Even before then, however, many of the Berkeley utilities would make their way into Stallman's GNU Project.

"I think it's highly unlikely that we ever would have gone as strongly as we did without the GNU influence," says Bostic, looking back. "It was clearly something where they were pushing hard and we liked the idea."

By the end of the 1980s, the GPL was beginning to exert a gravitational effect on the free software community. A program didn't have to carry the GPL to qualify as free software—witness the case of the BSD utilities—but putting a program under the GPL sent a definite message. "I think the very existence of the GPL inspired people to think through whether they were making free software, and how they would license it," says Bruce Perens, creator of Electric Fence, a popular Unix utility, and future leader of the Debian GNU/Linux development team. A few years after the release of the GPL, Perens says he decided to discard Electric Fence's homegrown license in favor of Stallman's lawyer-vetted copyright. "It was actually pretty easy to do," Perens recalls.

Rich Morin, the programmer who had viewed Stallman's initial GNU announcement with a degree of skepticism, recalls being impressed by the software that began to gather under the GPL umbrella. As the leader of a SunOS user group, one of Morin's primary duties during the 1980s had been to send out distribution tapes containing the best freeware or free software utilities. The job often mandated calling up original program authors to verify whether their programs were copyright protected or whether they had been consigned to the public domain. Around 1989, Morin says, he began to notice that the best software programs typically fell under the GPL license. "As a software distributor, as soon as I saw the word GPL, I knew I was home free," recalls Morin.

To compensate for the prior hassles that went into compiling distribution tapes to the Sun User Group, Morin had charged recipients a convenience fee. Now, with programs moving over to the GPL, Morin was suddenly getting his tapes put together in half the time, turning a tidy profit in the process. Sensing a commercial opportunity, Morin rechristened his hobby as a business: Prime Time Freeware.

Such commercial exploitation was completely within the confines of the free software agenda. "When we speak of free software, we are referring to freedom, not price," advised Stallman in the GPL's preamble. By the late 1980s, Stallman had refined it to a more simple mnemonic: "Don't think free as in free beer; think free as in free speech."

For the most part, businesses ignored Stallman's entreaties. Still, for a few entrepreneurs, the freedom associated with free software was the same freedom associated with free markets. Take software ownership out of the commercial equation, and you had a situation where even the smallest software company was free to compete against the IBMs and DECs of the world.

One of the first entrepreneurs to grasp this concept was Michael Tiemann, a software programmer and graduate student at Stanford University. During the 1980s, Tiemann had followed the GNU Project like an aspiring jazz musician following a favorite artist. It wasn't until the release of the GNU C Compiler in 1987, however, that he began to grasp the full potential of free software. Dubbing GCC a "bombshell," Tiemann says the program's own existence underlined Stallman's determination as a programmer.

"Just as every writer dreams of writing the great American novel, every programmer back in the 1980s talked about writing the great American compiler," Tiemman recalls. "Suddenly Stallman had done it. It was very humbling."

"You talk about single points of failure, GCC was it," echoes Bostic. "Nobody had a compiler back then, until GCC came along."

Rather than compete with Stallman, Tiemann decided to build on top of his work. The original version of GCC weighed in at 110,000 lines of code, but Tiemann recalls the program as surprisingly easy to understand. So easy in fact that Tiemann says it took less than five days to master and another week to port the software to a new hardware platform, National Semiconductor's 32032 microchip. Over the next year, Tiemann began playing around with the source code, creating a native compiler for the C+ programming language. One day, while delivering a lecture on the program at Bell Labs, Tiemann ran into some AT&T developers struggling to pull off the same thing.

"There were about 40 or 50 people in the room, and I asked how many people were working on the native code compiler," Tiemann recalls. "My host said the information was confidential but added that if I took a look around the room I might get a good general idea."

It wasn't long after, Tiemann says, that the light bulb went off in his head. "I had been working on that project for six months," Tiemann says. I just thought to myself, whether it's me or the code this is a level of efficiency that the free market should be ready to reward."

Tiemann found added inspiration in the GNU Manifesto, which, while excoriating the greed of some software vendors, encourages other vendors to consider the advantages of free software from a consumer point of view. By removing the power of monopoly from the commerical software question, the GPL makes it possible for the smartest vendors to compete on the basis of service and consulting, the two most profit-rich corners of the software marketplace.

In a 1999 essay, Tiemann recalls the impact of Stallman's Manifesto. "It read like a socialist polemic, but I saw something different. I saw a business plan in disguise."[7]

Teaming up with John Gilmore, another GNU Project fan, Tiemann launched a software consulting service dedicated to customizing GNU programs. Dubbed Cygnus Support, the company signed its first development contract in February, 1990. By the end of the year, the company had $725,000 worth of support and development contracts.

GNU Emacs, GDB, and GCC were the "big three" of developer-oriented tools, but they weren't the only ones developed by Stallman during the GNU Project's first half decade. By 1990, Stallman had also generated GNU versions of the Bourne Shell (rechristened the Bourne Again Shell, or BASH), YACC (rechristened Bison), and awk (rechristened gawk). Like GCC, every GNU program had to be designed to run on multiple systems, not just a single vendor's platform. In the process of making programs more flexible, Stallman and his collaborators often made them more useful as well.

Recalling the GNU universalist approach, Prime Time Freeware's Morin points to a critical, albeit mundane, software package called hello. "It's the hello world program which is five lines of C, packaged up as if it were a GNU distribution," Morin says. "And so it's got the Texinfo stuff and the configure stuff. It's got all the other software engineering goo that the GNU Project has come up with to allow packages to port to all these different environments smoothly. That's tremendously important work, and it affects not only all of [Stallman's] software, but also all of the other GNU Project software."

According to Stallman, improving software programs was secondary to building them in the first place. "With each piece I may or may not find a way to improve it," said Stallman to *Byte*. "To some extent I am getting the benefit of reimplementation, which makes many systems much better. To some extent it's because I have been in the field a long time and worked on many other systems. I therefore have many ideas to bring to bear."[8]

Nevertheless, as GNU tools made their mark in the late 1980s, Stallman's AI Lab–honed reputation for design fastidiousness soon became legendary throughout the entire software-development community.

Jeremy Allison, a Sun user during the late 1980s and programmer destined to run his own free software project, Samba, in the 1990s, recalls that reputation with a laugh. During the late 1980s, Allison began using Emacs. Inspired by the program's community-development model, Allison says he sent in a snippet of source code only to have it rejected by Stallman.

"It was like the *Onion* headline," Allison says. "'Child's prayers to God answered: No.'"

Stallman's growing stature as a software programmer, however, was balanced by his struggles as a project manager. Although the GNU Project moved from success to success in creation of developer-oriented tools, its inability to generate a working kernel—the central "traffic cop" program in all Unix systems that determines which devices and applications get access to the microprocessor and when—was starting to elicit grumbles as the 1980s came to a close. As with most GNU Project efforts, Stallman had started kernel development by looking for an existing program to modify. According to a January 1987 "Gnusletter," Stallman was already working to overhaul TRIX, a Unix kernel developed at MIT.

A review of GNU Project "GNUsletters" of the late 1980s reflects the management tension. In January, 1987, Stallman announced to the world that the GNU Project was working to overhaul TRIX, a Unix kernel developed at MIT. A year later, in February of 1988, the GNU Project announced that it had shifted its attentions to Mach, a lightweight "micro-kernel" developed at Carnegie Mellon. All told, however, official GNU Project kernel development wouldn't commence until 1990.[9]

The delays in kernel development were just one of many concerns weighing on Stallman during this period. In 1989, Lotus Development Corporation filed suit against rival software company, Paperback Software International, for copying menu commands in Lotus' popular 1-2-3 Spreadsheet program. Lotus' suit, coupled with the Apple-Microsoft "look and feel" battle, provided a troublesome backdrop for the GNU Project. Although both suits fell outside the scope of the GNU Project, both revolved around operating systems and software applications developed for the personal computer, not Unix-compatible hardware systems— they threatened to impose a chilling effect on the entire culture of software development. Determined to do something, Stallman recruited a few programmer friends and composed a magazine ad blasting the lawsuits. He then followed up the ad by helping to organize a group to protest the corporations filing the suit. Calling itself the League of Programming Freedom, the group held protests outside the offices of Lotus, Inc. and the Boston courtroom hosting the Lotus trial.

The protests were notable.[10] They document the evolving nature of software industry. Applications had quietly replaced operating systems as the primary corporate battleground. In its unfulfilled quest to build a free software operating system, the GNU Project seemed hopelessly behind the times. Indeed, the very fact that Stallman had felt it necessary to put together an entirely new group dedicated to battling the "look and feel" lawsuits reinforced that obsolescence in the eyes of some observers.

In 1990, the John D. and Catherine T. MacArthur Foundation cerified Stallman's genius status when it granted Stallman a MacArthur fellowship, therefore making him a recipient for the organization's so-called "genius grant." The grant, a $240,000 reward for launching the GNU Project and giving voice to the free software philosophy, relieved a number of short-term concerns. First and foremost, it gave Stallman, a nonsalaried employee of the FSF who had been supporting himself through consulting contracts, the ability to devote more time to writing GNU code.[11]

Ironically, the award also made it possible for Stallman to vote. Months before the award, a fire in Stallman's apartment house had consumed his few earthly possessions. By the time of the award, Stallman was listing himself as a "squatter"[12] at 545 Technology Square. "[The registrar of voters] didn't want to accept that as my address," Stallman would later recall. "A newspaper article about the MacArthur grant said that and then they let me register."[13]

Most importantly, the MacArthur money gave Stallman more freedom. Already dedicated to the issue of software freedom, Stallman chose to use the additional freedom to increase his travels in support of the GNU Project mission.

Interestingly, the ultimate success of the GNU Project and the free software movement in general would stem from one of these trips. In 1990, Stallman paid a visit to the Polytechnic University in Helsinki, Finland. Among the audience members was 21-year-old Linus Torvalds, future developer of the Linux kernel—the free software kernel destined to fill the GNU Project's most sizable gap.

A student at the nearby University of Helsinki at the time, Torvalds regarded Stallman with bemusement. "I saw, for the first time in my life, the stereotypical long-haired, bearded hacker type," recalls Torvalds in his 2001 autobiography *Just for Fun.* "We don't have much of them in Helsinki."14

While not exactly attuned to the "sociopolitical" side of the Stallman agenda, Torvalds nevertheless appreciated the agenda's underlying logic: no programmer writes error-free code. By sharing software, hackers put a program's improvement ahead of individual motivations such as greed or ego protection.

Like many programmers of his generation, Torvalds had cut his teeth not on mainframe computers like the IBM 7094, but on a motley assortment of home-built computer systems. As university student, Torvalds had made the step up from C programming to Unix, using the university's MicroVAX. This ladder-like progression had given Torvalds a different perspective on the barriers to machine access. For Stallman, the chief barriers were bureaucracy and privilege. For Torvalds, the chief barriers were geography and the harsh Helsinki winter. Forced to trek across the University of Helsinki just to log in to his Unix account, Torvalds quickly began looking for a way to log in from the warm confines of his off-campus apartment.

The search led Torvalds to the operating system Minix, a lightweight version of Unix developed for instructional purposes by Dutch university professor Andrew Tanenbaum. The program fit within the memory confines of a 386 PC, the most powerful machine Torvalds could afford, but still lacked a few necessary features. It most notably lacked terminal emulation, the feature that allowed Torvalds' machine to mimic a university terminal, making it possible to log in to the MicroVAX from home. During the summer of 1991, Torvalds rewrote Minix from the ground up, adding other features as he did so. By the end of the summer, Torvalds was referring to his evolving work as the "GNU/Emacs of terminal emulation programs."[15] Feeling confident, he solicited a Minix newsgroup for copies of the POSIX standards, the software blue prints that determined whether a program was Unix compatible. A few weeks later, Torvalds was posting a message eerily reminiscent of Stallman's original 1983 GNU posting:

Hello everybody out there using minix-

I'm doing a (free) operating system (just a hobby, won't be big and professional like gnu for 386 (486) AT clones). This has been brewing since April, and is starting to get ready. I'd like any feedback on things people like/dislike in minix, as my OS resembles it somewhat (same physical layout of the file-system (due to practical reasons) among other things).[16]

The posting drew a smattering of responses and within a month, Torvalds had posted a 0.01 version of the operating system—i.e., the earliest possible version fit for outside review—on an Internet FTP site. In the course of doing so, Torvalds had to come up with a name for the new system. On his own PC hard drive, Torvalds had saved the program as Linux, a name that paid its respects to the software convention of giving each Unix variant a name that ended with the letter X. Deeming the name too "egotistical," Torvalds changed it to Freax, only to have the FTP site manager change it back.

Although Torvalds had set out build a full operating system, both he and other developers knew at the time that most of the functional tools needed to do so were already available, thanks to the work of GNU, BSD, and other free software developers. One of the first tools the Linux development team took advantage of was the GNU C Compiler, a tool that made it possible to process programs written in the C programming language.

Integrating GCC improved the performance of Linux. It also raised issues. Although the GPL's "viral" powers didn't apply to the Linux kernel, Torvald's willingness to borrow GCC for the purposes of his own free software operating system indicated a certain obligation to let other users borrow back. As Torvalds would later put it: "I had hoisted myself up on the shoulders of giants."[17] Not surprisingly, he began to think about what would happen when other people looked to him for similar support. A decade after the decision, Torvalds echoes the Free Software Foundation's Robert Chassel when he sums up his thoughts at the time:

> *You put six months of your life into this thing and you want to make it available and you want to get something out of it, but you don't want people to take advantage of it. I wanted people to be able to see [Linux], and to make changes and improvements to their hearts' content. But I also wanted to make sure that what I got out of it was to see what they were doing. I wanted to always have access to the sources so that if they made improvements, I could make those improvements myself.[18]*

When it was time to release the 0.12 version of Linux, the first to include a fully integrated version of GCC, Torvalds decided to voice his allegiance with the free software movement. He discarded the old kernel license and replaced it with the GPL. The decision triggered a porting spree, as Torvalds and his collaborators looked to other GNU programs to fold into the growing Linux stew. Within three years, Linux developers were offering their first production release, Linux 1.0, including fully modified versions of GCC, GDB, and a host of BSD tools.

By 1994, the amalgamated operating system had earned enough respect in the hacker world to make some observers wonder if Torvalds hadn't given away the farm by switching to the GPL in the project's initial months. In the first issue of Linux Journal, publisher Robert Young sat down with Torvalds for an interview. When Young asked the Finnish programmer if he felt regret at giving up private ownership of the Linux source code,

Torvalds said no. "Even with 20/20 hindsight," Torvalds said, he considered the GPL "one of the very best design decisions" made during the early stages of the Linux project.[19] That the decision had been made with zero appeal or deference to Stallman and the Free Software Foundation speaks to the GPL's growing portability. Although it would take a few years to be recognized by Stallman, the explosiveness of Linux development conjured flashbacks of Emacs. This time around, however, the innovation triggering the explosion wasn't a software hack like Control-R but the novelty of running a Unix-like system on the PC architecture. The motives may have been different, but the end result certainly fit the ethical specifications: a fully functional operating system composed entirely of free software.

As his initial email message to the comp.os.minix newsgroup indicates, it would take a few months before Torvalds saw Linux as anything less than a holdover until the GNU developers delivered on the HURD kernel. This initial unwillingness to see Linux in political terms would represent a major blow to the Free Software Foundation.

As far as Torvalds was concerned, he was simply the latest in a long line of kids taking apart and reassembling things just for fun. Nevertheless, when summing up the runaway success of a project that could have just as easily spent the rest of its days on an abandoned computer hard drive, Torvalds credits his younger self for having the wisdom to give up control and accept the GPL bargain.

"I may not have seen the light," writes Torvalds, reflecting on Stallman's 1991 Polytechnic University speech and his subsequent decision to switch to the GPL. "But I guess something from his speech sunk in."[20]

ENDNOTES

1. See Hal Abelson, Mike Fischer, and Joanne Costello, "Software and Copyright Law," updated version (1998).

    http://www.swiss.ai.mit.edu/6805/articles/int-prop/software-copyright.html

2. See Trn Kit README.

    http://www.za.debian.org/doc/trn/trn-readme

3. See John Gilmore, quoted from email to author.

4. See Richard Stallman, et al., "GNU General Public License: Version 1," (February, 1989).

   http://www.gnu.org/copyleft/copying-1.0.html

5. See David Betz and Jon Edwards, "Richard Stallman discusses his public-domain [sic] Unix-compatible software system with BYTE editors," *BYTE* (July, 1996). (Reprinted on the GNU Project web site: *http://www.gnu.org/gnu/byte-interview.html.*)

   This interview offers an interesting, not to mention candid, glimpse at Stallman's political attitudes during the earliest days of the GNU Project. It is also helpful in tracing the evolution of Stallman's rhetoric.

   Describing the purpose of the GPL, Stallman says, "I'm trying to change the way people approach knowledge and information in general. I think that to try to own knowledge, to try to control whether people are allowed to use it, or to try to stop other people from sharing it, is sabotage."

   Contrast this with a statement to the author in August 2000: "I urge you not to use the term 'intellectual property' in your thinking. It will lead you to misunderstand things, because that term generalizes about copyrights, patents, and trademarks. And those things are so different in their effects that it is entirely foolish to try to talk about them at once. If you hear somebody saying something about intellectual property, without quotes, then he's not thinking very clearly and you shouldn't join."

6. The University of California's "obnoxious advertising clause" would later prove to be a problem. Looking for a less restrictive alternative to the GPL, some hackers used the University of California, replacing "University of California" with the name of their own instution. The result: free software programs that borrowed from dozens of other programs would have to cite dozens of institutions in advertisements. In 1999, after a decade of lobbying on Stallman's part, the University of California agreed to drop this clause.

   See "The BSD License Problem" at *http://www.gnu.org/philosophy/bsd.html.*

7. See Michael Tiemann, "Future of Cygnus Solutions: An Entrepreneur's Account," *Open Sources* (O'Reilly & Associates, Inc., 1999): 139.

8. See Richard Stallman, *BYTE* (1986).

9. See "HURD History."

   http://www.gnu.org/software/hurd/history.html

10. According to a League of Programming Freedom Press, the protests were notable for featuring the first hexadecimal protest chant:

    1-2-3-4, toss the lawyers out the door;

    5-6-7-8, innovate don't litigate;

    9-A-B-C, 1-2-3 is not for me;

    D-E-F-O, look and feel have got to go

    http://lpf.ai.mit.edu/Links/prep.ai.mit.edu/demo.final.release

11. I use the term "writing" here loosely. About the time of the MacArthur award, Stallman began suffering chronic pain in his hands and was dictating his work to FSF-employed typists. Although some have speculated that the hand pain was the result of repetitive stress injury, or RSI, an injury common among software programmers, Stallman is not 100% sure. "It was NOT carpal tunnel syndrome," he writes. "My hand problem was in the hands themselves, not in the wrists." Stallman has since learned to work without typists after switching to a keyboard with a lighter touch.

12. See Reuven Lerner, "Stallman wins $240,000 MacArthur award," MIT, *The Tech* (July 18, 1990).

    http://the-tech.mit.edu/V110/N30/rms.30n.html

13. See Michael Gross, "Richard Stallman: High School Misfit, Symbol of Free Software, MacArthur-certified Genius" (1999).

14. See Linus Torvalds and David Diamond, *Just For Fun: The Story of an Accidentaly Revolutionary* (HarperCollins Publishers, Inc., 2001): 58–59.

15. See Linus Torvalds and David Diamond, *Just For Fun: The Story of an Accidentaly Revolutionary* (HarperCollins Publishers, Inc., 2001): 78.

16. See "Linux 10th Anniversary."

    http://www.linux10.org/history/

17. See Linus Torvalds and David Diamond, *Just For Fun: The Story of an Accidentaly Revolutionary* (HarperCollins Publishers, Inc., 2001): 96–97.

18. See Linus Torvalds and David Diamond, *Just For Fun: The Story of an Accidentaly Revolutionary* (HarperCollins Publishers, Inc., 2001): 94–95.

19. See Robert Young, "Interview with Linus, the Author of Linux," *Linux Journal* (March 1, 1994).

    http://www.linuxjournal.com/article.php?sid=2736

20. See Linus Torvalds and David Diamond, *Just For Fun: The Story of an Accidentaly Revolutionary* (HarperCollins Publishers, Inc., 2001): 59.

CHAPTER 10

GNU/LINUX

By 1993, the free software movement was at a crossroads. To the optimistically inclined, all signs pointed toward success for the hacker cultur. *Wired* magazine, a funky, new publication offering stories on data encryption, Usenet, and software freedom, was flying off magazine racks. The Internet, once a slang term used only by hackers and research scientists, had found its way into mainstream lexicon. Even President Clinton was using it. The personal computer, once a hobbyist's toy, had grown to full-scale respectability, giving a whole new generation of computer users access to hacker-built software. And while the GNU Project had not yet reached its goal of a fully intact, free software operating system, curious users could still try Linux in the interim.

Any way you sliced it, the news was good, or so it seemed. After a decade of struggle, hackers and hacker values were finally gaining acceptance in mainstream society. People were getting it.

Or were they? To the pessimistically inclined, each sign of acceptance carried its own troubling countersign. Sure, being a hacker was suddenly cool, but was cool good for a community that thrived on alienation? Sure, the White House was saying all the right things about the Internet, even going so far as to register its own domain name, whitehouse.gov, but it was also meeting with the companies, censorship advocates, and law-enforcement officials looking to tame the Internet's Wild West culture. Sure, PCs were more powerful, but in commoditizing the PC marketplace with its chips, Intel had created a situation in which proprietary software vendors now held the power. For every new user won over to the free software cause via Linux, hundreds, perhaps thousands, were booting up Microsoft Windows for the first time.

Finally, there was the curious nature of Linux itself. Unrestricted by design bugs (like GNU) and legal disputes (like BSD), Linux' high-speed evolution had been so unplanned, its success so accidental, that programmers closest to the software code itself didn't know what to make of it. More compilation album than operating system, it was comprised of a hacker medley of greatest hits: everything from GCC, GDB, and glibc (the GNU Project's newly developed C Library) to X (a Unix-based graphic user interface developed by MIT's Laboratory for Computer Science) to BSD-developed tools such as BIND (the Berkeley Internet Naming Daemon, which lets users substitute easy-to-remember Internet domain names for numeric IP addresses) and TCP/IP. The arch's capstone, of course, was the Linux kernel—itself a bored-out, super-charged version of Minix. Rather than building their operating system from scratch, Torvalds and his rapidly expanding Linux development team had followed the old Picasso adage, "good artists borrow; great artists steal." Or as Torvalds himself would later translate it when describing the secret of his success: "I'm basically a very lazy person who likes to take credit for things other people actually do."[1]

Such laziness, while admirable from an efficiency perspective, was troubling from a political perspective. For one thing, it underlined the lack of an ideological agenda on Torvalds' part. Unlike the GNU developers, Torvalds hadn't built an operating system out of a desire to give his fellow hackers something to work with; he'd built it to have something he himself could play with. Like Tom Sawyer whitewashing a fence, Torvalds' genius lay less in the overall vision and more in his ability to recruit other hackers to speed the process.

That Torvalds and his recruits had succeeded where others had not raised its own troubling question: what, exactly, was Linux? Was it a manifestation of the free software philosophy first articulated by Stallman in the GNU Manifesto? Or was it simply an amalgamation of nifty software tools that any user, similarly motivated, could assemble on his own home system?

By late 1993, a growing number of Linux users had begun to lean toward the latter definition and began brewing private variations on the Linux theme. They even became bold enough to bottle and sell their variations—or "distributions"—to fellow Unix aficionados. The results were spotty at best.

"This was back before Red Hat and the other commercial distributions," remembers Ian Murdock, then a computer science student at Purdue University. "You'd flip through Unix magazines and find all these business card–sized ads proclaiming 'Linux.' Most of the companies were fly-by-night operations that saw nothing wrong with slipping a little of their own source code into the mix."

Murdock, a Unix programmer, remembers being "swept away" by Linux when he first downloaded and installed it on his home PC system. "It was just a lot of fun," he says. "It made me want to get involved." The explosion of poorly built distributions began to dampen his early enthusiasm, however. Deciding that the best way to get involved was to build a version of Linux free of additives, Murdock set about putting a list of the best free software tools available with the intention of folding them into his own distribution. "I wanted something that would live up to the Linux name," Murdock says.

In a bid to "stir up some interest," Murdock posted his intentions on the Internet, including Usenet's comp.os.linux newsgroup. One of the first responding email messages was from *rms@ai.mit.edu*. As a hacker, Murdock instantly recognized the address. It was Richard M. Stallman, founder of the GNU Project and a man Murdock knew even back then as "the hacker of hackers." Seeing the address in his mail queue, Murdock was puzzled. Why on Earth would Stallman, a person leading his own operating-system project, care about Murdock's gripes over Linux?

Murdock opened the message.

"He said the Free Software Foundation was starting to look closely at Linux and that the FSF was interested in possibly doing a Linux system, too. Basically, it looked to Stallman like our goals were in line with their philosophy."

The message represented a dramatic about-face on Stallman's part. Until 1993, Stallman had been content to keep his nose out of the Linux community's affairs. In fact, he had all but shunned the renegade operating system when it first appeared on the Unix programming landscape in 1991. After receiving the first notification of a Unix-like operating system that ran on PCs, Stallman says he delegated the task of examining the new operating system to a friend. Recalls Stallman, "He reported back that the software was modeled after System V, which was the inferior version of Unix. He also told me it wasn't portable."

The friend's report was correct. Built to run on 386-based machines, Linux was firmly rooted to its low-cost hardware platform. What the friend failed to report, however, was the sizable advantage Linux enjoyed as the only freely modifiable operating system in the marketplace. In other words, while Stallman spent the next three years listening to bug reports from his HURD team, Torvalds was winning over the programmers who would later uproot and replant the operating system onto new platforms.

By 1993, the GNU Project's inability to deliver a working kernel was leading to problems both within the GNU Project and within the free software movement at large. A March, 1993, a *Wired* magazine article by Simson Garfinkel described the GNU Project as "bogged down" despite the success of the project's many tools.[2] Those within the project and its nonprofit adjunct, the Free Software Foundation, remember the mood as being even worse than Garfinkel's article let on. "It was very clear, at least to me at the time, that there was a window of opportunity to introduce a new operating system," says Chassell. "And once that window was closed, people would become less interested. Which is in fact exactly what happened."[3]

Much has been made about the GNU Project's struggles during the 1990–1993 period. While some place the blame on Stallman for those struggles, Eric Raymond, an early member of the GNU Emacs team and later Stallman critic, says the problem was largely institutional. "The FSF got arrogant," Raymond says. "They moved away from the goal of doing a production-ready operating system to doing operating-system research." Even worse, "They thought nothing outside the FSF could affect them."

Murdock, a person less privy to the inner dealings of the GNU Project, adopts a more charitable view. "I think part of the problem is they were a little too ambitious and they threw good money after bad," he says. "Micro-kernels in the late 80s and early 90s were a hot topic. Unfortunately, that was about the time that the GNU Project started to design their kernel. They ended up with alot of baggage and it would have taken a lot of back-pedaling to lose it."

Stallman cites a number of issues when explaining the delay. The Lotus and Apple lawsuits had provided political distractions, which, coupled with Stallman's inability to type, made it difficult for Stallman to lend a helping hand to the HURD team. Stallman also cites poor communication between various portions of the GNU Project. "We had to do a lot of work to get the debugging environment to work," he recalls. "And the people maintaining GDB at the time were not that cooperative." Mostly, however, Stallman says he and the other members of the GNU Project team underestimated the difficulty of expanding the Mach microkernal into a full-fledged Unix kernel.

"I figured, OK, the [Mach] part that has to talk to the machine has already been debugged," Stallman says, recalling the HURD team's troubles in a 2000 speech. "With that head start, we should be able to get it done faster. But instead, it turned out that debugging these asynchronous multithreaded programs was really hard. There were timing books that would clobber the files, and that's no fun. The end result was that it took many, many years to produce a test version."[4]

Whatever the excuse, or excuses, the concurrent success of the Linux-kernel team created a tense situation. Sure, the Linux kernel had been licensed under the GPL, but as Murdock himself had noted, the desire to treat Linux as a purely free software operating system was far from uniform. By late 1993, the total Linux user population had grown from a dozen or so Minix enthusiasts to somewhere between 20,000 and 100,000.[5] What had once been a hobby was now a marketplace ripe for exploitation. Like Winston Churchill watching Soviet troops sweep into Berlin, Stallman felt an understandable set of mixed emotions when it came time to celebrate the Linux "victory."[6]

Although late to the party, Stallman still had clout. As soon as the FSF announced that it would lend its money and moral support to Murdock's software project, other offers of support began rolling in. Murdock dubbed the new project Debian—a compression of his and his wife, Deborah's, names—and within a few weeks was rolling out the first distribution. "[Richard's support] catapulted Debian almost overnight from this interesting little project to something people within the community had to pay attention to," Murdock says.

In January of 1994, Murdock issued the "Debian Manifesto." Written in the spirit of Stallman's "GNU Manifesto" from a decade before, it explained the importance of working closely with the Free Software Foundation. Murdock wrote:

> *The Free Software Foundation plays an extremely important role in the future of Debian. By the simple fact that they will be distributing it, a message is sent to the world that Linux is not a commercial product and that it never should be, but that this does not mean that Linux will never be able to compete commercially. For those of you who disagree, I challenge you to rationalize the success of GNU Emacs and GCC, which are not commercial software but which have had quite an impact on the commercial market regardless of that fact.*

The time has come to concentrate on the future of Linux rather than on the destructive goal of enriching oneself at the expense of the entire Linux community and its future. The development and distribution of Debian may not be the answer to the problems that I have outlined in the Manifesto, but I hope that it will at least attract enough attention to these problems to allow them to be solved.7

Shortly after the Manifesto's release, the Free Software Foundation made its first major request. Stallman wanted Murdock to call its distribution "GNU/Linux." At first, Murdock says, Stallman had wanted to use the term "Lignux"—"as in Linux with GNU at the heart of it"—but a sample testing of the term on Usenet and in various impromptu hacker focus groups had merited enough catcalls to convince Stallman to go with the less awkward GNU/Linux.

Although some would dismiss Stallman's attempt to add the "GNU" prefix as a belated quest for credit, Murdock saw it differently. Looking back, Murdock saw it as an attempt to counteract the growing tension between GNU Project and Linux-kernel developers. "There was a split emerging," Murdock recalls. "Richard was concerned."

The deepest split, Murdock says, was over glibc. Short for GNU C Library, glibc is the package that lets programmers make "system calls" directed at the kernel. Over the course of 1993–1994, glibc emerged as a troublesome bottleneck in Linux development. Because so many new users were adding new functions to the Linux kernel, the GNU Project's glibc maintainers were soon overwhelmed with suggested changes. Frustrated by delays and the GNU Project's growing reputation for foot-dragging, some Linux developers suggested creating a "fork"—i.e., a Linux-specific C Library parallel to glibc.

In the hacker world, forks are an interesting phenomenon. Although the hacker ethic permits a programmer to do anything he wants with a given program's source code, most hackers prefer to pour their innovations into a central source-code file or "tree" to ensure compatibility with other people's programs. To fork glibc this early in the development of Linux would have meant losing the potential input of hundreds, even thousands, of Linux developers. It would also mean growing incompatibility between Linux and the GNU system that Stallman and the GNU team still hoped to develop.

As leader of the GNU Project, Stallman had already experienced the negative effects of a software fork in 1991. A group of Emacs developers working for a software company named Lucid had a falling out over Stallman's unwillingness to fold changes back into the GNU Emacs code base. The fork had given birth to a parallel version, Lucid Emacs, and hard feelings all around.[8]

Murdock says Debian was mounting work on a similar fork in glibc source code that motivated Stallman to insist on adding the GNU prefix when Debian rolled out its software distribution. "The fork has since converged. Still, at the time, there was a concern that if the Linux community saw itself as a different thing as the GNU community, it might be a force for disunity."

Stallman seconds Murdock's recollection. In fact, he says there were nascent forks appearing in relation to every major GNU component. At first, Stallman says he considered the forks to be a product of sour grapes. In contrast to the fast and informal dynamics of the Linux-kernel team, GNU source-code maintainers tended to be slower and more circumspect in making changes that might affect a program's long-term viability. They also were unafraid of harshly critiquing other people's code. Over time, however, Stallman began to sense that there was an underlying lack of awareness of the GNU Project and its objectives when reading Linux developers' emails.

"We discovered that the people who considered themselves Linux users didn't care about the GNU Project," Stallman says. "They said, 'Why should I bother doing these things? I don't care about the GNU Project. It's working for me. It's working for us Linux users, and nothing else matters to us.' And that was quite surprising given that people were essentially using a variant of the GNU system, and they cared so little. They cared less than anybody else about GNU."

While some viewed descriptions of Linux as a "variant" of the GNU Project as politically grasping, Murdock, already sympathetic to the free software cause, saw Stallman's request to call Debian's version GNU/Linux as reasonable. "It was more for unity than for credit," he says.

Requests of a more technical nature quickly followed. Although Murdock had been accommodating on political issues, he struck a firmer pose when it came to the design and development model of the actual software. What had begun as a show of solidarity soon became of model of other GNU projects.

"I can tell you that I've had my share of disagreements with him," says Murdock with a laugh. "In all honesty Richard can be a fairly difficult person to work with."

In 1996, Murdock, following his graduation from Purdue, decided to hand over the reins of the growing Debian project. He had already been ceding management duties to Bruce Perens, the hacker best known for his work on Electric Fence, a Unix utility released under the GPL. Perens, like Murdock, was a Unix programmer who had become enamored of GNU/Linux as soon as the program's Unix-like abilities became manifest. Like Murdock, Perens sympathized with the political agenda of Stallman and the Free Software Foundation, albeit from afar.

"I remember after Stallman had already come out with the GNU Manifesto, GNU Emacs, and GCC, I read an article that said he was working as a consultant for Intel," says Perens, recalling his first brush with Stallman in the late 1980s. "I wrote him asking how he could be advocating free software on the one hand and working for Intel on the other. He wrote back saying, 'I work as a consultant to produce free software.' He was perfectly polite about it, and I thought his answer made perfect sense."

As a prominent Debian developer, however, Perens regarded Murdock's design battles with Stallman with dismay. Upon assuming leadership of the development team, Perens says he made the command decision to distance Debian from the Free Software Foundation. "I decided we did not want Richard's style of micro-management," he says.

According to Perens, Stallman was taken aback by the decision but had the wisdom to roll with it. "He gave it some time to cool off and sent a message that we really needed a relationship. He requested that we call it GNU/Linux and left it at that. I decided that was fine. I made the decision unilaterally. Everybody breathed a sigh of relief."

Over time, Debian would develop a reputation as the hacker's version of Linux, alongside Slackware, another popular distribution founded during the same 1993–1994 period. Outside the realm of hacker-oriented systems, however, Linux was picking up steam in the commercial Unix marketplace. In North Carolina, a Unix company billing itself as Red Hat was revamping its business to focus on Linux. The chief executive officer was Robert Young, the former *Linux Journal* editor who in 1994 had put the question to Linus Torvalds, asking whether he had any regrets about putting the kernel under the GPL. To Young, Torvalds' response had a "profound" impact on his own view toward Linux. Instead of looking for a way to corner the GNU/Linux market via traditional software tactics, Young began to consider what might happen if a company adopted the same approach as Debian—i.e., building an operating system completely out of free software parts. Cygnus Solutions, the company founded by Michael Tiemann and John Gilmore in 1990, was already demonstrating the ability to sell free software based on quality and customizability. What if Red Hat took the same approach with GNU/Linux?

"In the western scientific tradition we stand on the shoulders of giants," says Young, echoing both Torvalds and Sir Isaac Newton before him. "In business, this translates to not having to reinvent wheels as we go along. The beauty of [the GPL] model is you put your code into the public domain.[9] If you're an independent software vendor and you're trying to build some application and you need a modem-dialer, well, why reinvent modem dialers? You can just steal PPP off of Red Hat Linux and use that as the core of your modem-dialing tool. If you need a graphic tool set, you don't have to write your own graphic library. Just download

GTK. Suddenly you have the ability to reuse the best of what went before. And suddenly your focus as an application vendor is less on software management and more on writing the applications specific to your customer's needs."

Young wasn't the only software executive intrigued by the business efficiencies of free software. By late 1996, most Unix companies were starting to wake up and smell the brewing source code. The Linux sector was still a good year or two away from full commercial breakout mode, but those close enough to the hacker community could feel it: something big was happening. The Intel 386 chip, the Internet, and the World Wide Web had hit the marketplace like a set of monster waves, and Linux—and the host of software programs that echoed it in terms of source-code accessibility and permissive licensing—seemed like the largest wave yet.

For Ian Murdock, the programmer courted by Stallman and then later turned off by Stallman's micromanagement style, the wave seemed both a fitting tribute and a fitting punishment for the man who had spent so much time giving the free software movement an identity. Like many Linux aficionados, Murdock had seen the original postings. He'd seen Torvalds's original admonition that Linux was "just a hobby." He'd also seen Torvalds's admission to Minix creator Andrew Tanenbaum: "If the GNU kernel had been ready last spring, I'd not have bothered to even start my project."10 Like many, Murdock knew the opportunities that had been squandered. He also knew the excitement of watching new opportunities come seeping out of the very fabric of the Internet.

"Being involved with Linux in those early days was fun," recalls Murdock. "At the same time, it was something to do, something to pass the time. If you go back and read those old [comp.os.minix] exchanges, you'll see the sentiment: this is something we can play with until the HURD is ready. People were anxious. It's funny, but in a lot of ways, I suspect that Linux would never have happened if the HURD had come along more quickly."

By the end of 1996, however, such "what if" questions were already moot. Call it Linux, call it GNU/Linux; the users had spoken. The 36-month window had closed, meaning that even if the GNU Project had rolled out its HURD kernel, chances were slim anybody outside the hard-core hacker community would have noticed. The first Unix-like free software operating system was here, and it had momentum. All hackers had left to do was sit back and wait for the next major wave to come crashing down on their heads. Even the shaggy-haired head of one Richard M. Stallman.

Ready or not.

ENDNOTES

1. Torvalds has offered this quote in many different settings. To date, however, the quote's most notable appearance is in the Eric Raymond essay, "The Cathedral and the Bazaar" (May, 1997).

    http://www.tuxedo.org/~esr/writings/cathedral-bazaar/cathedral-bazaar/index. html

2. See Simson Garfinkel, "Is Stallman Stalled?" *Wired* (March, 1993).

3. Chassel's concern about there being a 36-month "window" for a new operating system is not unique to the GNU Project. During the early 1990s, free software versions of the Berkeley Software Distribution were held up by Unix System Laboratories' lawsuit restricting the release of BSD-derived software. While many users consider BSD offshoots such as FreeBSD and OpenBSD to be demonstrably superior to GNU/Linux both in terms of performance and security, the number of FreeBSD and OpenBSD users remains a fraction of the total GNU/Linux user population.

    To view a sample analysis of the relative success of GNU/Linux in relation to other free software operating systems, see the essay by New Zealand hacker, Liam Greenwood, "Why is Linux Successful" (1999).

4. See Maui High Performance Computing Center Speech.

5. GNU/Linux user-population numbers are sketchy at best, which is why I've provided such a broad range. The 100,000 total comes from the Red Hat "Milestones" site, *http://www.redhat.com/about/corporate/milestones.html*.

6. I wrote this Winston Churchill analogy before Stallman himself sent me his own unsolicited comment on Churchill:

    > *World War II and the determination needed to win it was a very strong memory as I was growing up. Statements such as Churchill's, "We will fight them in the landing zones, we will fight them on the beaches . . . we will never surrender," have always resonated for me.*

7. See Ian Murdock, "A Brief History of Debian," (January 6, 1994): Appendix A, "The Debian Manifesto."

    http://www.debian.org/doc/manuals/project-history/apA.html

8. Jamie Zawinski, a former Lucid programmer who would go on to head the Mozilla development team, has a web site that documents the Lucid/GNU Emacs fork, titled, "The Lemacs/FSFmacs Schism."

    http://www.jwz.org/doc/lemacs.html

9. Young uses the term "public domain" incorrectly here. Public domain means not protected by copyright. GPL-protected programs are by definition protected by copyright.

10. This quote is taken from the much-publicized Torvalds-Tanenbaum "flame war" following the initial release of Linux. In the process of defending his choice of a nonportable monolithic kernel design, Torvalds says he started working on Linux as a way to learn more about his new 386 PC. "If the GNU kernel had been ready last spring, I'd not have bothered to even start my project." See Chris DiBona et al., *Open Sources* (O'Reilly & Associates, Inc., 1999): 224.

OPEN SOURCE

In November, 1995, Peter Salus, a member of the Free Software Foundation and author of the 1994 book, *A Quarter Century of Unix*, issued a call for papers to members of the GNU Project's "system-discuss" mailing list. Salus, the conference's scheduled chairman, wanted to tip off fellow hackers about the upcoming Conference on Freely Redistributable Software in Cambridge, Massachusetts. Slated for February, 1996 and sponsored by the Free Software Foundation, the event promised to be the first engineering conference solely dedicated to free software and, in a show of unity with other free software programmers, welcomed papers on "any aspect of GNU, Linux, NetBSD, 386BSD, FreeBSD, Perl, Tcl/tk, and other tools for which the code is accessible and redistributable." Salus wrote:

> *Over the past 15 years, free and low-cost software has become ubiquitous. This conference will bring together implementers of several different types of freely redistributable software and publishers of such software (on various media). There will be tutorials and refereed papers, as well as keynotes by Linus Torvalds and Richard Stallman.*[1]

One of the first people to receive Salus' email was conference committee member Eric S. Raymond. Although not the leader of a project or company like the various other members of the list, Raymond had built a tidy reputation within the hacker community as a major contributor to GNU Emacs and as editor of *The New Hacker Dictionary*, a book version of the hacking community's decade-old Jargon File.

For Raymond, the 1996 conference was a welcome event. Active in the GNU Project during the 1980s, Raymond had distanced himself from the project in 1992, citing, like many others before him, Stallman's "micro-management" style. "Richard kicked up a fuss about my making unauthorized modifications when I was cleaning up the Emacs LISP libraries," Raymond recalls. "It frustrated me so much that I decided I didn't want to work with him anymore."

Despite the falling out, Raymond remained active in the free software community. So much so that when Salus suggested a conference pairing Stallman and Torvalds as keynote speakers, Raymond eagerly seconded the idea. With Stallman representing the older, wiser contingent of ITS/Unix hackers and Torvalds representing the younger, more energetic crop of Linux hackers, the pairing indicated a symbolic show of unity that could only be beneficial, especially to ambitious younger (i.e., below 40) hackers such as Raymond. "I sort of had a foot in both camps," Raymond says.

By the time of the conference, the tension between those two camps had become palpable. Both groups had one thing in common, though: the conference was their first chance to meet the Finnish *wunderkind* in the flesh. Surprisingly, Torvalds proved himself to be a charming, affable speaker. Possessing only a slight Swedish accent, Torvalds surprised audience members with his quick, self-effacing wit.[2] Even more surprising, says Raymond, was Torvalds' equal willingness to take potshots at other prominent hackers, including the most prominent hacker of all, Richard Stallman. By the end of the conference, Torvalds' half-hacker, half-slacker manner was winning over older and younger conference-goers alike.

"It was a pivotal moment," recalls Raymond. "Before 1996, Richard was the only credible claimant to being the ideological leader of the entire culture. People who dissented didn't do so in public. The person who broke that taboo was Torvalds."

The ultimate breach of taboo would come near the end of the show. During a discussion on the growing market dominance of Microsoft Windows or some similar topic, Torvalds admitted to being a fan of Microsoft's PowerPoint slideshow software program. From the perspective of old-line software purists, it was like a Mormon bragging in church about his fondness of whiskey. From the perspective of Torvalds and his growing band of followers, it was simply common sense. Why shun worthy proprietary software programs just to make a point? Being a hacker wasn't about suffering, it was about getting the job done.

"That was a pretty shocking thing to say," Raymond remembers. "Then again, he was able to do that, because by 1995 and 1996, he was rapidly acquiring clout."

Stallman, for his part, doesn't remember any tension at the 1996 conference, but he does remember later feeling the sting of Torvalds' celebrated cheekiness. "There was a thing in the Linux documentation which says print out the GNU coding standards and then tear them up," says Stallman, recalling one example. "OK, so he disagrees with some of our conventions. That's fine, but he picked a singularly nasty way of saying so. He could have just said 'Here's the way I think you should indent your code.' Fine. There should be no hostility there."

For Raymond, the warm reception other hackers gave to Torvalds' comments merely confirmed his suspicions. The dividing line separating Linux developers from GNU/Linux developers was largely generational. Many Linux hackers, like Torvalds, had grown up in a world of proprietary software. Unless a program was clearly inferior, most saw little reason to rail against a program on licensing issues alone. Somewhere in the universe of free software systems lurked a program that hackers might someday turn into a free software alternative to PowerPoint. Until then, why begrudge Microsoft the initiative of developing the program and reserving the rights to it?

As a former GNU Project member, Raymond sensed an added dynamic to the tension between Stallman and Torvalds. In the decade since launching the GNU Project, Stallman had built up a fearsome reputation as a programmer. He had also built up a reputation for intransigence both in terms of software design and people management. Shortly before the 1996 conference, the Free Software Foundation would experience a full-scale staff defection, blamed in large part on Stallman. Brian Youmans, a current FSF staffer hired by Salus in the wake of the resignations, recalls the scene: "At one point, Peter [Salus] was the only staff member working in the office."

For Raymond, the defection merely confirmed a growing suspicion: recent delays such as the HURD and recent troubles such as the Lucid-Emacs schism reflected problems normally associated with software project management, not software code development. Shortly after the Freely Redistributable Software Conference, Raymond began working on his own pet software project, a popmail utility called "fetchmail." Taking a cue from Torvalds, Raymond issued his program with a tacked-on promise to update the source code as early and as often as possible. When users began sending in bug reports and feature suggestions, Raymond, at first anticipating a tangled mess, found the resulting software surprisingly sturdy. Analyzing the success of the Torvalds approach, Raymond issued a quick analysis: using the Internet as his "petri dish" and the harsh scrutiny of the hacker community as a form of natural selection, Torvalds had created an evolutionary model free of central planning.

What's more, Raymond decided, Torvalds had found a way around Brooks' Law. First articulated by Fred P. Brooks, manager of IBM's OS/360 project and author of the 1975 book, *The Mythical Man-Month*, Brooks' Law held that adding developers to a project only resulted in further project delays. Believing as most hackers that software, like soup, benefits from a limited number of cooks, Raymond sensed something revolutionary at work. In inviting more and more cooks into the kitchen, Torvalds had actually found a way to make the resulting software *better*.[3]

Raymond put his observations on paper. He crafted them into a speech, which he promptly delivered before a group of friends and neighbors in Chester County, Pennsylvania. Dubbed "The Cathedral and the Bazaar," the speech contrasted the management styles of the GNU Project with the management style of Torvalds and the kernel hackers. Raymond says the response was enthusiastic, but not nearly as enthusiastic as the one he received during the 1997 Linux Kongress, a gathering of Linux users in Germany the next spring.

"At the Kongress, they gave me a standing ovation at the end of the speech," Raymond recalls. "I took that as significant for two reasons. For one thing, it meant they were excited by what they were hearing. For another thing, it meant they were excited even after hearing the speech delivered through a language barrier."

Eventually, Raymond would convert the speech into a paper, also titled "The Cathedral and the Bazaar." The paper drew its name from Raymond's central analogy. GNU programs were "cathedrals," impressive, centrally planned monuments to the hacker ethic, built to stand the test of time. Linux, on the other hand, was more like "a great babbling bazaar," a software program developed through the loose decentralizing dynamics of the Internet.

Implicit within each analogy was a comparison of Stallman and Torvalds. Where Stallman served as the classic model of the cathedral architect—i.e., a programming "wizard" who could disappear for 18 months and return with something like the GNU C Compiler—Torvalds was more like a genial dinner-party host. In letting others lead the Linux design discussion and stepping in only when the entire table needed a referee, Torvalds had created a development model very much reflective of his own laid-back personality. From the Torvalds' perspective, the most important managerial task was not imposing control but keeping the ideas flowing.

Summarized Raymond, "I think Linus's cleverest and most consequential hack was not the construction of the Linux kernel itself, but rather his invention of the Linux development model."[4]

In summarizing the secrets of Torvalds' managerial success, Raymond himself had pulled off a coup. One of the audience members at the Linux Kongress was Tim O'Reilly, publisher of O'Reilly & Associates, a company specializing in software manuals and software-related books (and the publisher of this book). After hearing Raymond's Kongress speech, O'Reilly promptly invited Raymond to deliver it again at the company's inaugural Perl Conference later that year in Monterey, California.

Although the conference was supposed to focus on Perl, a scripting language created by Unix hacker Larry Wall, O'Reilly assured Raymond that the conference would address other free software technologies. Given the growing commercial interest in Linux and Apache, a popular free software web server, O'Reilly hoped to use the event to publicize the role of free software in creating the entire infrastructure of the Internet. From web-friendly languages such as Perl and Python to back-room programs such as BIND (the Berkeley Internet Naming Daemon), a software tool that lets users replace arcane IP numbers with the easy-to-remember domain-name addresses (e.g., amazon.com), and sendmail, the most popular mail program on the Internet, free software had become an emergent phenomenon. Like a colony of ants creating a beautiful nest one grain of sand at a time, the only thing missing was the communal self-awareness. O'Reilly saw Raymond's speech as a good way to inspire that self-awareness, to drive home the point that free software development didn't start and end with the GNU Project. Programming languages, such as Perl and Python, and Internet software, such as BIND, sendmail, and Apache, demonstrated that free software was already ubiquitous and influential. He also assured Raymond an even warmer reception than the one at Linux Kongress.

O'Reilly was right. "This time, I got the standing ovation before the speech," says Raymond, laughing.

As predicted, the audience was stocked not only with hackers, but with other people interested in the growing power of the free software movement. One contingent included a group from

Netscape, the Mountain View, California startup then nearing the end game of its three-year battle with Microsoft for control of the web-browser market. Intrigued by Raymond's speech and anxious to win back lost market share, Netscape executives took the message back to corporate headquarters. A few months later, in January, 1998, the company announced its plan to publish the source code of its flagship Navigator web browser in the hopes of enlisting hacker support in future development.

When Netscape CEO Jim Barksdale cited Raymond's "Cathedral and the Bazaar" essay as a major influence upon the company's decision, the company instantly elevated Raymond to the level of hacker celebrity. Determined not to squander the opportunity, Raymond traveled west to deliver interviews, advise Netscape executives, and take part in the eventual party celebrating the publication of Netscape Navigator's source code. The code name for Navigator's source code was "Mozilla": a reference both to the program's gargantuan size—30 million lines of code—and to its heritage. Developed as a proprietary offshoot of Mosaic, the web browser created by Marc Andreessen at the University of Illinois, Mozilla was proof, yet again, that when it came to building new programs, most programmers preferred to borrow on older, modifiable programs.

While in California, Raymond also managed to squeeze in a visit to VA Research, a Santa Clara–based company selling workstations with the GNU/Linux operating system preinstalled. Convened by Raymond, the meeting was small. The invite list included VA founder Larry Augustin, a few VA employees, and Christine Peterson, president of the Foresight Institute, a Silicon Valley think tank specializing in nanotechnology.

"The meeting's agenda boiled down to one item: how to take advantage of Netscape's decision so that other companies might follow suit?" Raymond doesn't recall the conversation that took place, but he does remember the first complaint addressed. Despite the best efforts of Stallman and other hackers to remind people that the word "free" in free software stood for freedom and not price, the message still wasn't getting through. Most business executives, upon hearing the term for the first time, interpreted the word as synonymous with "zero cost," tuning out any follow up messages in short order. Until hackers found a way to get past this cognitive dissonance, the free software movement faced an uphill climb, even after Netscape.

Peterson, whose organization had taken an active interest in advancing the free software cause, offered an alternative: open source.

Looking back, Peterson says she came up with the open source term while discussing Netscape's decision with a friend in the public relations industry. She doesn't remember where she came upon the term or if she borrowed it from another field, but she does remember her friend disliking the term.[5]

At the meeting, Peterson says, the response was dramatically different. "I was hesitant about suggesting it," Peterson recalls. "I had no standing with the group, so started using it casually, not highlighting it as a new term." To Peterson's surprise, the term caught on. By the end of the meeting, most of the attendees, including Raymond, seemed pleased by it.

Raymond says he didn't publicly use the term "open source" as a substitute for free software until a day or two after the Mozilla launch party, when O'Reilly had scheduled a meeting to talk about free software. Calling his meeting "the Freeware Summit," O'Reilly says he wanted to direct media and community attention to the other deserving projects that had also encouraged Netscape to release Mozilla. "All these guys had so much in common, and I was surprised they didn't all know each other," says O'Reilly. "I also wanted to let the world know just how great an impact the free software culture had already made. People were missing out on a large part of the free software tradition."

In putting together the invite list, however, O'Reilly made a decision that would have long-term political consequences. He decided to limit the list to west-coast developers such as Wall, Eric Allman, creator of sendmail, and Paul Vixie, creator of BIND. There were exceptions, of course: Pennsylvania-resident Raymond, who was already in town thanks to the Mozilla launch, earned an quick invite. So did Virginia-resident Guido van Rossum, creator of Python. "Frank Willison, my editor in chief and champion of Python within the company, invited him without first checking in with me," O'Reilly recalls. "I was happy to have him there, but when I started, it really was just a local gathering."

For some observers, the unwillingness to include Stallman's name on the list qualified as a snub. "I decided not to go to the event because of it," says Perens, remembering the summit. Raymond, who did go, says he argued for Stallman's inclusion to no avail. The snub rumor gained additional strength from the fact that O'Reilly, the event's host, had feuded publicly with Stallman over the issue of software-manual copyrights. Prior to the meeting, Stallman had argued that free software manuals should be as freely copyable and modifiable as free software programs. O'Reilly, meanwhile, argued that a value-added market for non-free books increased the utility of free software by making it more accessible to a wider community. The two had also disputed the title of the event, with Stallman insisting on "Free Software" over the less politically laden "Freeware."

Looking back, O'Reilly doesn't see the decision to leave Stallman's name off the invite list as a snub. "At that time, I had never met Richard in person, but in our email interactions, he'd been inflexible and unwilling to engage in dialogue. I wanted to make sure the GNU tradition was represented at the meeting, so I invited John Gilmore and Michael Tiemann, whom I knew personally, and whom I knew were passionate about the value of the GPL but seemed more willing to engage in a frank back-and-forth about the strengths and weaknesses of the various free software projects and traditions. Given all the later brouhaha, I do wish I'd invited Richard as well, but I certainly don't think that my failure to do so should be interpreted as a lack of respect for the GNU Project or for Richard personally."

Snub or no snub, both O'Reilly and Raymond say the term "open source" won over just enough summit-goers to qualify as a success. The attendees shared ideas and experiences and brainstormed on how to improve free software's image. Of key concern was how to point out the successes of free software, particularly in the realm of Internet infrastructure, as opposed to playing up the GNU/Linux challenge to Microsoft Windows. But like the earlier meeting at VA, the discussion soon turned to the problems associated with the term "free software." O'Reilly, the summit host, remembers a particularly insightful comment from Torvalds, a summit attendee.

"Linus had just moved to Silicon Valley at that point, and he explained how only recently that he had learned that the word 'free' had two meanings—free as in 'libre' and free as in 'gratis'—in English."

Michael Tiemann, founder of Cygnus, proposed an alternative to the troublesome "free software" term: sourceware. "Nobody got too excited about it," O'Reilly recalls. "That's when Eric threw out the term 'open source.'"

Although the term appealed to some, support for a change in official terminology was far from unanimous. At the end of the one-day conference, attendees put the three terms—free software, open source, or sourceware—to a vote. According to O'Reilly, 9 out of the 15 attendees voted for "open source." Although some still quibbled with the term, all attendees agreed to use it in future discussions with the press. "We wanted to go out with a solidarity message," O'Reilly says.

The term didn't take long to enter the national lexicon. Shortly after the summit, O'Reilly shepherded summit attendees to a press conference attended by reporters from the *New York Times*, the *Wall Street Journal*, and other prominent publications. Within a few months, Torvalds' face was appearing on the cover of *Forbes* magazine, with the faces of Stallman, Perl creator Larry Wall, and Apache team leader Brian Behlendorf featured in the interior spread. Open source was open for business.

For summit attendees such as Tiemann, the solidarity message was the most important thing. Although his company had achieved a fair amount of success selling free software tools and services, he sensed the difficulty other programmers and entrepreneurs faced.

"There's no question that the use of the word free was confusing in a lot of situations," Tiemann says. "Open source positioned itself as being business friendly and business sensible. Free software positioned itself as morally righteous. For better or worse we figured it was more advantageous to align with the open source crowd.

For Stallman, the response to the new "open source" term was slow in coming. Raymond says Stallman briefly considered adopting the term, only to discard it. "I know because I had direct personal conversations about it," Raymond says.

By the end of 1998, Stallman had formulated a position: open source, while helpful in communicating the technical advantages of free software, also encouraged speakers to soft-pedal the issue of software freedom. Given this drawback, Stallman would stick with the term free software.

Summing up his position at the 1999 LinuxWorld Convention and Expo, an event billed by Torvalds himself as a "coming out party" for the Linux community, Stallman implored his fellow hackers to resist the lure of easy compromise.

"Because we've shown how much we can do, we don't have to be desperate to work with companies or compromise our goals," Stallman said during a panel discussion. "Let them offer and we'll accept. We don't have to change what we're doing to get them to help us. You can take a single step towards a goal, then another and then more and more and you'll actually reach your goal. Or, you can take a half measure that means you don't ever take another step and you'll never get there."

Even before the LinuxWorld show, however, Stallman was showing an increased willingness to alienate his more conciliatory peers. A few months after the Freeware Summit, O'Reilly hosted its second annual Perl Conference. This time around, Stallman was in attendance. During a panel discussion lauding IBM's decision to employ the free software Apache web server in its commercial offerings, Stallman, taking advantage of an audience microphone, disrupted the proceedings with a tirade against panelist John Ousterhout, creator of the Tcl scripting language. Stallman branded Ousterhout a "parasite" on the free software community for marketing a proprietary version of Tcl via Ousterhout's startup company, Scriptics. "I don't think Scriptics is necessary for the continued existence of Tcl," Stallman said to hisses from the fellow audience members.[5]

"It was a pretty ugly scene," recalls Prime Time Freeware's Rich Morin. "John's done some pretty respectable things: Tcl, Tk, Sprite. He's a real contributor."

Despite his sympathies for Stallman and Stallman's position, Morin felt empathy for those troubled by Stallman's discordant behavior.

Stallman's Perl Conference outburst would momentarily chase off another potential sympathizer, Bruce Perens. In 1998, Eric Raymond proposed launching the Open Source Initiative, or OSI, an organization that would police the use of the term "open source" and provide a definition for companies interested in making their own programs. Raymond recruited Perens to draft the definition.[6]

Perens would later resign from the OSI, expressing regret that the organization had set itself up in opposition to Stallman and the FSF. Still, looking back on the need for a free software definition outside the Free Software Foundation's auspices, Perens understands why other hackers might still feel the need for distance. "I really like and admire Richard," says Perens. "I do think Richard would do his job better if Richard had more balance. That includes going away from free software for a couple of months."

Stallman's monomaniacal energies would do little to counteract the public-relations momentum of open source proponents. In August of 1998, when chip-maker Intel purchased a stake in GNU/Linux vendor Red Hat, an accompanying *New York Times* article described the company as the product of a movement "known alternatively as free software and open source."[7] Six months later, a John Markoff article on Apple Computer was proclaiming the company's adoption of the "open source" Apache server in the article headline.[8]

Such momentum would coincide with the growing momentum of companies that actively embraced the "open source" term. By August of 1999, Red Hat, a company that now eagerly billed itself as "open source," was selling shares on Nasdaq. In December, VA Linux—formerly VA Research—was floating its own IPO to historical effect. Opening at $30 per share, the company's stock price exploded past the $300 mark in initial trading only to settle back down to the $239 level. Shareholders lucky enough to get in at the bottom and stay until the end experienced a 698% increase in paper wealth, a Nasdaq record.

Among those lucky shareholders was Eric Raymond, who, as a company board member since the Mozilla launch, had received 150,000 shares of VA Linux stock. Stunned by the realization that his essay contrasting the Stallman-Torvalds managerial styles had netted him $36 million in potential wealth, Raymond penned a follow-up essay. In it, Raymond mused on the relationship between the hacker ethic and monetary wealth:

> *Reporters often ask me these days if I think the open-source community will be corrupted by the influx of big money. I tell them what I believe, which is this: commercial demand for programmers has been so intense for so long that anyone who can be seriously distracted by money is already gone. Our community has been self-selected for caring about other things—accomplishment, pride, artistic passion, and each other.*[9]

Whether or not such comments allayed suspicions that Raymond and other open source proponents had simply been in it for the money, they drove home the open source community's ultimate message: all you needed to sell the free software concept is a friendly face and a sensible message. Instead of fighting the marketplace head-on as Stallman had done, Raymond, Torvalds, and other new leaders of the hacker community had adopted a more relaxed approach—ignoring the marketplace in some areas, leveraging it in others. Instead of playing the role of high-school outcasts, they had played the game of celebrity, magnifying their power in the process.

"On his worst days Richard believes that Linus Torvalds and I conspired to hijack his revolution," Raymond says. "Richard's rejection of the term open source and his deliberate creation of an ideological fissure in my view comes from an odd mix of idealism and territoriality. There are people out there who think it's all Richard's personal ego. I don't believe that. It's more that he so personally associates himself with the free software idea that he sees any threat to that as a threat to himself."

Ironically, the success of open source and open source advocates such as Raymond would not diminish Stallman's role as a leader. If anything, it gave Stallman new followers to convert. Still, the Raymond territoriality charge is a damning one. There are numerous instances of Stallman sticking to his guns more out of habit than out of principle: his initial dismissal of the Linux kernel, for example, and his current unwillingness as a political figure to venture outside the realm of software issues.

Then again, as the recent debate over open source also shows, in instances when Stallman has stuck to his guns, he's usually found a way to gain ground because of it. "One of Stallman's primary character traits is the fact he doesn't budge," says Ian Murdock. "He'll wait up to a decade for people to come around to his point of view if that's what it takes."

Murdock, for one, finds that unbudgeable nature both refreshing and valuable. Stallman may no longer be the solitary leader of the free software movement, but he is still the polestar of the free software community. "You always know that he's going to be consistent in his views," Murdock says. "Most people aren't like that. Whether you agree with him or not, you really have to respect that."

ENDNOTES

1. See Peter Salus, "FYI—Conference on Freely Redistributable Software, 2/2, Cambridge" (1995) (archived by Terry Winograd).

   http://hci.stanford.edu/pcd-archives/pcd-fyi/1995/0078.html

2. Although Linus Torvalds is Finnish, his mother tongue is Swedish. "The Rampantly Unofficial Linus FAQ" offers a brief explanation:

Finland has a significant (about 6%) Swedish-speaking minority population. They call themselves "finlandssvensk" or "finlandssvenskar" and consider themselves Finns; many of their families have lived in Finland for centuries. Swedish is one of Finland's two official languages.

http://tuxedo.org/~esr/faqs/linus/

3. Brooks' Law is the shorthand summary of the following quote taken from Brooks' book:

   Since software construction is inherently a systems effort—an exercise in complex interrelationships—communication effort is great, and it quickly dominates the decrease in individual task time brought about by partitioning. Adding more men then lengthens, not shortens, the schedule.

   See Fred P. Brooks, *The Mythical Man-Month* (Addison Wesley Publishing, 1995)

4. See Eric Raymond, "The Cathredral and the Bazaar" (1997).

5. See Malcolm Maclachlan, "Profit Motive Splits Open Source Movement," *TechWeb News* (August 26, 1998).

   http://content.techweb.com/wire/story/TWB19980824S0012

6. See Bruce Perens et al., "The Open Source Definition," The Open Source Initiative (1998).

   http://www.opensource.org/docs/definition.html

7. See Amy Harmon, "For Sale: Free Operating System," *New York Times* (September 28, 1998).

   http://www.nytimes.com/library/tech/98/09/biztech/articles/28linux.html

8. See John Markoff, "Apple Adopts 'Open Source' for its Server Computers," *New York Times* (March 17, 1999).

   http://www.nytimes.com/library/tech/99/03/biztech/articles/17apple.html

9. See Eric Raymond, "Surprised by Wealth," *Linux Today* (December 10, 1999).

   http://linuxtoday.com/news_story.php3?ltsn=1999-12-10-001-05-NW-LF

CHAPTER 12

A BRIEF JOURNEY THROUGH
HACKER HELL

Richard Stallman stares, unblinking, through the windshield of a rental car, waiting for the light to change as we make our way through downtown Kihei.

The two of us are headed to the nearby town of Pa'ia, where we are scheduled to meet up with some software programmers and their wives for dinner in about an hour or so.

It's about two hours after Stallman's speech at the Maui High Performance Center, and Kihei, a town that seemed so inviting before the speech, now seems profoundly uncooperative. Like most beach cities, Kihei is a one-dimensional exercise in suburban sprawl. Driving down its main drag, with its endless succession of burger stands, realty agencies, and bikini shops, it's hard not to feel like a steel-coated morsel passing through the alimentary canal of a giant commercial tapeworm. The feeling is exacerbated by the lack of side roads. With nowhere to go but forward, traffic moves in spring-like lurches. 200 yards ahead, a light turns green. By the time we are moving, the light is yellow again.

For Stallman, a lifetime resident of the east coast, the prospect of spending the better part of a sunny Hawaiian afternoon trapped in slow traffic is enough to trigger an embolism. Even worse is the knowledge that, with just a few quick right turns a quarter mile back, this whole situation easily could have been avoided. Unfortunately, we are at the mercy of the driver ahead of us, a programmer from the lab who knows the way and who has decided to take us to Pa'ia via the scenic route instead of via the nearby Pilani Highway.

"This is terrible," says Stallman between frustrated sighs. "Why didn't we take the other route?"

Again, the light a quarter mile ahead of us turns green. Again, we creep forward a few more car lengths. This process continues for another 10 minutes, until we finally reach a major crossroad promising access to the adjacent highway.

The driver ahead of us ignores it and continues through the intersection.

"Why isn't he turning?" moans Stallman, throwing up his hands in frustration. "Can you believe this?"

I decide not to answer either. I find the fact that I am sitting in a car with Stallman in the driver seat, in Maui no less, unbelievable enough. Until two hours ago, I didn't even know Stallman knew how to drive. Now, listening to Yo-Yo Ma's cello playing the mournful bass notes of "Appalachian Journey" on the car stereo and watching the sunset pass by on our left, I do my best to fade into the upholstery.

When the next opportunity to turn finally comes up, Stallman hits his right turn signal in an attempt to cue the driver ahead of us. No such luck. Once again, we creep slowly through the intersection, coming to a stop a good 200 yards before the next light. By now, Stallman is livid.

"It's like he's deliberately ignoring us," he says, gesturing and pantomiming like an air craft carrier landing-signals officer in a futile attempt to catch our guide's eye. The guide appears unfazed, and for the next five minutes all we see is a small portion of his head in the rearview mirror.

I look out Stallman's window. Nearby Kahoolawe and Lanai Islands provide an ideal frame for the setting sun. It's a breathtaking view, the kind that makes moments like this a bit more bearable if you're a Hawaiian native, I suppose. I try to direct Stallman's attention to it, but Stallman, by now obsessed by the inattentiveness of the driver ahead of us, blows me off.

When the driver passes through another green light, completely ignoring a "Pilani Highway Next Right," I grit my teeth. I remember an early warning relayed to me by BSD programmer Keith Bostic. "Stallman does not suffer fools gladly," Bostic warned me. "If somebody says or does something stupid, he'll look them in the eye and say, 'That's stupid.'"

Looking at the oblivious driver ahead of us, I realize that it's the stupidity, not the inconvenience, that's killing Stallman right now.

"It's as if he picked this route with absolutely no thought on how to get there efficiently," Stallman says.

The word "efficiently" hangs in the air like a bad odor. Few things irritate the hacker mind more than inefficiency. It was the inefficiency of checking the Xerox laser printer two or three times a day that triggered Stallman's initial inquiry into the printer source code. It was the inefficiency of rewriting software tools hijacked by commercial software vendors that led Stallman to battle Symbolics and to launch the GNU Project. If, as Jean Paul Sartre once opined, hell is other people, hacker hell is duplicating other people's stupid mistakes, and it's no exaggeration to say that Stallman's entire life has been an attempt to save mankind from these fiery depths.

This hell metaphor becomes all the more apparent as we take in the slowly passing scenery. With its multitude of shops, parking lots, and poorly timed street lights, Kihei seems less like a city and more like a poorly designed software program writ large. Instead of rerouting traffic and distributing vehicles through side streets and expressways, city planners have elected to run everything through a single main drag. From a hacker perspective, sitting in a car amidst all this mess is like listening to a CD rendition of nails on a chalkboard at full volume.

"Imperfect systems infuriate hackers," observes Steven Levy, another warning I should have listened to before climbing into the car with Stallman. "This is one reason why hackers generally hate driving cars—the system of randomly programmed red lights and oddly laid out one-way streets causes delays which are so goddamn *unnecessary* [Levy's emphasis] that the impulse is to rearrange signs, open up traffic-light control boxes . . . redesign the entire system."[1]

More frustrating, however, is the duplicity of our trusted guide. Instead of searching out a clever shortcut—as any true hacker would do on instinct—the driver ahead of us has instead chosen to play along with the city planners' game. Like Virgil in Dante's *Inferno*, our guide is determined to give us the full guided tour of this hacker hell whether we want it or not.

Before I can make this observation to Stallman, the driver finally hits his right turn signal. Stallman's hunched shoulders relax slightly, and for a moment the air of tension within the car dissipates. The tension comes back, however, as the driver in front of us slows down. "Construction Ahead" signs line both sides of the street, and even though the Pilani Highway lies less than a quarter mile off in the distance, the two-lane road between us and the highway is blocked by a dormant bulldozer and two large mounds of dirt.

It takes Stallman a few seconds to register what's going on as our guide begins executing a clumsy five-point U-turn in front of us. When he catches a glimpse of the bulldozer and the "No Through Access" signs just beyond, Stallman finally boils over.

"Why, why, why?" he whines, throwing his head back. "You should have known the road was blocked. You should have known this way wouldn't work. You did this deliberately."

The driver finishes the turn and passes us on the way back toward the main drag. As he does so, he shakes his head and gives us an apologetic shrug. Coupled with a toothy grin, the driver's gesture reveals a touch of mainlander frustration but is tempered with a protective dose of islander fatalism. Coming through the sealed windows of our rental car, it spells out a succinct message: "Hey, it's Maui; what are you gonna do?"

Stallman can take it no longer.

"Don't you fucking smile!" he shouts, fogging up the glass as he does so. "It's your fucking fault. This all could have been so much easier if we had just done it my way."

Stallman accents the words "my way" by gripping the steering wheel and pulling himself towards it twice. The image of Stallman's lurching frame is like that of a child throwing a temper tantrum in a car seat, an image further underlined by the tone of Stallman's voice. Halfway between anger and anguish, Stallman seems to be on the verge of tears.

Fortunately, the tears do not arrive. Like a summer cloudburst, the tantrum ends almost as soon as it begins. After a few whiny gasps, Stallman shifts the car into reverse and begins executing his own U-turn. By the time we are back on the main drag, his face is as impassive as it was when we left the hotel 30 minutes earlier.

It takes less than five minutes to reach the next cross-street. This one offers easy highway access, and within seconds, we are soon speeding off toward Pa'ia at a relaxing rate of speed. The sun that once loomed bright and yellow over Stallman's left shoulder is now burning a cool orange-red in our rearview mirror. It lends its color to the gauntlet wili wili trees flying past us on both sides of the highway.

For the next 20 minutes, the only sound in our vehicle, aside from the ambient hum of the car's engine and tires, is the sound of a cello and a violin trio playing the mournful strains of an Appalachian folk tune.

ENDNOTE

1.   See Steven Levy, *Hackers* (Penguin USA [paperback], 1984): 40.

CHAPTER 13

CONTINUING THE FIGHT

For Richard Stallman, time may not heal all wounds, but it does provide a convenient ally.

Four years after "The Cathedral and the Bazaar," Stallman still chafes over the Raymond critique. He also grumbles over Linus Torvalds' elevation to the role of world's most famous hacker. He recalls a popular T-shirt that began showing at Linux tradeshows around 1999. Designed to mimic the original promotional poster for Star Wars, the shirt depicted Torvalds brandishing a lightsaber like Luke Skywalker, while Stallman's face rides atop R2D2. The shirt still grates on Stallmans nerves not only because it depicts him as a Torvalds' sidekick, but also because it elevates Torvalds to the leadership role in the free software/open source community, a role even Torvalds himself is loath to accept. "It's ironic," says Stallman mournfully. "Picking up that sword is exactly what Linus refuses to do. He gets everybody focusing on him as the symbol of the movement, and then he won't fight. What good is it?"

Then again, it is that same unwillingness to "pick up the sword," on Torvalds part, that has left the door open for Stallman to bolster his reputation as the hacker community's ethical arbiter. Despite his grievances, Stallman has to admit that the last few years have been quite good, both to himself and to his organization. Relegated to the periphery by the unforeseen success of

GNU/Linux, Stallman has nonetheless successfully recaptured the initiative. His speaking schedule between January 2000 and December 2001 included stops on six continents and visits to countries where the notion of software freedom carries heavy overtones—China and India, for example.

Outside the bully pulpit, Stallman has also learned how to leverage his power as costeward of the GNU General Public License (GPL). During the summer of 2000, while the air was rapidly leaking out of the 1999 Linux IPO bubble, Stallman and the Free Software Foundation scored two major victories. In July, 2000, Troll Tech, a Norwegian software company and developer of Qt, a valuable suite of graphics tools for the GNU/Linux operating system, announced it was licensing its software under the GPL. A few weeks later, Sun Microsystems, a company that, until then, had been warily trying to ride the open source bandwagon without giving up total control of its software properties, finally relented and announced that it, too, was dual licensing its new OpenOffice application suite under the Lesser GNU Public License (LGPL) and the Sun Industry Standards Source License (SISSL).

Underlining each victory was the fact that Stallman had done little to fight for them. In the case of Troll Tech, Stallman had simply played the role of free software pontiff. In 1999, the company had come up with a license that met the conditions laid out by the Free Software Foundation, but in examining the license further, Stallman detected legal incompatibles that would make it impossible to bundle Qt with GPL-protected software programs. Tired of battling Stallman, Troll Tech management finally decided to split the Qt into two versions, one GPL-protected and one QPL-protected, giving developers a way around the compatibility issues cited by Stallman.

In the case of Sun, they desired to play according to the Free Software Foundation's conditions. At the 1999 O'Reilly Open Source Conference, Sun Microsystems cofounder and chief scientist Bill Joy defended his company's "community source" license, essentially a watered-down compromise letting users copy and modify Sun-owned software but not charge a fee for said software without negotiating a royalty agreement with Sun. A year after Joy's speech, Sun Microsystems vice president Marco Boerries was appearing on the same stage spelling out the company's new licensing compromise in the case of OpenOffice, an office-application suite designed specifically for the GNU/Linux operating system.

"I can spell it out in three letters," said Boerries. "GPL."

At the time, Boerries said his company's decision had little to do with Stallman and more to do with the momentum of GPL-protected programs. "What basically happened was the recognition that different products attracted different communities, and the license you use depends on what type of community you want to attract," said Boerries. "With [OpenOffice], it was clear we had the highest correlation with the GPL community."[1]

Such comments point out the under-recognized strength of the GPL and, indirectly, the political genius of man who played the largest role in creating it. "There isn't a lawyer on earth who would have drafted the GPL the way it is," says Eben Moglen, Columbia University law professor and Free Software Foundation general counsel. "But it works. And it works because of Richard's philosophy of design."

A former professional programmer, Moglen traces his pro bono work with Stallman back to 1990 when Stallman requested Moglen's legal assistance on a private affair. Moglen, then working with encryption expert Phillip Zimmerman during Zimmerman's legal battles with the National Security Administration, says he was honored by the request. "I told him I used Emacs every day of my life, and it would take an awful lot of lawyering on my part to pay off the debt."

Since then, Moglen, perhaps more than any other individual, has had the best chance to observe the crossover of Stallman's hacker philosophies into the legal realm. Moglen says the difference between Stallman's approach to legal code and software code are largely the same. "I have to say, as a lawyer, the idea that what you should do with a legal document is to take out all the bugs doesn't make much sense," Moglen says. "There is uncertainty in every legal process, and what most lawyers want to do is to capture the benefits of uncertainty for their client. Richard's goal is the complete opposite. His goal is to remove uncertainty, which is inherently impossible. It is inherently impossible to draft one license to control all circumstances in all legal systems all over the world. But if you were to go at it, you would have to go at it his way. And the resulting elegance, the resulting simplicity in design almost achieves what it has to achieve. And from there a little lawyering will carry you quite far."

As the person charged with pushing the Stallman agenda, Moglen understands the frustration of would-be allies. "Richard is a man who does not want to compromise over matters that he thinks of as fundamental," Moglen says, "and he does not take easily the twisting of words or even just the seeking of artful ambiguity, which human society often requires from a lot of people."

Because of the Free Software Foundation's unwillingness to weigh in on issues outside the purview of GNU development and GPL enforcement, Moglen has taken to devoting his excess energies to assisting the Electronic Frontier Foundation, the organization providing legal aid to recent copyright defendants such as Dmitri Skylarov. In 2000, Moglen also served as direct counsel to a collection of hackers that were joined together from circulating the DVD decryption program deCSS. Despite the silence of his main client in both cases, Moglen has learned to appreciate the value of Stallman's stubbornness. "There have been times over the years where I've gone to Richard and said, 'We have to do this. We have to do that. Here's the strategic situation. Here's the next move. Here's what he have to do.' And Richard's response has always been, 'We don't have to do anything.' Just wait. What needs doing will get done."

"And you know what?" Moglen adds. "Generally, he's been right."

Such comments disavow Stallman's own self-assessment: "I'm not good at playing games," Stallman says, addressing the many unseen critics who see him as a shrewd strategist. "I'm not good at looking ahead and anticipating what somebody else might do. My approach has always been to focus on the foundation, to say 'Let's make the foundation as strong as we can make it.'"

The GPL's expanding popularity and continuing gravitational strength are the best tributes to the foundation laid by Stallman and his GNU colleagues. While no longer capable of billing himself as the "last true hacker," Stallman nevertheless can take sole credit for building the free software movement's ethical framework. Whether or not other modern programmers feel comfortable working inside that framework is immaterial. The fact that they even have a choice at all is Stallman's greatest legacy.

Discussing Stallman's legacy at this point seems a bit premature. Stallman, 48 at the time of this writing, still has a few years left to add to or subtract from that legacy. Still, the autopilot nature of the free software movement makes it tempting to examine Stallman's life outside the day-to-day battles of the software industry and within a more august, historical setting.

To his credit, Stallman refuses all opportunities to speculate. "I've never been able to work out detailed plans of what the future was going to be like," says Stallman, offering his own premature epitaph. "I just said 'I'm going to fight. Who knows where I'll get?'"

There's no question that in picking his fights, Stallman has alienated the very people who might otherwise have been his greatest champions. It is also a testament to his forthright, ethical nature that many of Stallman's erstwhile political opponents still manage to put in a few good words for him when pressed. The tension between Stallman the ideologue and Stallman the hacker genius, however, leads a biographer to wonder: how will people view Stallman when Stallman's own personality is no longer there to get in the way?

In early drafts of this book, I dubbed this question the "100 year" question. Hoping to stimulate an objective view of Stallman and his work, I asked various software-industry luminaries to take themselves out of the current timeframe and put themselves in a position of a historian looking back on the free software movement 100 years in the future. From the current vantage point, it is easy to see similarities between Stallman and past Americans who, while somewhat marginal during their lifetime, have attained heightened historical importance in relation to their age. Easy comparisons include Henry David Thoreau, transcendentalist philosopher and author of *On Civil Disobedience*, and John Muir, founder of the Sierra Club and progenitor of the modern environmental movement. It is also easy to see similarities in men like William Jennings Bryan, a.k.a. "The Great Commoner," leader of the populist movement, enemy of monopolies, and a man who, though powerful, seems to have faded into historical insignificance.

Although not the first person to view software as public property, Stallman is guaranteed a footnote in future history books thanks to the GPL. Given that fact, it seems worthwhile to step back and examine Richard Stallman's legacy outside the current time frame. Will the GPL still be something software programmers use in the year 2102, or will it have long since fallen by the wayside? Will the term "free software" seem as politically quaint as "free silver" does today, or will it seem eerily prescient in light of later political events?

Predicting the future is risky sport, but most people, when presented with the question, seemed eager to bite. "One hundred years from now, Richard and a couple of other people are going to deserve more than a footnote," says Moglen. "They're going to be viewed as the main line of the story."

The "couple other people" Moglen nominates for future textbook chapters include John Gilmore, Stallman's GPL advisor and future founder of the Electronic Frontier Foundation, and Theodor Holm Nelson, a.k.a. Ted Nelson, author of the 1982 book, *Literary Machines*. Moglen says Stallman, Nelson, and Gilmore each stand out in historically significant, nonoverlapping ways. He credits Nelson, commonly considered to have coined the term "hypertext," for identifying the predicament of information ownership in the digital age. Gilmore and Stallman, meanwhile, earn notable credit for identifying the negative political effects of information control and building organizations—the Electronic Frontier Foundation in the case of Gilmore and the Free Software Foundation in the case of Stallman—to counteract those effects. Of the two, however, Moglen sees Stallman's activities as more personal and less political in nature.

"Richard was unique in that the ethical implications of unfree software were particularly clear to him at an early moment," says Moglen. "This has a lot to do with Richard's personality, which lots of people will, when writing about him, try to depict as epiphenomenal or even a drawback in Richard Stallman's own life work."

Gilmore, who describes his inclusion between the erratic Nelson and the irascible Stallman as something of a "mixed honor," nevertheless seconds the Moglen argument. Writes Gilmore:

> My guess is that Stallman's writings will stand up as well as Thomas Jefferson's have; he's a pretty clear writer and also clear on his principles ... Whether Richard will be as influential as Jefferson will depend on whether the abstractions we call "civil rights" end up more important a hundred years from now than the abstractions that we call "software" or "technically imposed restrictions."

Another element of the Stallman legacy not to be overlooked, Gilmore writes, is the collaborative software-development model pioneered by the GNU Project. Although flawed at times, the model has nevertheless evolved into a standard within the software-development industry. All told, Gilmore says, this collaborative software-development model may end up being even more influential than the GNU Project, the GPL License, or any particular software program developed by Stallman:

> Before the Internet, it was quite hard to collaborate over distance on software, even among teams that know and trust each other. Richard pioneered collaborative development of software, particularly by disorganized volunteers who seldom meet each other. Richard didn't build any of the basic tools for doing this (the TCP protocol, email lists, diff and patch, tar files, RCS or CVS or remote-CVS), but he used the ones that were available to form social groups of programmers who could effectively collaborate.

Lawrence Lessig, Stanford law professor and author of the 2001 book, *The Future of Ideas*, is similarly bullish. Like many legal scholars, Lessig sees the GPL as a major bulwark of the current so-called "digital commons," the vast agglomeration of community-owned software programs, network and telecommunication standards that have triggered the Internet's exponential growth over the last three decades. Rather than connect Stallman with other Internet pioneers, men such as Vannevar Bush, Vinton Cerf, and J. C. R. Licklider who convinced others to see computer technology on a wider scale, Lessig sees Stallman's impact as more personal, introspective, and, ultimately, unique:

> *[Stallman] changed the debate from is to ought. He made people see how much was at stake, and he built a device to carry these ideals forward . . . That said, I don't quite know how to place him in the context of Cerf or Licklider. The innovation is different. It is not just about a certain kind of code, or enabling the Internet. [It's] much more about getting people to see the value in a certain kind of Internet. I don't think there is anyone else in that class, before or after.*

Not everybody sees the Stallman legacy as set in stone, of course. Eric Raymond, the open source proponent who feels that Stallman's leadership role has diminished significantly since 1996, sees mixed signals when looking into the 2102 crystal ball:

> *I think Stallman's artifacts (GPL, Emacs, GCC) will be seen as revolutionary works, as foundation-stones of the information world. I think history will be less kind to some of the theories from which RMS operated, and not kind at all to his personal tendency towards territorial, cult-leader behavior.*

As for Stallman himself, he, too, sees mixed signals:

> *What history says about the GNU Project, twenty years from now, will depend on who wins the battle of freedom to use public knowledge. If we lose, we will be just a footnote. If we win, it is uncertain whether people will know the role of the GNU operating system—if they think the system is "Linux," they will build a false picture of what happened and why.*

But even if we win, what history people learn a hundred years from now is likely to depend on who dominates politically.

Searching for his own 19th-century historical analogy, Stallman summons the figure of John Brown, the militant abolitionist regarded as a hero on one side of the Mason Dixon line and a madman on the other.

John Brown's slave revolt never got going, but during his subsequent trial he effectively roused national demand for abolition. During the Civil War, John Brown was a hero; 100 years after, and for much of the 1900s, history textbooks taught that he was crazy. During the era of legal segregation, while bigotry was shameless, the US partly accepted the story that the South wanted to tell about itself, and history textbooks said many untrue things about the Civil War and related events.

Such comparisons document both the self-perceived peripheral nature of Stallman's current work and the binary nature of his current reputation. Although it's hard to see Stallman's reputation falling to the level of infamy as Brown's did during the post-Reconstruction period—Stallman, despite his occasional war-like analogies, has done little to inspire violence—it's easy to envision a future in which Stallman's ideas wind up on the ash-heap. In fashioning the free software cause not as a mass movement but as a collection of private battles against the forces of proprietary temptation, Stallman seems to have created a unwinnable situation, especially for the many acolytes with the same stubborn will.

Then again, it is that very will that may someday prove to be Stallman's greatest lasting legacy. Moglen, a close observer over the last decade, warns those who mistake the Stallman personality as counter-productive or epiphenomenal to the "artifacts" of Stalllman's life. Without that personality, Moglen says, there would be precious few artifiacts to discuss. Says Moglen, a former Supreme Court clerk:

Look, the greatest man I ever worked for was Thurgood Marshall. I knew what made him a great man. I knew why he had been able to change the world in his possible way. I would be going out on a limb a little bit if I were to make a comparison, because they could not be more different. Thurgood Marshall

*was a man in society, representing an outcast society to the
society that enclosed it, but still a man in society. His skill was
social skills. But he was all of a piece, too. Different as they
were in every other respect, that the person I most now compare him to in that sense, all of a piece, compact, made of the
substance that makes stars, all the way through, is Stallman.*

In an effort to drive that image home, Moglen reflects on a shared
moment in the spring of 2000. The success of the VA Linux IPO
was still resonating in the business media, and a half dozen free
software–related issues were swimming through the news. Surrounded by a swirling hurricane of issues and stories each begging
for comment, Moglen recalls sitting down for lunch with Stallman
and feeling like a castaway dropped into the eye of the storm. For
the next hour, he says, the conversation calmly revolved around a
single topic: strengthening the GPL.

"We were sitting there talking about what we were going to
do about some problems in Eastern Europe and what we were
going to do when the problem of the ownership of content began
to threaten free software," Moglen recalls. "As we were talking, I
briefly thought about how we must have looked to people passing
by. Here we are, these two little bearded anarchists, plotting and
planning the next steps. And, of course, Richard is plucking the
knots from his hair and dropping them in the soup and behaving
in his usual way. Anybody listening in on our conversation would
have thought we were crazy, but I knew: I knew the revolution's
right here at this table. This is what's making it happen. And this
man is the person making it happen."

Moglen says that moment, more than any other, drove home
the elemental simplicity of the Stallman style.

"It was funny," recalls Moglen. "I said to him, 'Richard, you
know, you and I are the two guys who didn't make any money
out of this revolution.' And then I paid for the lunch, because I
knew he didn't have the money to pay for it.'"

ENDNOTE

1.   See Marco Boerries, interview with author (July, 2000).

CRUSHING LONELINESS

Writing the biography of a living person is a bit like producing a play. The drama in front of the curtain often pales in comparison to the drama backstage. In *The Autobiography of Malcolm X*, Alex Haley gives readers a rare glimpse of that backstage drama. Stepping out of the ghostwriter role, Haley delivers the book's epilogue in his own voice. The epilogue explains how a freelance reporter originally dismissed as a "tool" and "spy" by the Nation of Islam spokesperson managed to work through personal and political barriers to get Malcolm X's life story on paper.

While I hesitate to compare this book with *The Autobiography of Malcolm X*, I do owe a debt of gratitude to Haley for his candid epilogue. Over the last 12 months, it has served as a sort of instruction manual on how to deal with a biographical subject who has built an entire career on being disagreeable. From the outset, I envisioned closing this biography with a similar epilogue, both as an homage to Haley and as a way to let readers know how this book came to be.

The story behind this story starts in an Oakland apartment, winding its way through the various locales mentioned in the book—Silicon Valley, Maui, Boston, and Cambridge. Ultimately, however, it is a tale of two cities: New York, New York, the book-publishing capital of the world, and Sebastopol, California, the book-publishing capital of Sonoma County.

The story starts in April, 2000. At the time, I was writing stories for the ill-fated BeOpen web site (*http://www.beopen.com*). One of my first assignments was a phone interview with Richard M. Stallman. The interview went well, so well that Slashdot (*http://www.slashdot.org*), the popular "news for nerds" site owned by VA Software, Inc. (formerly VA Linux Systems and before that, VA Research), gave it a link in its daily list of feature stories. Within hours, the web servers at BeOpen were heating up as readers clicked over to the site.

For all intents and purposes, the story should have ended there. Three months after the interview, while attending the O'Reilly Open Source Conference in Monterey, California, I received the following email message from Tracy Pattison, foreign-rights manager at a large New York publishing house:

```
To: sam@BeOpen.com
Subject: RMS Interview
Date: Mon, 10 Jul 2000 15:56:37 -0400
Dear Mr. Williams,

I read your interview with Richard Stallman on BeOpen with great
interest. I've been intrigued by RMS and his work for some time now
and was delighted to find your piece which I really think you did a
great job of capturing some of the spirit of what Stallman is
trying to do with  GNU-Linux and the Free Software Foundation.

What I'd love to do, however, is read more - and I don't think I'm
alone. Do you think there is more information and/or sources out
there to expand and update your interview and adapt it into more of
a profile of Stallman? Perhaps including some more anecdotal
information about his personality and background that might really
interest and enlighten  readers outside the more hardcore
programming scene?
```

The email asked that I give Tracy a call to discuss the idea further. I did just that. Tracy told me her company was launching a new electronic book line, and it wanted stories that appealed to an early-adopter audience. The e-book format was 30,000 words, about 100 pages, and she had pitched her bosses on the idea of profiling a major figure in the hacker community. Her bosses liked the idea, and in the process of searching for interesting people to profile, she had come across my BeOpen interview with Stallman. Hence her email to me.

That's when Tracy asked me: would I be willing to expand the interview into a full-length feature profile? My answer was instant: yes. Before accepting it, Tracy suggested I put together a story proposal she could show her superiors. Two days later, I sent her a polished proposal. A week later, Tracy sent me a follow up email. Her bosses had given it the green light.

I have to admit, getting Stallman to participate in an e-book project was an afterthought on my part. As a reporter who covered the open source beat, I knew Stallman was a stickler. I'd already received a half dozen emails at that point upbraiding me for the use of "Linux" instead of "GNU/Linux."

Then again, I also knew Stallman was looking for ways to get his message out to the general public. Perhaps if I presented the project to him that way, he would be more receptive. If not, I could always rely upon the copious amounts of documents, interviews, and recorded online conversations Stallman had left lying around the Internet and do an unauthorized biography.

During my research, I came across an essay titled "Freedom—Or Copyright?" Written by Stallman and published in the June, 2000, edition of the MIT Technology Review, the essay blasted e-books for an assortment of software sins. Not only did readers have to use proprietary software programs to read them, Stallman lamented, but the methods used to prevent unauthorized copying were overly harsh. Instead of downloading a transferable HTML or PDF file, readers downloaded an encrypted file. In essence, purchasing an e-book meant purchasing a nontransferable key to unscramble the encrypted content. Any attempt to open a book's content without an authorized key constituted a criminal violation of the Digital Millennium Copyright Act, the 1998 law designed to bolster copyright enforcement on the Internet. Similar penalties held for readers who converted a book's content into an open file format, even if their only intention was to read the book on a different computer in their home. Unlike a normal book, the reader no longer held the right to lend, copy, or resell an e-book. They only had the right to read it on an authorized machine, warned Stallman:

> *We still have the same old freedoms in using paper books. But if e-books replace printed books, that exception will do little good. With "electronic ink," which makes it possible to download new text onto an apparently printed piece of paper, even newspapers could become ephemeral. Imagine: no more used book stores; no more lending a book to your friend; no more borrowing one from the public library—no more "leaks" that might give someone a chance to read without paying. (And judging from the ads for Microsoft Reader, no more anonymous purchasing of books either.) This is the world publishers have in mind for us.*[1]

Needless to say, the essay caused some concern. Neither Tracy nor I had discussed the software her company would use nor had we discussed the type of copyright that would govern the e-book's usage. I mentioned the Technology Review article and asked if she could give me information on her company's e-book policies. Tracy promised to get back to me.

Eager to get started, I decided to call Stallman anyway and mention the book idea to him. When I did, he expressed immediate interest and immediate concern. "Did you read my essay on e-books?" he asked.

When I told him, yes, I had read the essay and was waiting to hear back from the publisher, Stallman laid out two conditions: he didn't want to lend support to an e-book licensing mechanism he fundamentally opposed, and he didn't want to come off as lending support. "I don't want to participate in anything that makes me look like a hypocrite," he said.

For Stallman, the software issue was secondary to the copyright issue. He said he was willing to ignore whatever software the publisher or its third-party vendors employed just so long as the company specified within the copyright that readers were free to make and distribute verbatim copies of the e-book's content.

Stallman pointed to Stephen King's *The Plant* as a possible model. In June, 2000, King announced on his official web site that he was self-publishing *The Plant* in serial form. According to the announcement, the book's total cost would be $13, spread out over a series of $1 installments. As long as at least 75% of the readers paid for each chapter, King promised to continue releasing new installments. By August, the plan seemed to be working, as King had published the first two chapters with a third on the way.

"I'd be willing to accept something like that," Stallman said. "As long as it also permitted verbatim copying."

I forwarded the information to Tracy. Feeling confident that she and I might be able to work out an equitable arrangement, I called up Stallman and set up the first interview for the book. Stallman agreed to the interview without making a second inquiry into the status issue. Shortly after the first interview, I raced to set up a second interview (this one in Kihei), squeezing it in before Stallman headed off on a 14-day vacation to Tahiti.

It was during Stallman's vacation that the bad news came from Tracy. Her company's legal department didn't want to adjust its copyright notice on the e-books. Readers who wanted to make their books transferable would either have to crack the encryption code or convert the book to an open format such as HTML. Either way, the would be breaking the law and facing criminal penalties.

With two fresh interviews under my belt, I didn't see any way to write the book without resorting to the new material. I quickly set up a trip to New York to meet with my agent and with Tracy to see if there was a compromise solution.

When I flew to New York, I met my agent, Henning Guttman. It was our first face-to-face meeting, and Henning seemed pessimistic about our chances of forcing a compromise, at least on the publisher's end. The large, established publishing houses already viewed the e-book format with enough suspicion and weren't in the mood to experiment with copyright language that made it easier for readers to avoid payment. As an agent who specialized in technology books, however, Henning was intrigued by the novel nature of my predicament. I told him about the two interviews I'd already gathered and the promise not to publish the book in a way that made Stallman "look like a hypocrite." Agreeing that I was in an ethical bind, Henning suggested we make that our negotiating point.

Barring that, Henning said, we could always take the carrot-and-stick approach. The carrot would be the publicity that came with publishing an e-book that honored the hacker community's internal ethics. The stick would be the risks associated with publishing an e-book that didn't. Nine months before Dmitri Skylarov became an Internet cause célèbre, we knew it was only a matter of time before an enterprising programmer revealed how to hack e-books. We also knew that a major publishing house releasing an encryption-protected e-book on Richard M. Stallman was the software equivalent of putting "Steal This E-Book" on the cover.

After my meeting with Henning, I put a call into Stallman. Hoping to make the carrot more enticing, I discussed a number of potential compromises. What if the publisher released the book's content under a split license, something similar to what Sun Microsystems had done with Open Office, the free software desktop applications suite? The publisher could then release commercial versions of the e-book under a normal format, taking advantage of all the bells and whistles that went with the e-book software, while releasing the copyable version under a less aesthetically pleasing HTML format.

Stallman told me he didn't mind the split-license idea, but he did dislike the idea of making the freely copyable version inferior to the restricted version. Besides, he said, the idea was too cumbersome. Split licenses worked in the case of Sun's Open Office only because he had no control over the decision making. In this case, Stallman said, he did have a way to control the outcome. He could refuse to cooperate.

I made a few more suggestions with little effect. About the only thing I could get out of Stallman was a concession that the e-book's copyright restrict all forms of file sharing to "noncommercial redistribution."

Before I signed off, Stallman suggested I tell the publisher that I'd promised Stallman that the work would be free. I told Stallman I couldn't agree to that statement but that I did view the book as unfinishable without his cooperation. Seemingly satisfied, Stallman hung up with his usual sign-off line: "Happy hacking."

Henning and I met with Tracy the next day. Tracy said her company was willing to publish copyable excerpts in a unencrypted format but would limit the excerpts to 500 words. Henning informed her that this wouldn't be enough for me to get around my ethical obligation to Stallman. Tracy mentioned her own company's contractual obligation to online vendors such as Amazon.com. Even if the company decided to open up its e-book content this one time, it faced the risk of its partners calling it a breach of contract. Barring a change of heart in the executive suite or on the part of Stallman, the decision was up to me. I could use the interviews and go against my earlier agreement with Stallman, or I could plead journalistic ethics and back out of the verbal agreement to do the book.

Following the meeting, my agent and I relocated to a pub on Third Ave. I used his cell phone to call Stallman, leaving a message when nobody answered. Henning left for a moment, giving me time to collect my thoughts. When he returned, he was holding up the cell phone.

"It's Stallman," Henning said.

The conversation got off badly from the start. I relayed Tracy's comment about the publisher's contractual obligations.

"So," Stallman said bluntly. "Why should I give a damn about their contractual obligations?"

Because asking a major publishing house to risk a legal battle with its vendors over a 30,000 word e-book is a tall order, I suggested.

"Don't you see?" Stallman said. "That's exactly why I'm doing this. I want a signal victory. I want them to make a choice between freedom and business as usual."

As the words "signal victory" echoed in my head, I felt my attention wander momentarily to the passing foot traffic on the sidewalk. Coming into the bar, I had been pleased to notice that the location was less than half a block away from the street corner memorialized in the 1976 Ramones song, "53rd and 3rd," a song I always enjoyed playing in my days as a musician. Like the perpetually frustrated street hustler depicted in that song, I could feel things falling apart as quickly as they had come together. The irony was palpable. After weeks of gleefully recording other people's laments, I found myself in the position of trying to pull off the rarest of feats: a Richard Stallman compromise.

When I continued hemming and hawing, pleading the publisher's position and revealing my growing sympathy for it, Stallman, like an animal smelling blood, attacked.

"So that's it? You're just going to screw me? You're just going to bend to their will?"

I brought up the issue of a dual-copyright again.

"You mean license," Stallman said curtly.

"Yeah, license. Copyright. Whatever," I said, feeling suddenly like a wounded tuna trailing a rich plume of plasma in the water.

"Aw, why didn't you just fucking do what I told you to do!" he shouted.

I must have been arguing on behalf of the publisher to the very end, because in my notes I managed to save a final Stallman chestnut: "I don't care. What they're doing is evil. I can't support evil. Good-bye."

As soon as I put the phone down, my agent slid a freshly poured Guinness to me. "I figured you might need this," he said with a laugh. "I could see you shaking there towards the end."

I was indeed shaking. The shaking wouldn't stop until the Guinness was more than halfway gone. It felt weird, hearing myself characterized as an emissary of "evil." It felt weirder still, knowing that three months before, I was sitting in an Oakland apartment trying to come up with my next story idea. Now, I was sitting in a part of the world I'd only known through rock songs, taking meetings with publishing executives and drinking beer with an agent I'd never even laid eyes on until the day before. It was all too surreal, like watching my life reflected back as a movie montage.

About that time, my internal absurdity meter kicked in. The initial shaking gave way to convulsions of laughter. To my agent, I must have looked like a another fragile author undergoing an untimely emotional breakdown. To me, I was just starting to appreciate the cynical beauty of my situation. Deal or no deal, I already had the makings of a pretty good story. It was only a matter of finding a place to tell it. When my laughing convulsions finally subsided, I held up my drink in a toast.

"Welcome to the front lines, my friend," I said, clinking pints with my agent. "Might as well enjoy it."

If this story really were a play, here's where it would take a momentary, romantic interlude. Disheartened by the tense nature of our meeting, Tracy invited Henning and I to go out for drinks with her and some of her coworkers. We left the bar on Third Ave., headed down to the East Village, and caught up with Tracy and her friends.

Once there, I spoke with Tracy, careful to avoid shop talk. Our conversation was pleasant, relaxed. Before parting, we agreed to meet the next night. Once again, the conversation was pleasant, so pleasant that the Stallman e-book became almost a distant memory.

When I got back to Oakland, I called around to various journalist friends and acquaintances. I recounted my predicament. Most upbraided me for giving up too much ground to Stallman in the preinterview negotiation. A former j-school professor suggested I ignore Stallman's "hypocrite" comment and just write the story. Reporters who knew of Stallman's media-savviness expressed sympathy but uniformly offered the same response: it's your call.

I decided to put the book on the back burner. Even with the interviews, I wasn't making much progress. Besides, it gave me a chance to speak with Tracy without running things past Henning first. By Christmas we had traded visits: she flying out to the west coast once, me flying out to New York a second time. The day before New Year's Eve, I proposed. Deciding which coast to live on, I picked New York. By February, I packed up my laptop computer and all my research notes related to the Stallman biography, and we winged our way to JFK Airport. Tracy and I were married on May 11. So much for failed book deals.

During the summer, I began to contemplate turning my interview notes into a magazine article. Ethically, I felt in the clear doing so, since the original interview terms said nothing about traditional print media. To be honest, I also felt a bit more comfortable writing about Stallman after eight months of radio silence. Since our telephone conversation in September, I'd only received two emails from Stallman. Both chastised me for using "Linux" instead of "GNU/Linux" in a pair of articles for the web magazine *Upside Today*. Aside from that, I had enjoyed the silence. In June, about a week after the New York University speech, I took a crack at writing a 5,000-word magazine-length story about Stallman. This time, the words flowed. The distance had helped restore my lost sense of emotional perspective, I suppose.

In July, a full year after the original email from Tracy, I got a call from Henning. He told me that O'Reilly & Associates, a publishing house out of Sebastopol, California, was interested in the running the Stallman story as a biography. The news pleased me. Of all the publishing houses in the world, O'Reilly, the same company that had published Eric Raymond's *The Cathedral and the Bazaar*, seemed the most sensitive to the issues that had killed the earlier e-book. As a reporter, I had relied heavily on the O'Reilly book *Open Sources* as a historical reference. I also knew that various chapters of the book, including a chapter written by Stallman, had been published with copyright notices that permitted redistribution. Such knowledge would come in handy if the issue of electronic publication ever came up again.

Sure enough, the issue did come up. I learned through Henning that O'Reilly intended to publish the biography both as a book and as part of its new Safari Tech Books Online subscription service. The Safari user license would involve special restrictions,[1] Henning warned, but O'Reilly was willing to allow for a copyright that permitted users to copy and share and the book's text regardless of medium. Basically, as author, I had the choice between two licenses: the Open Publication License or the GNU Free Documentation License.

I checked out the contents and background of each license. The Open Publication License (OPL)[2] gives readers the right to reproduce and distribute a work, in whole or in part, in any medium "physical or electronic," provided the copied work retains the Open Publication License. It also permits modification of a work, provided certain conditions are met. Finally, the Open Publication License includes a number of options, which, if selected by the author, can limit the creation of "substantively modified" versions or book-form derivatives without prior author approval.

The GNU Free Documentation License (GFDL),[3] meanwhile, permits the copying and distribution of a document in any medium, provided the resulting work carries the same license. It also permits the modification of a document provided certain conditions. Unlike the OPL, however, it does not give authors the option to restrict certain modifications. It also does not give authors the right to reject modifications that might result in a competitive book product. It does require certain forms of front- and back-cover information if a party other than the copyright holder wishes to publish more than 100 copies of a protected work, however.

In the course of researching the licenses, I also made sure to visit the GNU Project web page titled "Various Licenses and Comments About Them."[4] On that page, I found a Stallman critique of the Open Publication License. Stallman's critique related to the creation of modified works and the ability of an author to select either one of the OPL's options to restrict modification. If an author didn't want to select either option, it was better to use the GFDL instead, Stallman noted, since it minimized the risk of the nonselected options popping up in modified versions of a document.

The importance of modification in both licenses was a reflection of their original purpose—namely, to give software-manual owners a chance to improve their manuals and publicize those improvements to the rest of the community. Since my book wasn't a manual, I had little concern about the modification clause in either license. My only concern was giving users the freedom to exchange copies of the book or make copies of the content, the same freedom they would have enjoyed if they purchased a hardcover book. Deeming either license suitable for this purpose, I signed the O'Reilly contract when it came to me.

Still, the notion of unrestricted modification intrigued me. In my early negotiations with Tracy, I had pitched the merits of a GPL-style license for the e-book's content. At worst, I said, the license would guarantee a lot of positive publicity for the e-book. At best, it would encourage readers to participate in the book-writing process. As an author, I was willing to let other people amend my work just so long as my name always got top billing. Besides, it might even be interesting to watch the book evolve. I pictured later editions looking much like online versions of the *Talmud*, my original text in a central column surrounded by illuminating, third-party commentary in the margins.

My idea drew inspiration from Project Xanadu *(http://www. xanadu.com)*, the legendary software concept originally conceived by Ted Nelson in 1960. During the O'Reilly Open Source Conference in 1999, I had seen the first demonstration of the project's open source offshoot Udanax and had been wowed by the result. In one demonstration sequence, Udanax displayed a parent document and a derivative work in a similar two-column, plain-text format. With a click of the button, the program introduced lines linking each sentence in the parent to its conceptual offshoot in the derivative. An e-book biography of Richard M. Stallman didn't have to be Udanax-enabled, but given such technological possibilities, why not give users a chance to play around?[5]

When Laurie Petrycki, my editor at O'Reilly, gave me a choice between the OPL or the GFDL, I indulged the fantasy once again. By September of 2001, the month I signed the contract, e-books had become almost a dead topic. Many publishing houses, Tracy's included, were shutting down their e-book imprints for lack of interest. I had to wonder. If these companies had treated e-books not as a form of publication but as a form of community building, would those imprints have survived?

After I signed the contract, I notified Stallman that the book project was back on. I mentioned the choice O'Reilly was giving me between the Open Publication License and the GNU Free Documentation License. I told him I was leaning toward the OPL, if only for the fact I saw no reason to give O'Reilly's competitors a chance to print the same book under a different cover. Stallman wrote back, arguing in favor of the GFDL, noting that O'Reilly had already used it several times in the past. Despite the events of the past year, I suggested a deal. I would choose the GFDL if it gave me the possibility to do more interviews and if Stallman agreed to help O'Reilly publicize the book. Stallman agreed to participate in more interviews but said that his participation in publicity-related events would depend on the content of the book. Viewing this as only fair, I set up an interview for December 17, 2001 in Cambridge.

I set up the interview to coincide with a business trip my wife Tracy was taking to Boston. Two days before leaving, Tracy suggested I invite Stallman out to dinner.

"After all," she said, "he is the one who brought us together."

I sent an email to Stallman, who promptly sent a return email accepting the offer. When I drove up to Boston the next day, I met Tracy at her hotel and hopped the T to head over to MIT. When we got to Tech Square, I found Stallman in the middle of a conversation just as we knocked on the door.

"I hope you don't mind," he said, pulling the door open far enough so that Tracy and I could just barely hear Stallman's conversational counterpart. It was a youngish woman, mid-20s I'd say, named Sarah.

"I took the liberty of inviting somebody else to have dinner with us," Stallman said, matter-of-factly, giving me the same cat-like smile he gave me back in that Palo Alto restaurant.

To be honest, I wasn't too surprised. The news that Stallman had a new female friend had reached me a few weeks before, courtesy of Stallman's mother. "In fact, they both went to Japan last month when Richard went over to accept the Takeda Award," Lippman told me at the time.[6]

On the way over to the restaurant, I learned the circumstances of Sarah and Richard's first meeting. Interestingly, the circumstances were very familiar. Working on her own fictional book, Sarah said she heard about Stallman and what an interesting character he was. She promptly decided to create a character in her book on Stallman and, in the interests of researching the character, set up an interview with Stallman. Things quickly went from there. The two had been dating since the beginning of 2001, she said.

"I really admired the way Richard built up an entire political movement to address an issue of profound personal concern," Sarah said, explaining her attraction to Stallman.

My wife immediately threw back the question: "What was the issue?"

"Crushing loneliness."

During dinner, I let the women do the talking and spent most of the time trying to detect clues as to whether the last 12 months had softened Stallman in any significant way. I didn't see anything to suggest they had. Although more flirtatious than I remembered—a flirtatiousness spoiled somewhat by the number of times Stallman's eyes seemed to fixate on my wife's chest—Stallman retained the same general level of prickliness. At one point, my wife uttered an emphatic "God forbid" only to receive a typical Stallman rebuke.

"I hate to break it to you, but there is no God," Stallman said.

Afterwards, when the dinner was complete and Sarah had departed, Stallman seemed to let his guard down a little. As we walked to a nearby bookstore, he admitted that the last 12 months had dramatically changed his outlook on life. "I thought I was going to be alone forever," he said. "I'm glad I was wrong."

Before parting, Stallman handed me his "pleasure card," a business card listing Stallman's address, phone number, and favorite pastimes ("sharing good books, good food and exotic music and dance") so that I might set up a final interview.

sharing good books, good food and exotic music and dance
tender embraces
unusual sense of humor

Richard Stallman

545 Tech Square, rm. 425, Cambridge, MA 02139

rms@gnu.org   (617) 253-███

Stallman's "pleasure" card, handed to me the night of our dinner.

The next day, over another meal of dim sum, Stallman seemed
even more lovestruck than the night before. Recalling his debates
with Currier House dorm maters over the benefits and drawbacks
of an immortality serum, Stallman expressed hope that scientists
might some day come up with the key to immortality. "Now that
I'm finally starting to have happiness in my life, I want to have
more," he said.

When I mentioned Sarah's "crushing loneliness" comment,
Stallman failed to see a connection between loneliness on a physical or spiritual level and loneliness on a hacker level. "The
impulse to share code is about friendship but friendship at a much
lower level," he said. Later, however, when the subject came up
again, Stallman did admit that loneliness, or the fear of perpetual
loneliness, had played a major role in fueling his determination
during the earliest days of the GNU Project.

"My fascination with computers was not a consequence of
anything else," he said. "I wouldn't have been less fascinated with
computers if I had been popular and all the women flocked to me.
However, it's certainly true the experience of feeling I didn't have
a home, finding one and losing it, finding another and having it
destroyed, affected me deeply. The one I lost was the dorm. The
one that was destroyed was the AI Lab. The precariousness of not

having any kind of home or community was very powerful. It made me want to fight to get it back."

After the interview, I couldn't help but feel a certain sense of emotional symmetry. Hearing Sarah describe what attracted her to Stallman and hearing Stallman himself describe the emotions that prompted him to take up the free software cause, I was reminded of my own reasons for writing this book. Since July, 2000, I have learned to appreciate both the seductive and the repellent sides of the Richard Stallman persona. Like Eben Moglen before me, I feel that dismissing that persona as epiphenomenal or distracting in relation to the overall free software movement would be a grievous mistake. In many ways the two are so mutually defining as to be indistinguishable.

While I'm sure not every reader feels the same level of affinity for Stallman—indeed, after reading this book, some might feel zero affinity—I'm sure most will agree. Few individuals offer as singular a human portrait as Richard M. Stallman. It is my sincere hope that, with this initial portrait complete and with the help of the GFDL, others will feel a similar urge to add their own perspective to that portrait.

ENDNOTES

1. See "Safari Tech Books Online; Subscriber Agreement: Terms of Service." *http://safari.oreilly.com/mainhlp.asp?help=service*

2. See "The Open Publication License: Draft v1.0" (June 8, 1999). *http://opencontent.org/openpub/*

3. See "The GNU Free Documentation License: Version 1.1" (March, 2000). *http://www.gnu.org/copyleft/fdl.html*

4. See *http://www.gnu.org/philosophy/license-list.html*

5. Anybody willing to "port" this book over to Udanax, the free software version of Xanadu, will receive enthusiastic support from me. To find out more about this intriguing technology, visit *http://www.udanax.com*.

6. Alas, I didn't find out about the Takeda Foundation's decision to award Stallman, along with Linus Torvalds and Ken Sakamura, with its first-ever award for "Techno-Entrepreneurial Achievement for Social/Economic Well-Being" until after Stallman had made the trip to Japan to accept the award. For more information about the award and its accompanying $1 million prize, visit the Takeda site, *http://www.takeda-foundation.jp*.

TERMINOLOGY

For the most part, I have chosen to use the term GNU/Linux in reference to the free software operating system and Linux when referring specifically to the kernel that drives the operating system. The most notable exception to this rule comes in Chapter 9. In the final part of that chapter, I describe the early evolution of Linux as an offshoot of Minix. It is safe to say that during the first two years of the project's development, the operating system Torvalds and his colleagues were working on bore little similarity to the GNU system envisioned by Stallman, even though it gradually began to share key components, such as the GNU C Compiler and the GNU Debugger.

This decision further benefits from the fact that, prior to 1993, Stallman saw little need to insist on credit.

Some might view the decision to use GNU/Linux for later versions of the same operating system as arbitrary. I would like to point out that it was in no way a prerequisite for gaining Stallman's cooperation in the making of this book. I came to it of my own accord, partly because of the operating system's modular nature and the community surrounding it, and partly because of the apolitical nature of the Linux name. Given that this is a biography of Richard Stallman, it seemed inappropriate to define the operating system in apolitical terms.

In the final phases of the book, when it became clear that O'Reilly & Associates would be the book's publisher, Stallman did make it a condition that I use "GNU/Linux" instead of Linux if O'Reilly expected him to provide promotional support for the book after publication. When informed of this, I relayed my earlier decision and left it up to Stallman to judge whether the resulting book met this condition or not. At the time of this writing, I have no idea what Stallman's judgment will be.

A similar situation surrounds the terms "free software" and "open source." Again, I have opted for the more politically laden "free software" term when describing software programs that come with freely copyable and freely modifiable source code. Although more popular, I have chosen to use the term "open source" only when referring to groups and businesses that have championed its usage. But for a few instances, the terms are completely interchangeable, and in making this decision I have followed the advice of Christine Peterson, the person generally credited with coining the term. "The 'free software' term should still be used in circumstances where it works better," Peterson writes. "['Open source'] caught on mainly because a new term was greatly needed, not because it's ideal."

Hack, Hackers, and Hacking

To understand the full meaning of the word "hacker," it helps to examine the word's etymology over the years.

The New Hacker Dictionary, an online compendium of software-programmer jargon, officially lists nine different connotations of the word "hack" and a similar number for "hacker." Then again, the same publication also includes an accompanying essay that quotes Phil Agre, an MIT hacker who warns readers not to be fooled by the word's perceived flexibility. "Hack has only one meaning," argues Agre. "An extremely subtle and profound one which defies articulation."

Regardless of the width or narrowness of the definition, most modern hackers trace the word back to MIT, where the term bubbled up as popular item of student jargon in the early 1950s. In 1990 the MIT Museum put together a journal documenting the hacking phenomenon. According to the journal, students who attended the institute during the fifties used the word "hack" the way a modern student might use the word "goof." Hanging a jalopy out a dormitory window was a "hack," but anything harsh or malicious—e.g., egging a rival dorm's windows or defacing a campus statue—fell outside the bounds. Implicit within the definition of "hack" was a spirit of harmless, creative fun.

This spirit would inspire the word's gerund form: "hacking." A 1950s student who spent the better part of the afternoon talking on the phone or dismantling a radio might describe the activity as "hacking." Again, a modern speaker would substitute the verb form of "goof"—"goofing" or "goofing off"—to describe the same activity.

As the 1950s progressed, the word "hack" acquired a sharper, more rebellious edge. The MIT of the 1950s was overly competitive, and hacking emerged as both a reaction to and extension of that competitive culture. Goofs and pranks suddenly became a way to blow off steam, thumb one's nose at campus administration, and indulge creative thinking and behavior stifled by the Institute's rigorous undergraduate curriculum. With its myriad hallways and underground steam tunnels, the Institute offered plenty of exploration opportunities for the student undaunted by locked doors and "No Trespassing" signs. Students began to refer to their off-limits explorations as "tunnel hacking." Above ground, the campus phone system offered similar opportunities. Through casual experimentation and due diligence, students learned how to perform humorous tricks. Drawing inspiration from the more traditional pursuit of tunnel hacking, students quickly dubbed this new activity "phone hacking."

The combined emphasis on creative play and restriction-free exploration would serve as the basis for the future mutations of the hacking term. The first self-described computer hackers of the 1960s MIT campus originated from a late 1950s student group called the Tech Model Railroad Club. A tight clique within the club was the Signals and Power (S&P) Committee—the group behind the railroad club's electrical circuitry system. The system was a sophisticated assortment of relays and switches similar to the kind that controlled the local campus phone system. To control it, a member of the group simply dialed in commands via a connected phone and watched the trains do his bidding.

The nascent electrical engineers responsible for building and maintaining this system saw their activity as similar in spirit to phone hacking. Adopting the hacking term, they began refining it even further. From the S&P hacker point of view, using one less relay to operate a particular stretch of track meant having one more relay for future play. Hacking subtly shifted from a synonym for idle play to a synonym for idle play that improved the overall performance or efficiency of the club's railroad system at the same time. Soon S&P committee members proudly referred to the entire activity of improving and reshaping the track's underlying circuitry as "hacking" and to the people who did it as "hackers."

Given their affinity for sophisticated electronics—not to mention the traditional MIT-student disregard for closed doors and "No Trespassing" signs—it didn't take long before the hackers caught wind of a new machine on campus. Dubbed the TX-0, the machine was one of the first commercially marketed computers. By the end of the 1950s, the entire S&P clique had migrated en masse over to the TX-0 control room, bringing the spirit of creative play with them. The wide-open realm of computer programming would encourage yet another mutation in etymology. "To hack" no longer meant soldering unusual looking circuits, but cobbling together software programs with little regard to "official" methods or software-writing procedures. It also meant improving the efficiency and speed of already-existing programs that tended to hog up machine resources. True to the word's roots, it also meant writing programs that served no other purpose than to amuse or entertain.

A classic example of this expanded hacking definition is the game Spacewar, the first interactive video game. Developed by MIT hackers in the early 1960s, Spacewar had all the traditional hacking definitions: it was goofy and random, serving little useful purpose other than providing a nightly distraction for the dozen or so hackers who delighted in playing it. From a software perspective, however, it was a monumental testament to innovation of programming skill. It was also completely free. Because hackers had built it for fun, they saw no reason to guard their creation, sharing it extensively with other programmers. By the end of the 1960s, Spacewar had become a favorite diversion for mainframe programmers around the world.

This notion of collective innovation and communal software ownership distanced the act of computer hacking in the 1960s from the tunnel hacking and phone hacking of the 1950s. The latter pursuits tended to be solo or small-group activities. Tunnel and phone hackers relied heavily on campus lore, but the off-limits nature of their activity discouraged the open circulation of new discoveries. Computer hackers, on the other hand, did their work amid a scientific field biased toward collaboration and the rewarding of innovation. Hackers and "official" computer scientists weren't always the best of allies, but in the rapid evolution of the field, the two species of computer programmer evolved a cooperative—some might say symbiotic—relationship.

It is a testament to the original computer hackers' prodigious skill that later programmers, including Richard M. Stallman, aspired to wear the same hacker mantle. By the mid to late 1970s, the term "hacker" had acquired elite connotations. In a general sense, a computer hacker was any person who wrote software code for the sake of writing software code. In the particular sense, however, it was a testament to programming skill. Like the term "artist," the meaning carried tribal overtones. To describe a fellow programmer as hacker was a sign of respect. To describe oneself as a hacker was a sign of immense personal confidence. Either way, the original looseness of the computer-hacker appellation diminished as computers became more common.

As the definition tightened, "computer" hacking acquired additional semantic overtones. To be a hacker, a person had to do more than write interesting software; a person had to belong to the hacker "culture" and honor its traditions the same way a medieval wine maker might pledge membership to a vintners' guild. The social structure wasn't as rigidly outlined as that of a guild, but hackers at elite institutions such as MIT, Stanford, and Carnegie Mellon began to speak openly of a "hacker ethic": the yet-unwritten rules that governed a hacker's day-to-day behavior. In the 1984 book *Hackers*, author Steven Levy, after much research and consultation, codified the hacker ethic as five core hacker tenets.

In many ways, the core tenets listed by Levy continue to define the culture of computer hacking. Still, the guild-like image of the hacker community was undermined by the overwhelmingly populist bias of the software industry. By the early 1980s, computers were popping up everywhere, and programmers who once would have had to travel to top-rank institutions or businesses just to gain access to a machine suddenly had the ability to rub elbows with major-league hackers via the ARPAnet. The more these programmers rubbed elbows, the more they began to appropriate the anarchic philosophies of the hacker culture in places like MIT. Lost within the cultural transfer, however, was the native MIT cultural taboo against malicious behavior. As younger programmers began employing their computer skills to harmful ends—creating and disseminating computer viruses, breaking into military computer systems, deliberately causing machines such as MIT Oz, a popular ARPAnet gateway, to crash—the term "hacker" acquired a punk, nihilistic edge. When police and businesses began tracing computer-related crimes back to a few renegade programmers who cited convenient portions of the hacking ethic in defense of their activities, the word "hacker" began appearing in newspapers and magazine stories in a negative light. Although books like *Hackers* did much to document the original spirit of exploration that gave rise to the hacking culture, for most news reporters, "computer hacker" became a synonym for "electronic burglar."

Although hackers have railed against this perceived misusage for nearly two decades, the term's rebellious connotations dating back to the 1950s make it hard to discern the 15-year-old writing software programs that circumvent modern encryption programs from the 1960s college student, picking locks and battering down doors to gain access to the lone, office computer terminal. One person's creative subversion of authority is another person's security headache, after all. Even so, the central taboo against malicious or deliberately harmful behavior remains strong enough that most hackers prefer to use the term "cracker"—i.e., a person who deliberately cracks a computer security system to steal or vandalize data—to describe the subset of hackers who apply their computing skills maliciously.

This central taboo against maliciousness remains the primary cultural link between the notion of hacking in the early 21st century and hacking in the 1950s. It is important to note that, as the idea of computer hacking has evolved over the last four decades, the original notion of hacking—i.e., performing pranks or exploring underground tunnels—remains intact. In the fall of 2000, the MIT Museum paid tradition to the Institute's age-old hacking tradition with a dedicated exhibit, the Hall of Hacks. The exhibit includes a number of photographs dating back to the 1920s, including one involving a mock police cruiser. In 1993, students paid homage to the original MIT notion of hacking by placing the same police cruiser, lights flashing, atop the Institute's main dome. The cruiser's vanity license plate read IHTFP, a popular MIT acronym with many meanings. The most noteworthy version, itself dating back to the pressure-filled world of MIT student life in the 1950s, is "I hate this fucking place." In 1990, however, the Museum used the acronym as a basis for a journal on the history of hacks. Titled, The Institute for Hacks Tomfoolery and Pranks, the journal offers an adept summary of the hacking.

"In the culture of hacking, an elegant, simple creation is as highly valued as it is in pure science," writes *Boston Globe* reporter Randolph Ryan in a 1993 article attached to the police car exhibit. "A Hack differs from the ordinary college prank in that the event usually requires careful planning, engineering and finesse, and has an underlying wit and inventiveness," Ryan writes. "The unwritten rule holds that a hack should be good-natured, non-destructive and safe. In fact, hackers sometimes assist in dismantling their own handiwork."

The urge to confine the culture of computer hacking within the same ethical boundaries is well-meaning but impossible. Although most software hacks aspire to the same spirit of elegance and simplicity, the software medium offers less chance for reversibility. Dismantling a police cruiser is easy compared with dismantling an idea, especially an idea whose time has come. Hence the growing distinction between "black hat" and "white hat"—i.e., hackers who turn new ideas toward destructive, malicious ends versus hackers who turn new ideas toward positive or, at the very least, informative ends.

Once a vague item of obscure student jargon, the word "hacker" has become a linguistic billiard ball, subject to political spin and ethical nuances. Perhaps this is why so many hackers and journalists enjoy using it. Where that ball bounces next, however, is anybody's guess.

GNU Free Documentation License (GFDL)

GNU Free Documentation License
Version 1.1, March 2000
Copyright © 2000 Free Software Foundation, Inc.
59 Temple Place, Suite 330, Boston, MA 02111-1307 USA
Everyone is permitted to copy and distribute verbatim copies of this license document, but changing it is not allowed.

0. PREAMBLE

The purpose of this License is to make a manual, textbook, or other written document "free" in the sense of freedom: to assure everyone the effective freedom to copy and redistribute it, with or without modifying it, either commercially or noncommercially. Secondarily, this License preserves for the author and publisher a way to get credit for their work, while not being considered responsible for modifications made by others.

This License is a kind of "copyleft," which means that derivative works of the document must themselves be free in the same sense. It complements the GNU General Public License, which is a copyleft license designed for free software.

We have designed this License in order to use it for manuals for free software, because free software needs free documentation: a free program should come with manuals providing the same freedoms that the software does. But this License is not limited to software manuals; it can be used for any textual work, regardless of subject matter or whether it is published as a printed book. We recommend this License principally for works whose purpose is instruction or reference.

1. APPLICABILITY AND DEFINITIONS

This License applies to any manual or other work that contains a notice placed by the copyright holder saying it can be distributed under the terms of this License. The "Document", below, refers to any such manual or work. Any member of the public is a licensee, and is addressed as "you."

A "Modified Version" of the Document means any work containing the Document or a portion of it, either copied verbatim, or with modifications and/or translated into another language.

A "Secondary Section" is a named appendix or a front-matter section of the Document that deals exclusively with the relationship of the publishers or authors of the Document to the Document's overall subject (or to related matters) and contains nothing that could fall directly within that overall subject. (For example, if the Document is in part a textbook of mathematics, a Secondary Section may not explain any mathematics.) The relationship could be a matter of historical connection with the subject or with related matters, or of legal, commercial, philosophical, ethical or political position regarding them.

The "Invariant Sections" are certain Secondary Sections whose titles are designated, as being those of Invariant Sections, in the notice that says that the Document is released under this License.

The "Cover Texts" are certain short passages of text that are listed, as Front-Cover Texts or Back-Cover Texts, in the notice that says that the Document is released under this License.

A "Transparent" copy of the Document means a machine-readable copy, represented in a format whose specification is available to the general public, whose contents can be viewed and edited directly and straightforwardly with generic text editors or (for images composed of pixels) generic paint programs or (for drawings) some widely available drawing editor, and that is suitable for input to text formatters or for automatic translation to a variety of formats suitable for input to text formatters. A copy made in an otherwise Transparent file format whose markup has been designed to thwart or discourage subsequent modification by readers is not Transparent. A copy that is not "Transparent" is called "Opaque."

Examples of suitable formats for Transparent copies include plain ASCII without markup, Texinfo input format, LaTeX input format, SGML or XML using a publicly available DTD, and standard-conforming simple HTML designed for human modification. Opaque formats include PostScript, PDF, proprietary formats that can be read and edited only by proprietary word processors, SGML or XML for which the DTD and/or processing tools are not generally available, and the machine-generated HTML produced by some word processors for output purposes only.

The "Title Page" means, for a printed book, the title page itself, plus such following pages as are needed to hold, legibly, the material this License requires to appear in the title page. For works in formats which do not have any title page as such, "Title Page" means the text near the most prominent appearance of the work's title, preceding the beginning of the body of the text.

2. VERBATIM COPYING

You may copy and distribute the Document in any medium, either commercially or noncommercially, provided that this License, the copyright notices, and the license notice saying this License applies to the Document are reproduced in all copies, and that you add no other conditions whatsoever to those of this License. You may not use technical measures to obstruct or control the reading or further copying of the copies you make or distribute. However, you may accept compensation in exchange for copies. If you distribute a large enough number of copies you must also follow the conditions in section 3.

You may also lend copies, under the same conditions stated above, and you may publicly display copies.

3. COPYING IN QUANTITY

If you publish printed copies of the Document numbering more than 100, and the Document's license notice requires Cover Texts, you must enclose the copies in covers that carry, clearly and legibly, all these Cover Texts: Front-Cover Texts on the front cover, and Back-Cover Texts on the back cover. Both covers must also clearly and legibly identify you as the publisher of these copies. The front cover must present the full title with all words of the title equally prominent and visible. You may add other material on the covers in addition. Copying with changes limited to the covers, as long as they preserve the title of the Document and satisfy these conditions, can be treated as verbatim copying in other respects.

If the required texts for either cover are too voluminous to fit legibly, you should put the first ones listed (as many as fit reasonably) on the actual cover, and continue the rest onto adjacent pages.

If you publish or distribute Opaque copies of the Document numbering more than 100, you must either include a machine-readable Transparent copy along with each Opaque copy, or state in or with each Opaque copy a publicly-accessible computer-network location containing a complete Transparent copy of the Document, free of added material, which the general network-using public has access to download anonymously at no charge using public-standard network protocols. If you use the latter option, you must take reasonably prudent steps, when you begin distribution of Opaque copies in quantity, to ensure that this Transparent copy will remain thus accessible at the stated location until at least one year after the last time you distribute an Opaque copy (directly or through your agents or retailers) of that edition to the public.

It is requested, but not required, that you contact the authors of the Document well before redistributing any large number of copies, to give them a chance to provide you with an updated version of the Document.

4. MODIFICATIONS

You may copy and distribute a Modified Version of the Document under the conditions of sections 2 and 3 above, provided that you release the Modified Version under precisely this License, with the Modified Version filling the role of the Document, thus licensing distribution and modification of the Modified Version to whoever possesses a copy of it. In addition, you must do these things in the Modified Version:

A. Use in the Title Page (and on the covers, if any) a title distinct from that of the Document, and from those of previous versions (which should, if there were any, be listed in the History section of the Document). You may use the same title as a previous version if the original publisher of that version gives permission.

B. List on the Title Page, as authors, one or more persons or entities responsible for authorship of the modifications in the Modified Version, together with at least five of the principal authors of the Document (all of its principal authors, if it has less than five).

C. State on the Title page the name of the publisher of the Modified Version, as the publisher.

D. Preserve all the copyright notices of the Document.

E. Add an appropriate copyright notice for your modifications adjacent to the other copyright notices.

F. Include, immediately after the copyright notices, a license notice giving the public permission to use the Modified Version under the terms of this License, in the form shown in the Addendum below.

G. Preserve in that license notice the full lists of Invariant Sections and required Cover Texts given in the Document's license notice.

H. Include an unaltered copy of this License.

I. Preserve the section entitled "History," and its title, and add to it an item stating at least the title, year, new authors, and publisher of the Modified Version as given on the Title Page. If there is no section entitled "History" in the Document, create one stating the title, year, authors, and publisher of the Document as given on its Title Page, then add an item describing the Modified Version as stated in the previous sentence.

J. Preserve the network location, if any, given in the Document for public access to a Transparent copy of the Document, and likewise the network locations given in the Document for previous versions it was based on. These may be placed in the "History" section. You may omit a network location for a work that was published at least four years before the Document itself, or if the original publisher of the version it refers to gives permission.

K. In any section entitled "Acknowledgements" or "Dedications," preserve the section's title, and preserve in the section all the substance and tone of each of the contributor acknowledgements and/or dedications given therein.

L. Preserve all the Invariant Sections of the Document, unaltered in their text and in their titles. Section numbers or the equivalent are not considered part of the section titles.

M. Delete any section entitled "Endorsements." Such a section may not be included in the Modified Version.

N. Do not retitle any existing section as "Endorsements" or to conflict in title with any Invariant Section.

If the Modified Version includes new front-matter sections or appendices that qualify as Secondary Sections and contain no material copied from the Document, you may at your option designate some or all of these sections as invariant. To do this, add their titles to the list of Invariant Sections in the Modified Version's license notice. These titles must be distinct from any other section titles.

You may add a section entitled "Endorsements," provided it contains nothing but endorsements of your Modified Version by various parties—for example, statements of peer review or that the text has been approved by an organization as the authoritative definition of a standard.

You may add a passage of up to five words as a Front-Cover Text, and a passage of up to 25 words as a Back-Cover Text, to the end of the list of Cover Texts in the Modified Version. Only one passage of Front-Cover Text and one of Back-Cover Text may be added by (or through arrangements made by) any one entity. If the Document already includes a cover text for the same cover, previously added by you or by arrangement made by the same entity you are acting on behalf of, you may not add another; but you may replace the old one, on explicit permission from the previous publisher that added the old one.

The author(s) and publisher(s) of the Document do not by this License give permission to use their names for publicity for or to assert or imply endorsement of any Modified Version.

5. COMBINING DOCUMENTS

You may combine the Document with other documents released under this License, under the terms defined in section 4 above for modified versions, provided that you include in the combination all of the Invariant Sections of all of the original documents, unmodified, and list them all as Invariant Sections of your combined work in its license notice.

The combined work need only contain one copy of this License, and multiple identical Invariant Sections may be replaced with a single copy. If there are multiple Invariant Sections with the same name but different contents, make the title of each such section unique by adding at the end of it, in parentheses, the name of the original author or publisher of that section if known, or else a unique number. Make the same adjustment to the section titles in the list of Invariant Sections in the license notice of the combined work.

In the combination, you must combine any sections entitled "History" in the various original documents, forming one section entitled "History"; likewise combine any sections entitled "Acknowledgements," and any sections entitled "Dedications." You must delete all sections entitled "Endorsements."

6. COLLECTIONS OF DOCUMENTS

You may make a collection consisting of the Document and other documents released under this License, and replace the individual copies of this License in the various documents with a single copy that is included in the collection, provided that you follow the rules of this License for verbatim copying of each of the documents in all other respects.

You may extract a single document from such a collection, and distribute it individually under this License, provided you insert a copy of this License into the extracted document, and follow this License in all other respects regarding verbatim copying of that document.

7. AGGREGATION WITH INDEPENDENT WORKS

A compilation of the Document or its derivatives with other separate and independent documents or works, in or on a volume of a storage or distribution medium, does not as a whole count as a Modified Version of the Document, provided no compilation copyright is claimed for the compilation. Such a compilation is called an "aggregate," and this License does not apply to the other self-contained works thus compiled with the Document, on account of their being thus compiled, if they are not themselves derivative works of the Document.

If the Cover Text requirement of section 3 is applicable to these copies of the Document, then if the Document is less than one quarter of the entire aggregate, the Document's Cover Texts may be placed on covers that surround only the Document within the aggregate. Otherwise they must appear on covers around the whole aggregate.

8. TRANSLATION

Translation is considered a kind of modification, so you may distribute translations of the Document under the terms of section 4. Replacing Invariant Sections with translations requires special permission from their copyright holders, but you may include translations of some or all Invariant Sections in addition to the original versions of these Invariant Sections. You may include a translation of this License provided that you also include the original English version of this License. In case of a disagreement between the translation and the original English version of this License, the original English version will prevail.

9. TERMINATION

You may not copy, modify, sublicense, or distribute the Document except as expressly provided for under this License. Any other attempt to copy, modify, sublicense or distribute the Document is void, and will automatically terminate your rights under this License. However, parties who have received copies, or rights, from you under this License will not have their licenses terminated so long as such parties remain in full compliance.

10. FUTURE REVISIONS OF THIS LICENSE

The Free Software Foundation may publish new, revised versions of the GNU Free Documentation License from time to time. Such new versions will be similar in spirit to the present version, but may differ in detail to address new problems or concerns. See *http://www.gnu.org/copyleft/*.

Each version of the License is given a distinguishing version number. If the Document specifies that a particular numbered version of this License "or any later version" applies to it, you have the option of following the terms and conditions either of that specified version or of any later version that has been published (not as a draft) by the Free Software Foundation. If the Document does not specify a version number of this License, you may choose any version ever published (not as a draft) by the Free Software Foundation.

ADDENDUM: *How to Use This License for Your Documents*

To use this License in a document you have written, include a copy of the License in the document and put the following copyright and license notices just after the title page:

> Copyright © YEAR YOUR NAME.
>
> *Permission is granted to copy, distribute and/or modify this document under the terms of the GNU Free Documentation License, Version 1.1 or any later version published by the Free Software Foundation; with the Invariant Sections being LIST THEIR TITLES, with the Front-Cover Texts being LIST, and with the Back-Cover Texts being LIST. A copy of the license is included in the section entitled "GNU Free Documentation License".*

If you have no Invariant Sections, write "with no Invariant Sections" instead of saying which ones are invariant. If you have no Front-Cover Texts, write "no Front-Cover Texts" instead of "Front-Cover Texts being LIST"; likewise for Back-Cover Texts.

If your document contains nontrivial examples of program code, we recommend releasing these examples in parallel under your choice of free software license, such as the GNU General Public License, to permit their use in free software.

INDEX

The cover of this book was designed and produced in Adobe Photoshop 5.5 and QuarkXPress 4.1 with Interstate and Sabon fonts. The cover photograph of Richard Stallman was taken by Sam Ogden/Photo Researchers, Inc.

The interior of the book is set in Adobe's Sabon font and was produced in FrameMaker 5.5.6. Sabon was designed by Jan Tschichold in 1964. The roman design is based on Garamond; the italic is based on typefaces created by Robert Granjon, one of Garamond's contemporaries. Sabon is a registered trademark of Linotype-Hell AG and/or its subsidiaries.

Many people contributed to this project, including Tim O'Reilly, Laurie Petrycki, Jeffrey Holcomb, Edie Freedman, Hanna Dyer, Emma Colby, Melanie Wang, David Futato, Sheryl Avruch, Claire Cloutier, Joe Wizda, Rachel Wheeler, and Leanne Soylemez.